D1715093

Florida A&M University, Tallahassee
Florida Atlantic University, Boca Raton
Florida Gulf Coast University, Ft. Myers
Florida International University, Miami
Florida State University, Tallahassee
University of Central Florida, Orlando
University of Florida, Gainesville
University of North Florida, Jacksonville
University of South Florida, Tampa
University of West Florida, Pensacola

America's Palestine

Popular and Official Perceptions from Balfour
to Israeli Statehood

Lawrence Davidson

University Press of Florida
Gainesville · Tallahassee · Tampa · Boca Raton
Pensacola · Orlando · Miami · Jacksonville · Ft. Myers

Copyright 2001 by Lawrence Davidson
Printed in the United States of America on acid-free paper
All rights reserved

06 05 04 03   6 5 4 3 2

Library of Congress Cataloging-in-Publication Data
Davidson, Lawrence, 1945–
America's Palestine : popular and official perceptions
from Balfour to Israeli statehood / Lawrence Davidson.
p. cm.
Includes bibliographical references and index.
ISBN 0-8130-2421-8 (cloth : alk. paper)
1. Palestine—Foreign public opinion, American. 2. Public opinion—
United States. 3. Palestine—History—1917–1948. 4. Missions,
American—Palestine. I. Title.
DS 126 .D28   2001
956.94—dc21   2001027176

The University Press of Florida is the scholarly publishing agency for the
State University System of Florida, comprising Florida A&M University,
Florida Atlantic University, Florida Gulf Coast University, Florida Inter-
national University, Florida State University, University of Central Flor-
ida, University of Florida, University of North Florida, University of
South Florida, and University of West Florida.

University Press of Florida
15 Northwest 15th Street
Gainesville, FL 32611–2079
http://www.upf.com

Contents

This book is dedicated to Janet Kestenberg Amighi and Hisham Sharabi. Good friends and advisers, they strive to make the world a more just and humane place.

1

Our Palestine

The nineteenth century, and a good part of the twentieth, constituted an age of empire. About the year 1870, the European powers increased the pace of imperial expansion until they had captured most of the non-Western world. The United States also participated in this imperial race for territory.

The Basis of America's Perception of Palestine

The cultural and political views that supported imperialism can be understood in terms of a prevailing paradigm of the time that divided the world in a bipolar fashion. The world was divided into two parts—the civilized West, possessed of technological know-how and representing progress, efficiency, and good government; and the backward East, in need of "development" and guidance. Within this perceptual framework the spread of Western civilization was considered both inevitable and beneficial. Imperialism thus became altruistic.

> Take up the White Man's burden
> Send forth the best ye breed
> Go bind your sons to exile
> To serve your captive's needs;
> To wait in heavy harness,
> On fluttered fold and wild
> Your new caught, sullen peoples,
> Half devil and half child.

A good number of Americans would have agreed with Rudyard Kipling's words in this famous 1899 poem. They had adopted its sentiments to rationalize their expansion across the American continent and beyond to such American colonial possessions as the Philippine Islands, Hawaii, and Puerto Rico.[1] As with their European cousins, the bipolar worldview and its corollary of altruistic imperialism shaped their views of the non-Western world.

There was a second corollary to the bipolar worldview paradigm, and this had to do with religion. Not only was the civilized West in possession of superior technology and all the physical accoutrements of progress that it brought. It was also in possession of an alleged superior religion—Christianity. Here the notion that the West had a duty to bring the primitive East progress in the form of good government and the hardware of high civilization was melded to the proselytizing zeal of the Protestant Christian missionary.[2] Americans also felt this zeal and went abroad to bring the "word of God to the heathen."

American popular perceptions of Palestine were shaped by these paradigmatic forces. Palestine had always been a special place for both American Christians and Jews, owing to its biblical associations. Yet this religious identification was also understood within the context of the bipolar worldview. Palestine, being the birthplace of Jesus and the ancient homeland of the Jews, had, for a long time, been lost within the sphere of the primitive and "pagan" East. By the early nineteenth century, there was a feeling in the United States that the time had now come when this place, which was of the utmost spiritual importance to the Christian West, had to be redeemed, both spiritually and developmentally, by the work of American Protestant missionaries.

The nineteenth century was a particularly propitious time for this sort of outlook. America had been undergoing a religious revival in the Second Great Awakening.[3] Particularly swept up in this century-long religious revival were the New England Protestant churches: Presbyterian, Congregationalist, and the like, as well as their affiliated seminaries and colleges, such as Harvard, Yale, Williams, Amherst, and Andover. Here we find many young men dedicating themselves to a missionary profession the aim of which was to "morally renovate the world." What that translated into was an effort to "Christianize the world in one generation" or, in any case, before the turn of the century.[4]

Behind this American missionary effort to Christianize and morally renovate not only the peoples of the Near East and Palestine, but various other unenlightened folks on the far side of the bipolar divide, was a series of assumptions. These went beyond the missionary community and were shared by believing Protestants generally. They were that there was one true religion and Protestant Christians were in possession of it; that such possession brought with it an obligation to spread the "word" to the unenlightened; and that spreading the word constituted a divinely sanctioned mission on the success of which depended the salvation of the world.[5]

This effort at saving the world through Protestant evangelical proselytizing was then married, by these New England crusaders, to the notion of American manifest destiny. This latter outlook was seen as having the concomitant assumptions that the political and economic systems of the United States represented the greatest achievements of mankind and had created a superior civilization; this superior American civilization was God-blessed; those who represent this superior civilization have an obligation to expand it for the sake of mankind (as they were doing across America's western frontier); and this effort to expand American ways was also sanctified by God.

And so one has the coming together of two gospels, the Protestant and the American.[6] One can hear the melding of these two worldviews in the sermon, given to a gathering of supporters of American missions abroad, by the Reverend John Codman in Boston in 1836. "How can we better testify our appreciation of [America's] free institutions, than by laboring to plant them in other lands? For where the Gospel goes in its purity and power, there will follow in its train the blessings of civilization, liberty and good government. . . . Coming himself from a land of freedom, he [the missionary] will naturally spread around him an atmosphere of liberty."[7]

That this whole point of view ignored a multitude of sins on the part of American civilization (that, for instance, Codman made his speech in a country that stood as the last major Western nation to maintain slavery as a legal institution) did not make it any any less effective. As the century wore on, Americans would ignore their own shortcomings, and, following Codman's lead, use the need to Christianize and Americanize the natives as a single rationalization for becoming an imperialist power in their own right.[8] By the end of the century many Americans could blithely criticize European imperialist methods while categorizing American control of the Philippines and other colonies as a service to mankind. The same attitude would be affixed to their missionary efforts in the Muslim world. As one Congregationalist minister put it after returning from a trip to the Near East, "America is God's last dispensation towards the world."[9]

The American Missionary Effort in the Near East

The origins of the Protestant evangelical missionary movement can be found in New England and especially at the Andover Theological Seminary in Massachusetts. There, about 1810, a fraternity was formed the members of which pledged themselves to become missionaries abroad. Over the next one hundred years some 250 young men would choose such a career as part of this effort. Out of this enterprise also came the formation of the American Board of Commissioners for Foreign Missions, founded in 1810. The American Board (or ABCFM) served as a steering committee for this missionary effort, setting its goals and seeking the necessary funds. Spurred on by religious and patriotic convictions, it would turn out to be a successful and long-lived enterprise.

The ABCFM sent out its first missionaries to the Near East in 1819 reportedly with "a pledge of full protection from Secretary of State John Quincy Adams."[10] These men, two recent graduates of Andover, were instructed to learn the local languages, distribute Bibles and other religious tracts, and discreetly instruct in the Gospel, avoiding offense to local laws and customs.[11] Over time this missionary effort became headquartered at Beirut and spread out from there into Anatolia, Syria, Palestine, and beyond.

By 1900 there would be more Americans—mostly missionaries—in the Near East than any other Western nationality except the British. And while they spread the Gospel to the locals, often in a more zealous fashion than their early instructions called for, they simultaneously furnished Americans back home with their principal source of information and misinformation on contemporary Palestine.[12] As Edward Earle, professor of history at Columbia University and one of the first researchers of the American missionary enterprise, put it in the April 1929 issue of *Foreign Affairs,* "For almost a century American public opinion concerning the Near East was formed by the missionaries. If American opinion has been uninformed, misinformed and prejudiced, the missionaries are largely to blame. Interpreting history in terms of the advance of Christianity, they have given an inadequate, distorted, and occasionally a grotesque picture of Moslems and Islam."[13]

In the nineteenth century, Americans knew almost nothing about the actual Palestine and its Muslim-majority population, both of which were then part of the Ottoman Empire.[14] However, they knew a great deal about a romanticized and theocratized version of that land. They drew this version from a combination of Bible study (the Bible was assumed to relate historical fact), romantic fiction, and the occasional travelogue. As Fuad Sha'ban has shown in his work, *Islam and Arabs in Early American Thought,* for all intents and purposes a mythical Palestine, constructed in terms of Judeo-Christian theology, had displaced the real Palestine in the consciousness of Americans.[15] What the missionaries now added in terms of lecture tours, newsletters, and their own published diaries and accounts fit completely into this standard, theocratized version governing Western perception of the Holy Land.

The assumptions underlying the theocratized picture of Palestine went like this: Palestine was the land of the Bible, the birthplace of Jesus and the ancient homeland of the Jews. This meant that it was a Judeo-Christian place, which, in the modern age, really made it an important extension of the West. That it was geographically located beyond the borders of Western civilization lent it an exotic air, but was ultimately secondary to the fact that, religiously, it was as important to the West as Rome, Canterbury, or the Puritan meeting hall. Unfortunately, in the dim past this sacred place had been captured by infidel hordes and ruled ever since by despoiling "Mohammedans." Thus the "land of milk and honey" had been turned into a "land of dust."

News of—as the missionary Eli Smith put it—"the misery of the present scene"[16] only produced shock and dismay that the Palestine described by Western visitors fell so short of the idealized biblical picture. Protestant missionary work, therefore, was portrayed and accepted as part of an effort to redeem this holy place, to reclaim it by converting its occupants to the true religion and a better societal model that were both essentially Western and American. In relaying back information to the public, the American missionaries, steeped in these assumptions, only reinforced the demand that the real Palestine become a modernized version of the biblical holy land.

Religiously defined assumptions were not the only factors influencing American missionary behavior. Coming from a culture that separated church and state, and made religion a personal choice, the first generation of missionaries were ignorant of, and unprepared to work in, a culture that divided itself into "millets," or religiously defined communities. In the Ottoman Empire the religion of your birth affixed you to a residential community that was more or less self-contained. Minority groups, such as the Greek Orthodox, Catholics, Coptic Christians, and Jews, among others, lived within their own communal enclaves and were governed by their own religious and lay leaders, laws, and courts. As long as they paid their taxes and made no trouble they were usually left alone by the Muslim majority. It was a rare thing that one abandoned one's religion, for to do so meant abandoning one's family and community. For Muslims this could be a dangerous move in that apostasy was one of the few acts that carried a death penalty under Sharia law (Muslim holy law).

It seems that the early American missionaries knew nothing of this and, as is so often the case, simply worked on the assumption that their own cultural norms were universal. One can imagine the reaction of the local ulema (Muslim religious leaders), priests, and rabbis when New England evangelicals showed up "zealously advertising their brand of Christianity."[17] That the missionaries were not expelled outright by the authorities of the Ottoman Empire attests to the fact that they worked closely with British missionaries, and thereby obtained the protection of British consular officials (the United States had little diplomatic representation in the area before the twentieth century), whose own intrusive influence in the Near East was strong and growing.[18] Nonetheless, as one missionary complained, "Mohammedans, Muscovites [the Greek Orthodox] and Monks [Catholics] furnish their full quota of opposition."[19]

The greatest resistance, however, came from the Muslim and Jewish communities. As a consequence, in 1831, the ABCFM directed its Near Eastern missionaries to abandon efforts to convert Muslims and to concentrate their energies on "the degenerate Churches of the East" (for instance the Catholic and Greek Orthodox Churches).[20] Over time particular attention would be paid to the Armenians of Anatolia and the Arab Christians of greater Syria. At the same time a tactical shift occurred from straight proselytizing activities to the establishment of schools and clinics. These were fateful decisions. The creation of schools such as the Syrian Protestant College (now American University) at Beirut and Roberts College (now Bogazici University) in Istanbul began the dissemination of two types of information. One type came in the form of scientific training, for which there was an increasing demand throughout the Near East. The other was more ideological, and came in the form of an idealized picture of American society as a role model for future development and liberation. However, the decision to concentrate efforts upon Christian minority communities meant that, at least until the end of the nineteenth century, Muslim attendance at these institutions was minimal. What was going on here was the training in Western knowledge of an elite among the region's religious minorities. Eventually, this elite would grow increasingly dissatisfied with the nature of Ottoman society and their status within it.

The Ottoman government and the Muslim community, of course, saw what was happening and often interpreted it in the worst of lights.[21] This is particularly true in the case of the Anatolian Armenians, amongst whom the American missionaries were quite active. The Armenians always had an inclination toward independence which, if not incited by the missionaries, was certainly encouraged by missionary support of a national self-consciousness among this and other Ottoman subgroups (Arabs, Bulgarians, Albanians, etc). By the latter part of the nineteenth century the Ottoman authorities were becoming frightened by what they interpreted to be increasing separatist tendencies among the Armenians in particular. The fear took a paranoid turn during the reign of Sultan Abdul Hamid II (1876–1909), who was convinced that "foreigners whipped up disloyalty"[22] and was willing to use ruthless measures to counteract it. Not able to simply expel the foreigners because of their protection by Western powers, he engineered a series of pogroms against the Armenians between 1894 and 1896. During these attacks American missionary property was also destroyed. With the coming of World War I renewed attacks on Armenians would assume a genocidal character.

Missionary reaction to these events further elaborated the bipolar worldview held by Americans of the Near East. "The terrible Turks" and, by extension, Muslims in general, were cast as savages and barbarians in an American missionary campaign to raise funds for Armenian victims. So successful was the "negative campaigning" that in 1914 the Turkish ambassador to the United States, Ahmed Rustem, complained publicly that "For years past, Turkey has been the object of systematic attacks on the part of the press of the United States. These attacks, conceived very frequently in the most outrageous language, spare her in none of her feelings. Her religion, her nationality, her customs, her past, her present are reviled. She is represented as being a sink of iniquity."[23] The missionary portrayal of the Armenians and Arab Christians, on the other hand, was as peoples of biblical origin being mistreated by "the Mohammedans."[24] As the Muslims had desecrated the Holy Land, they now despoiled the Christian minorities who, the missionaries asserted, were really among the most worthy people of the empire. That is, unlike the incorrigible Muslims, they were subject to conversion not only to evangelical Protestantism, but also to American ways.

Thus, as World War I approached, Americans perceived a Near East in turmoil. The ruling Muslim element was seen as behaving badly toward Christians and Jews as well (the "biblical peoples"). The historical context for Ottoman and Muslim attitudes, which was, at least in part, shaped by Western expansionist policies that had long been negatively impacting the political, economic, and cultural stability of the Ottoman Empire, was largely unknown in America. In any case, that context could not easily constitute an operative aspect of the average American's history of the Holy Land. There was no point of reference for it within the conceptual framework that made up their ersatz history of Palestine and assigned an altrusitic motive to Western imperialism in that region. Rather, theirs was a theocratized Palestine in which biblical mythology transformed the area into an extension of the Judeo-Christian West, and where a contemporary drive toward redemption through missionary work now prevailed. Such was the bipolar worldview as it applied to the Holy Land. The result was a sustained dislike for Muslims that, beyond its current causes, had deep roots going back to the Crusades. Indeed, as we shall see, Allied actions in Palestine during World War I would be pictured as a modern-day crusade.

The Zionist Connection

Many of the same American Protestants who supported missionary work in the Near East also had a fascination with the Jews. This was particularly true of the millenarian sects in the United States. This interest was (and still is) related to their interpretation of biblical prophecy, which, they believed, predicted the in-gathering of the Jews in Palestine as a prelude to the second coming of Christ.[25]

By the mid nineteenth century, supporters of a Jewish restoration to Palestine could be found among most American Protestant denominations. Perhaps the best known is William Eugene Blackstone, a lay Bible preacher, prolific writer, and tireless campaigner for a modern reincarnation of ancient Israel. In 1891 Blackstone drew up a petition addressed to President Benjamin Harrison and Secretary of State James G. Blaine asking for the "use of their good offices and influence with the governments of the European world to secure the holding at an early date of an international conference to consider the condition of the Israelites and their claims to Palestine as their ancient home." It was signed by 413 well-known Americans, including the Speaker of the House of Representatives, the Chief Justice of the Supreme Court, J. P. Morgan, and John D. Rockefeller.[26] Here we have an early sign of the power of this subject to attract a wide range of influential people. Blackstone would go on to become a friend and supporter of the Zionist movement, and he is today revered in Israel. His interest in the Jews, however, was religiously inspired. It flowed from a Christian fundamentalist belief that a return of the Jews to Palestine was an imminent part of the working out of prophecy. In his book *The Roots of Fundamentalism*, Ernest R. Sandeen captures a sense of this anticipation when he writes, "millenarians [those fundamentalist Protestants looking to the second coming of Christ] watched in fascination the formation of Zionism under Theodor Herzl and the meeting of the first Zionist Congress in Basel in 1897, and millenarians correctly, almost instinctively, grasped the significance of Allenby's capture of Jerusalem and celebrated the event as the fulfillment of prophecy."[27]

Against this backdrop of prophetic expectation, those with millenarian inclinations connected Zionism with the fate of theocratized Palestine. More generally, the Jews were among the "biblical peoples" who had been put forth by the missionary organizations as truly worthy, indigenous residents of the Holy Land. Thus, come World War I and the subsequent British capture of Jerusalem, American Protestants in general would assume the right of the Jews, led by an active Zionist movement, to "return to their homeland." And if such a return set the stage for the fulfillment of prophecy, all the better. Therefore, it seemed logical for the American Presbyterian General Assembly in 1916 to pass a resolution supporting a Jewish homeland in Palestine.[28]

There resulted then a convergence of a set of perceptions that led Protestant fundamentalists, missionaries, Zionists, and and other interested Americans as well to support the "redemption" of the Holy Land. One can summarize these perceptions and their consequences as follows: (1) The theocratized picture of Palestine put emphasis on its "biblical people," the Christians and Jews. (2) The Muslim majority was reduced to usurpers who had ruined a place sacred to the Judeo-Christian West. (3) In essence this outlook erased the demographic and cultural realities of the Holy Land, replacing it with an alternative picture more compatible with biblical tradition. The culture, traditions, towns, and villages of the Muslim majority were simply held to be of no account. In modern terms, one can understand it as "perceptual depopulation," a form of ethnic cleansing on the conceptual level. (4) Given the American perception of Palestine as a Judeo-Christian homeland and the threatened status of its "biblical people," popular opinion held that an effort to redeem the land under Western guidance was justified. The prevailing bipolar worldview supported this judgment and allowed it to appear consistent with the altruistic nature of imperialism. The missionary effort was seen as part of this process. (5) Many Americans would also come to see the Zionist movement as a compatible and parallel effort in this same great venture.

Given the cultural paradigm that governed American perceptions of Palestine, World War I was bound to be seen as a seminal event by both Protestant Christians and Zionist Jews. The war brought about the final collapse of the Ottoman Empire and opened the way for Allied occupation of the Middle East. There was now a real prospect that Great Britain, a Western Christian power sympathetic to both Protestant missionary work and Zionism, would come into possession of Palestine. The stage was thus set for the long-awaited redemption of the Holy Land and, along with it, the return of the Jews. It is at this point that Britain's foreign secretary, Lord Arthur Balfour, and his famous declaration entered the picture.

2

America and the Balfour Declaration

On November 2, 1917, Sir Arthur James Balfour, the British foreign secretary in the wartime cabinet of Prime Minister David Lloyd George, issued what has since become known as the Balfour Declaration. An exercise in studied ambiguity brought forth after months of negotiation between the British government and the World Zionist Organization (WZO), the declaration read as follows:

> His Majesty's Government view with favour the establishment in Palestine of a national home for the Jewish people, and will use their best endeavours to facilitate the achievement of this object, it being clearly understood that nothing shall be done which may prejudice the civil and religious rights of the existing non-Jewish communities in Palestine, or the rights and political status enjoyed by Jews in any other country.[1]

A British-Zionist Alliance

Though it was presented as a humanitarian gesture, and thus appeared to fit within the parameters of altruistic imperialism, the Balfour Declaration was in truth much more. Jointly drafted by negotiators representing both parties, the declaration bound the British to facilitate the establishment of a "national home" for the Jews, in return for Zionist aid for the ongoing British war effort. The mutual obligation that underlay the arrangement was made clear in a memorandum to the British Cabinet in 1923. In that year, while debating future policy in Palestine, the colonial secretary, Lord Cavendish, reminded his colleagues,

> The object [of the Balfour Declaration] was to enlist the sympathies on the Allied side of influential Jews and Jewish organizations all over the world . . . [and] it is arguable that the negotiations with the Zionists . . . did in fact have considerable effect in advancing the date at which the United States Government intervened in the war. How-

ever that might be, it must be always remembered that the Declaration was made at a time of extreme peril to the cause of the Allies. . . . The Balfour Declaration was a war measure . . . designed to secure tangible benefits which it was hoped could contribute to the ultimate victory of the Allies. The benefits may or may not have been worth securing or may or may not have been actually secured; but the objections to going back on a promise made under such conditions are obvious. . . .The Jews would naturally regard it as an act of baseness if, having appealed to them in our hour of peril, we were to throw them over when the danger was past.[2]

The unsatisfactory state of the war effort against the Central Powers was the engine driving the British search for assistance. In 1915–17 things were so precarious that the British were not at all sure they were going to win. Fighting on the western front had ground down to a series of stalemated exercises in mutual slaughter. On the Russian front, the Allies were losing. The Russians thus appeared to be on their way out of the war, while the Americans (whom the British were earnestly wooing and who represented the Allies' real hope of military salvation) were not quite on their way in. It was indeed, as Cavendish noted, a "time of extreme peril."

The only bright spot on the military map was the Middle East. Here the Arabs had decided to ally themselves with the British and, in June of 1916, rose up against their Turkish overlords, who were, in turn, allied with the Germans. The British negotiations that led to this Arab revolt had been conducted with Sherif Husayn of Mecca, in the same vein as negotiations with the Zionists. They had begun in the fall of 1915, when Sir Henry McMahon, the British high commissioner in Cairo, began the exchange of a series of letters with Husayn giving a British pledge to support the creation of an independent Arab state in the Middle East. Husayn had sought a state that occupied all the territory from the Persian border in the east to the Mediterranean and Red Seas in the west. The British agreed, excepting, as McMahon rather vaguely put it in his correspondence, those "portions of Syria lying to the west of the districts [*wilayats*, or provinces in Arabic] of Homs, Hama, and Aleppo [which] cannot be said to be purely Arab."[3] Later, there would be much dispute over what the term "districts" meant in this context. While the definitions subsequently argued over may have indeed exempted Lebanon, it is hard to see how they precluded Palestine, which is found considerably to the south of the area "lying to the west of Homs, Hama, and Aleppo."

Nonetheless, when the British began conquering the Ottoman realms of the Middle East, they would assert just that, and thereby remove Palestine from the promised "independent" Arab state. By doing so, Prime Minister Lloyd George and Balfour gave conscious preference to the Zionists who, as fellow Europeans, shared a Judeo-Christian biblical tradition with the British. It was a policy decision quite in line with the bipolar worldview. However, the British had other ways of rationalizing this move. As Lord Cavendish explained, "whatever may be thought of our case [for separating out Palestine] . . . the Arabs as a whole have acquired a freedom undreamed of before the war. Considering what they owe to us, they may surely let us have our way in one small area, which we do not admit to be covered by our pledges, and which in any case, for historical and other reasons, stands on wholly different footing from the rest of the Arab countries."[4] The "wholly different footing" was, as we shall see, the assumption, detailed in chapter 1, that Western religious sentiments for the biblical Holy Land essentially took precedence over the rights of the majority Muslim population.

The British had conveniently forgotten the Arab contribution to their war effort, as witnessed by the colonial secretary's emphasis on what the Arabs "owe to us." But in truth, in 1916 and 1917, the Arabs were doing more damage to Britain's enemies than were the Zionists. And again, in 1917, if the British wanted to see progress on the ground they could not look to the WZO; they rather had to look across the Suez to the actions of the British and Arab armies. As a consequence, the Arabs ended up feeling toward the British exactly as Lord Cavendish speculated the Jews would feel if the Balfour Declaration had been ignored. That is, that the British were "going back on a promise." And thus the Arabs "naturally . . . regarded [this] as an act of baseness," because "having appealed to them in our hour of peril, [the British] were to throw them over when the danger was past."

What the Arabs failed to realize was that, during the war, the British-Zionist alliance played for bigger stakes. The Arabs might have had some regional military potential, but the Jews, supposedly, had enormous, worldwide financial and political potential. Here the old stereotype of the Jews being capable of worldwide conspiratorial machinations must have unconsciously come into play. The British fantasized that the Zionists had great influence in both the United States and Russia. They believed that Jews could encourage the Americans into the war while discouraging the Russians from leaving it.[5]

Such was the desperation of the hour that the British were willing, as a form of wartime strategy, to promise both parties, the Zionists and the Arabs, almost anything they wanted. It was not quite a blank check; British postwar imperial interests had to be kept in mind; and there were French ambitions in Syria that had already been secretly conceded at the January 3, 1916, signing of the Sykes-Picot Agreement. But these concerns, and the contradictions they represented to British promises made to both Arabs and Jews, could be worked out at a later, and safer time. For the moment studied ambiguity would have to do. And, of course, at this time, there was really no cost to any of this. The British were leveraging their promises with their enemy's land.

The American Connection

The United States finally declared war on Germany on April 6, 1917, and, as Lord Cavendish suggested, the British government believed that the Zionists had somehow been helpful in bringing about this vital act. Later that same month Arthur Balfour traveled to the United States. Part of his mission was to encourage continued American Jewish support for the war effort as well as a postwar British Palestine. Among those individuals Balfour cultivated at White House receptions and private interviews was Louis Brandeis, a member of the Supreme Court and a confidant of President Woodrow Wilson. He was also the leader of the Zionist Organization of America (ZOA).

Balfour seemed to take to Brandeis right away, perhaps projecting onto this man his general fascination with the Jews. Balfour felt the Jews had been repeatedly wronged: by Babylonians, by Romans, and, in the modern era, by European anti-Semites. He wanted to help right those wrongs. "My anxiety is simply to find some means by which the present dreadful state of so large a proportion of the Jewish race . . . may be brought to an end" he once stated while campaigning for Parliament. And "if a home was to be found for the Jewish people . . . it was in vain to seek it anywhere but in Palestine."[6] Thus we have a European statesman seeking to cure a European problem by exporting the victims to a non-European site. It was a problem-solving approach that could best be pursued in an age of imperialism. In any case, in 1917, it must have seemed truly serendipitous to Balfour that, as foreign secretary, he could now simultaneously pursue this private cause and forward Britain's wartime interests.

Brandeis probably sensed much of this. Just before Balfour's arrival, he had received information from the Zionists in Britain that they and the British government were discussing the possibility of a British protectorate over Palestine.[7] When the two men met, Balfour assured Brandeis of his personal approval of the Zionist cause and proceeded to propose an official British statement of support for Zionism. Brandeis responded positively and asserted his own and the ZOA's enthusiasm for postwar British control over Palestine. This link having been made explicit, the American Zionists joined the WZO-British alliance.[8]

The implications of all this must have been clear to the American Zionists. The road to a Jewish Palestine lay through a British victory. Thus, the Jews of the United States would have to be encouraged to support the allied war effort and a postwar British protectorate of the Holy Land. If this formula sounds simple today, it was not apparently so at the time. Some American Jews held antiwar and isolationist positions. There was also the fact that the social and economic elite of the Jewish community were of German ancestry. To this might be added the apprehension, felt by the British and the French, that the German government was contemplating its own announcement in support of Zionism. How serious these complications were is questionable. A German pro-Zionist stand would have run counter to the national interests of her Ottoman ally. And in the United States, German Americans were increasingly intimidated into silence as Germany's relations with the United States deteriorated. Sauerkraut was about to become "liberty cabbage."

According to State Department records, there is no evidence that Balfour raised the issue of Palestine in his meetings with President Wilson. However, after finally seeing a draft of the proposed British statement of support for Zionism, Brandeis spoke about Palestine to Wilson on May 4 and again on May 6. It was Brandeis who came away from his conversations with the president's pledge of support for both the proposed British protectorate and Zionist aims in Palestine. However, for reasons that will be made clear later, the president would only express this support discreetly. Brandeis understood this and, much to the frustration of many other American Zionists, also worked for the cause in a relatively discreet fashion.[9] Brandeis reported Wilson's positive attitude to his colleagues in London, and to the visiting Balfour. For Balfour it was mission accomplished, and before he left for home, he enthusiastically reaffirmed for Brandeis that "I am a Zionist."[10] And, indeed, he was about to have his name go down in history in just such a fashion.

Woodrow Wilson and the Zionist Cause

What of Woodrow Wilson's attitude toward Zionism? There can be little doubt that he too was supportive of the movement, and so Brandeis was, essentially, conferring with an ally when he took Balfour's ideas to the president in May of 1917.[11] Wilson was raised as a fundamentalist Christian of the Presbyterian faith. For him Palestine was the Holy Land, which meant that, as with most Americans who thought about this region, biblical Palestine was much more real than the modern, Muslim-dominated, version. And, of course, biblical Palestine was a Jewish place. Wilson's friendship with Zionists such as Brandeis and Rabbi Stephen Wise cemented his sympathies for the cause that was so ardently attempting to "bring the Jews home." He was flattered by the prospect that he might be able to play a role in what appeared to be the fulfillment of biblical prophecy. As Wilson told Wise in 1916, "To think that I, a son of the manse, should be able to help restore the Holy Land to its people."[12]

So the issue of a Jewish Palestine was important to Woodrow Wilson, but it was not as high a priority for him as for the American Zionists. Later, this difference in levels of priority would lead to misunderstanding and disappointment, as some American Zionists complained that Wilson was not public enough, or adamant enough, in his support for their cause.[13]

Alas, Wilson had other things on his mind, and in 1916 and 1917, neither Palestine nor Zionism rated as an immediate issue. Wilson was, after all, president of a country that was about to commit itself to a raging European war. There were also domestic political measures, such as the Federal Farm Loan Act, the Child Labor Act, the eight-hour workday, and other progressive domestic bills to be managed in the Congress. In foreign policy, there were the ongoing problems with Mexico and Japan. The whole issue of neutral rights on the high seas still festered, and German submarine warfare tactics were about to make matters worse. After April 1917, the need to prepare the country for entry into World War I on the side of England was an immediate demand.

It was this very full agenda that helps explain Wilson's delayed response to the British request for preapproval of the Balfour Declaration. Working through Wilson's adviser and confidant, Edward House, the British sought the president's agreement to the wording of the document that would be the Balfour Declaration. In a memo of September 7, 1917, House asked Wilson, "Have you made up your mind regarding what answer you will give Cecil [Sir Cecil Arthur Spring-Rice, British ambassador in Washington] concerning the Zionist Movement? It seems to me that there are many dangers lurking in it."[14] The Zionists added their own pressure for a positive response to the British draft, again through House, until he complained to Wilson in a note of October 3, 1917, that "the Jews from every tribe have descended in force, and they are determined to break in with a jimmy if they are not let in."[15] Finally, on October 13, 1917, the president literally rediscovered the issue amidst all the other problems he daily confronted. On that day he memoed House, "I find in my pocket the memorandum you gave me about the Zionist movement. I am afraid I did not say to you that I concurred in the formula suggested from the other side [the wording of the British draft of the Balfour Declaration]. I do, and would be obliged if you would let them know it."[16] So Wilson, rather offhandedly, gave his blessings to the Balfour Declaration.

It is to be noted that Wilson seems to have given his approval for the Balfour Declaration without serious consultation with the State Department.[17] This is a pattern that would persist over time and create repeated confusion over U.S. foreign policy for Palestine. Thus years later, when the State Department was reviewing all its documents referring to the Balfour Declaration, it could conclude that "there is no confirmatory evidence of [President Wilson's support for the declaration] in the records of the Department. . . . On the contrary it would appear . . . that this Government was not kept officially informed of negotiations leading up to the Balfour Declaration."[18] From the beginning the State Department stood apart from, and often uninformed about, presidential thinking on the subjects of Zionism and Palestine.

However incomplete the records of the State Department, Woodrow Wilson was in fact favorably disposed toward the Zionist cause. The Zionists, however, were not the only Americans with a strong interest in the Middle East who had the president's ear. There was another party, the American Protestant missionaries. Just as the president's evangelicalism predisposed him to the Zionists, it led him to support the work of the American Board of Commissioners for Foreign Missions. This organization had, as we have seen, extensive missionary interests and investments throughout the Ottoman Empire.

In the case of the missionaries, just as with the Zionists, personal friendships reinforced Wilson's commitment. The principal connection here was with Cleveland Dodge, head of Dodge Phelps Corporation, and a longtime leader and benefactor of the American Board. Dodge had known Wilson since 1875, and their friendship would last until Wilson's death. At the beginning of World War I, Wilson wrote to Dodge, "I know of no other friend like you. . . . Thank God that it is so, and that there is room somewhere for perfect trust!"[19] Dodge, along with James Barton, the secretary of the American Board, had ready access to Wilson during the war years. They used this access to ensure the government's cooperation in helping to protect and preserve the American Board's property and personnel in the Middle East. It was not difficult for them to convince Wilson to assist in this regard, for it was the president's opinion that "it would be a real misfortune . . . if the missionary program for the world should be interrupted. . . . that the work undertaken should be . . . at its full force, seems to me of capital necessity."[20]

How was this to be accomplished on the eve of an American declaration of war against Germany and its allies? The answer to this question, as it turned out, would create a problem for Wilson's support of Zionism. The way Wilson sought to protect the interests of the American Board was by exempting the Ottoman Empire from the war declaration bill. I am "trying to hold Congress back from following its inclination," Wilson wrote Dodge, "to include all the allies of Germany in its declaration of a state of war. I hope with all my heart that I can succeed."[21] The point man in this regard was Secretary of State Robert Lansing. He was given the job of dissuading Senator William H. King of Utah from including the Turks in the declaration of war bill he was about to introduce into the Senate. "The primary result" of their inclusion, Lansing told King, "would be the confiscation of church, school, and humanitarian institutions set up by American Protestants in the Near East."[22]

How did this stand complicate Wilson's support for the Zionists? It did so by requiring the president to express his approval of their efforts to secure a national home in Palestine in only private and discreet ways. For to publicly advocate the Zionist cause would be to overtly support a British protectorate for Palestine and the eventual introduction into that land of large numbers of European settlers. This clearly would necessitate the detachment of the Holy Land from the Ottoman Empire. But for the U.S. president to advocate the dismemberment of a nation with which his country was not at war was not at all proper. And to do so would certainly bring reprisals upon the American missionary establishment resident there. How clearly the American Zionists understood this dilemma is open to question. Most likely Brandeis understood, and so did not pressure Wilson to take a public stand beyond a rather general statement in praise of the "reconstructive work" of Zionists in Palestine issued by the president in August of 1918.[23]

While the needs of the American Protestant missionaries often took precedence over Zionist solicitations for public support, they never negated Wilson's sympathy for Zionist goals. And, at least in the years leading up to the Paris Peace Conference, it did not appear to Wilson, and other fundamentalist Protestants, that there was any inherent conflict between the two causes. After all, the Presbyterian General Assembly (and we have to remember that Wilson was a devout Presbyterian who read the Bible daily) had passed a resolution in 1916 in support of the idea of a Jewish homeland in Palestine. Toward the end of the war, however, things would become more complicated, when some of the American Protestant missionaries actually resident in the Middle East would throw their weight behind the right of self-determination for the Arab peoples, including those of Palestine.

The Dilemma of Self-Determination

The end of the war, and the issue of what to do with the territory and peoples of the conquered Ottoman Empire, would present Wilson with yet another and more profound dilemma. The pledge of self-determination was one of his own great ideas, enshrined in the very war aims (his Fourteen Points) by which he rallied the United States to the side of the Allies. While the war was being waged the cause of self-determination was a fine rallying cry. It stirred the hearts of millions of eastern Europeans as well as the subject peoples of the Ottoman Empire. But in 1919, with the Paris Peace Conference now having to deal with the realities of a "new world order," the idea of self-determination for all was one which, as Secretary of State Lansing put it, was "simply loaded with dynamite. It will raise hopes which can never be realized. It will, I fear, cost thousands of lives."[24]

It was only at the peace conference that Wilson had to face the issues raised by his own idealism. As it turned out, self-determination was to be unquestionably granted to many of the peoples of eastern Europe. However, the same right for the Arab peoples was not forthcoming. The reason was, in part, the Western racism inherent in the bipolar worldview. But more immediately, self-determination for Middle Eastern peoples threatened to get in the way of British and French imperial designs in that region and Zionist ambitions in Palestine. Wilson and his British and French allies finessed this problem by establishing "the mandate system." Various properties of the defeated Central Powers would be distributed to the victors as mandates. The "mandatory power" would then have the responsibility of tutoring (under League of Nations supervision) their mandate subjects in the art of self-government until such time as they were able to rule themselves. This arrangement fit well with the prevailing bipolar worldview that defined imperialism as an altruistic endeavor because it brought with it modern ways of doing things, including modern methods of governance.

However, many American Protestant missionaries stationed in the

Middle East came to support self-determination for the Arab peoples. If there had to be a mandatory, they wanted it to be the United States. This position was put forth by Howard Bliss, an eminent missionary and son of Daniel Bliss, the founder of the Syrian Protestant College in Beirut (later the American University of Beirut). Bliss had succeeded his father as president of that institution in 1902 and was, by 1919, as one historian of the period has put it, "the most influential American in the Middle East."[25]

Bliss showed up in Paris in February of 1919 as an official member of the Syrian delegation sent to argue for an independent Arab state before the peace conference. Unable to achieve this goal outright, he was able to persuade Wilson and the American delegation to at least inquire as to the political preferences of the local populations of the area. It was a request that was hard for the champions of self-determination to turn down, and so this project slowly took shape in the form of the King-Crane Commission. In the end this effort would make little difference to the fate of the Arabs in Palestine or elsewhere, but at the time Bliss was lobbying for it, it sent collective chills through the British, French, and Zionist delegations. After all, despite lip service paid to tutoring the natives in self-government, for the British and French to control the area required the de facto denial of real democratic processes.

For their part, the Zionists were adamantly against democracy for Palestine until they had achieved a majority in the country. Chaim Weizmann, leader of the World Zionist Organization, put it this way: "the democratic principle, which reckons with the relative numerical strength and the brutal numbers, operates against us, for there are five Arabs to one Jew." Democracy, therefore, would be manipulated by "the treacherous Arab" to prevent the takeover of Palestine by the Zionists.[26] There is no evidence that American Zionists took any exception to this line of reasoning. Indeed, the influential American Zionist leader Stephen Wise wrote to the Jewish philanthropist Nathan Straus on April 22, 1920, that "the whole of Asia Minor is to be ceded to the Allies and disposition will later be made. In any event, for the present we are freed from the horror of Arab suzerainty, an indignity and dishonor which Jews could not have tolerated."[27] There were, however, many non-Zionist, liberal Jews who were bothered by such an antidemocratic stand.[28]

The dilemma the principle of self-determination presented in the case of Palestine was thus clear to all concerned. Both Secretary of State Lansing and David Hunter Miller, the legal adviser to the American delegation, told Wilson that, in Hunter's words, "the rule of self-determination would prevent the establishment of a Jewish state in Palestine."[29] Nonetheless, there seems to have been an unofficial consensus reached among Wilson, the British, French, and Zionists, that Palestine would simply constitute an exception to the rule—which in any case was already considerably watered down outside of Europe by the imposition of the mandate system. Woodrow Wilson, "son of the manse," agreed with and acted upon the position put forth by Lord Balfour in a revealing internal Foreign Office memo of August 11, 1919. Here Balfour explained that the Great Powers were committed to Zionism. And "Zionism, be it right or wrong, good or bad, is rooted in age-long traditions, in present needs, in future hopes, of far profounder import than the desires and prejudices of 700,000 Arabs who now inhabit that ancient land. . . . Whatever deference should be paid to the views of those who live there, the Powers . . . do not propose, as I understood the matter, to consult them."[30] Thus it was at a March 2, 1919, meeting with Zionist leaders that Woodrow Wilson told Stephen Wise, "Don't Worry Dr. Wise, Palestine is yours."[31]

Popular Perceptions of Palestine as Revealed in the Press

Peter Grose, in his book *Israel in the Mind of America,* has written that Americans took no great note of the Balfour Declaration.[32] This, however, does not tell us much. We know that most Americans do not pay attention to foreign affairs unless it somehow directly impacts upon them or calls upon their sympathies. The more important question is, of those Americans who did pay attention to Palestine, who cared enough to hold and express an opinion, what was their stand? It turns out that their opinions were very much in tune with the position of Lord Balfour.

There were no public opinion pollsters at the time when the Balfour Declaration was announced, and so popular attitudes have to be ascertained in a more indirect fashion. One way of determining these is to go to the newspapers, a source that at once reflected and influenced public opinion of the day. Here we shall focus on the *New York Times,* the paper which covered Palestine in the most consistent and complete manner. To supplement *Times* coverage, and get a sense of opinion in the rest of the United States, we shall also look at the *Washington Post, Chicago Tribune,* and *Los Angeles Times.* In 1917 these four newspapers together published some 150 articles on Palestine and/or the Zionist movement—the bulk of the coverage coming toward the latter part of the year, after the November 2 issuance of the Balfour Declaration, and the December 10 capture of Jerusalem by the forces of the British general Edmund Allenby.

The newspaper writing of the day was markedly different from that of modern reporting. The language used was flamboyant and, in terms of expressing prevailing cultural and religious prejudices, uncensored. It was not uncommon for reporters to editorialize as they reported a story. For our purposes this style proves helpful, as there will be little need to read between lines. It also must be kept in mind that in 1917 Palestine was a theater of war where the British engaged the Turks, who were the allies of Germany. By this year American attitudes toward the Turks were well defined and overwhelmingly negative. Turkish treatment of the Armenian and other "biblical people" of the Ottoman Empire had brought on a prolonged campaign by American missionaries for philanthropic aid. That campaign had successfully cast all Turks as unmitigated barbarians. And because most Americans did not know an Arab from a Turk, this stereotype tended to cast the Muslim Arab inhabitants of Palestine as also barbaric.

As discussed above, this general negative attitude toward the native inhabitants of the Middle East fit neatly into the bipolar worldview that structured American and European relations with the non-Western World. It had helped rationalize imperialism before the war and, despite Wilson's talk of self-determination, continued to do so, in the form of mandates, after the war. The assumption was that the peoples of the Ottoman Empire were sufficiently inferior that they needed Western tutoring before they could rule themselves. The reporters and editors of the American newspapers were as immersed in this worldview as were their readers, and thus, the information they did gather about the Palestinians was selective and packaged according to accepted norms. This filtration and contextualization process was repeated by the reader. In addition, the land of Palestine had long ago been "theocratized" into the "Holy Land" and had, essentially, been made into an extension of the Judeo-Christian West. All of this tended to predetermine how the newspapers would tell the Palestine story. As a result some basic questions were rarely or never asked: Who were the native Palestinians? What was the nature of their culture and civilization? And most of all, what were their hopes and desires for the immediate postwar future? It is likely that these omissions were not committed consciously. Rather, the questions probably never were thought of by most reporters and editors. Again, Balfour's judgment on the issue of native "desires and prejudices" was ubiquitous and an unconscious part of the larger way of seeing the non-Western World.

The basic picture of Palestine offered by the press in 1917 coalesced around two themes. First, contemporary Palestine was the same Palestine of the Bible. Three thousand years of history had not changed its essence, only overlayed it with a distorting facade of alien culture. Thus it was first and foremost the birthplace of Jesus and the ancient homeland of the Jews. Therefore, it properly belonged to the civilized, that is, the Western, Judeo-Christian world. Second, while Palestine had long suffered under the yoke of an alien and distortive culture—the latest manifestation of which was the oppressive regime of the Turks—it was now being liberated and redeemed by a "modern Crusade." General Allenby was literally picking up where Richard the Lionhearted had left off.

A good example of the Crusader theme that emerges from the press coverage was pictorially displayed by a large (5 by 6.5 inches) front-page political cartoon appearing in the *Chicago Tribune* on November 18, 1917. Under the title "The Holy City," there appears a two-story building in Jerusalem, beyond which the Turkish and British forces battle. In front of the building stands a Turkish soldier armed with both rifle and sword. At the balcony window on the second story of the building there is a woman leaning out with her right arm extended and an anguished look on her face. She wears a flowing scarf on which is written CHRISTIANITY. One is left with the impression that, in Jerusalem, there are three main constituents: the Turks, the British, and the Christian population whom the British have come to rescue. Given the highly sensitized state of awareness the Armenian massacres had created in the American public, there can be little doubt that most readers would interpret the cartoon as meaning that the Christian population of Jerusalem was held captive and in danger. The local Muslim population is omitted, or worse, subsumed into the image of the Turk. The Jewish population is also absent from the picture, but they could, as a "biblical people," be associated with the Christian image. Pictorially ("a picture is worth a thousand words") the message is clear: the "Holy City" is a Christian place in need of rescue by a Christian, civilized force—the British crusaders.[33]

A month later a similar message was given by yet another large (5 by 9 inches) front-page political cartoon appearing in the *Los Angeles Times* of December 23, 1917. In this picture, which bears the title "Christmas Greetings," we find a brick wall with Middle East–style buildings visible beyond. On the wall is printed in capital letters the word JERUSALEM. Standing on top of the wall is the oversized figure of a knight in armor blowing a long horn and carrying a great shield bearing the sign of the cross. In front of the wall carrying a Turkish flag are diminutive figures each with a long hooked nose and wearing a fez. They are all slinking away. It is tempting to speculate that the *Los Angeles Times* artist had seen the earlier *Chicago Tribune* cartoon, for the second cartoon finishes the story begun by the first. The threatening Turk is replaced by the hero crusader knight. The capture of Jerusalem is not just a victory of the Allies over the Central Powers; it has been transformed into the victory of Christianity over an alien people.[34] Again, the only Muslim presence shown is that of the Turks.

The message given by these front-page cartoons—that the war in the Near East is a fulfillment of the Crusades, and that the only significant Muslim presence in the Holy Land is an enemy of the civilized world—were reinforced by numerous articles appearing in all four of the newspapers under consideration. The following quotes are typical of the overall reportage. An October 28 editorial appearing in the *Washington Post* stated that "some of the greatest nobles of France and England have sought service there [Palestine] . . . in emulation of their crusader forebears."[35] In the November 20 issue of the same paper we learn that "millions of ardent Christians are fervently hoping that the near future will witness the Holy Land reclaimed from the control of the Moslem who for centuries has held uninterrupted sway over the birthplace of the Christian religion. . . . That event will be the cause of general rejoicing throughout the civilized world."[36] Again on December 11 the *Post* editorialized, "Jerusalem has been wrested from the Turk and Christendom once more possesses its holy city. To millions of devout worshippers this triumph is the greatest fact of the war."[37] On December 24 the same paper quoted the Speaker of the House of Representatives, Champ Clark, as concluding, "so far as war operations are concerned, the one thing that pleases most people most is the capture of Jerusalem, 'The Holy City.' That rejoices the hearts of Jews and Christians. . . . After these hundreds of years the dream of Peter the Hermit, Richard Coeur de Lion and their fellow crusaders is an accomplished fact."[38]

The *Los Angeles Times* played the story to the same refrain. On November 11 the paper reported that "today the British forces are traversing the same territory over which Richard Coeur De Leon [sic] fought in the crusades of old." The British are then characterized as "the twentieth century crusaders." Their goal is Jerusalem, and soon the "holy city of the Jewish and Christian religions alike" will be "delivered from the thousand year dominion of the infidel."[39] On December 12 an *L.A. Times* editorial stated that for "twenty centuries the conquering Moslem left the trail of his bloodstained sandal in cruel patterns on every road of that sacred soil. . . . and now for all mankind a great light has suddenly dawned. The dream of centuries has been realized. Jerusalem has been redeemed. . . . Never again will its sacred stones be defiled by the rule of the infidel and pagan."[40]

The *Chicago Tribune* of November 19, 1917, took a similar though somewhat less vitriolic approach. In an article entitled "British Seize Jaffa, City of Biblical Fame," Jaffa is described not as a contemporary Arab city but, as the headline emphasized, as "Solomon's port and . . . the place from which Jonah took passage to Tarshish." In the same piece we learn that "The belief is strongly held at the Vatican that the Turkish crescent no longer flies over the Holy land. The Pope is eagerly awaiting confirmation of news to that effect. . . . He considers the recovery of the Holy Land one of the greatest triumphs of Christianity."[41] A week later, on November 27, the *Tribune* reinforced this message by explaining to its readers that Allied military action in Palestine was designed, in part, to "liberate Jerusalem from Mohammedan rule."[42]

In an editorial on March 9, 1917, the *New York Times* wrote, in reference to Jerusalem, "the grievance that so moved the Crusaders—the ruling of the city considered holy by more people than any other, by a race to whose members its associations are subjects of scorn—would at last be removed if the Turks were expelled."[43] The *Times* waxed poetic on this subject on March 14, with the publication of a poem by O. C. A. Child entitled "Jerusalem":

> Again the Briton nears the ancient gates!
> The city of the Holy Sepulchre . . .
> . . . .
> Perchance the ghost of grim Saladin
> A scimitar across their path may fling
> Yet shall one wave them onward till they win—
> The wraith of England's Lion-Hearted King![44]

The *New York Times* would end the year still melding the present war in the Holy Land with a romanticized version of the Crusader past. On December 11, it explained the British war effort in the area this way: "So, first under Maxwell, and then under Murray, and now under Allenby, a new crusade to recover the Holy Sepulchre and all that it materially and symbolically stands for was conceived, put into execution and carried out."[45]

There are numerous additional examples of reporting in which Palestine is similarly presented as a biblical land somehow transformed into the present and rescued from the Muslim "infidel" by a latter-day Crusade.[46]

There were, in turn, only a few exceptions to this presentation. In an interesting piece on December 11, 1917, a *New York Times* reporter, referring to the British "crusade" in Palestine, commented: "paradoxical as it may seem, the auxiliaries in this new crusade are coreligionists of the Turks—the fellahin of Egypt and the Arabs of the new Kingdom of the Hejaz, who, having recovered the Moslem holy places [the reporter is referring to Mecca and Medina in Arabia], are ready to aid Christians to recover theirs."[47] Even with this rare exception to the rule, where Arabs are differentiated from the Turks, they are absented from Palestine. And Jerusalem, the third-holiest city in Islam, is reserved exclusively for the Christian (Western) world. Other occasional references produced the same effect, describing Arabs within the context of the anti-Turkish revolt of the sherif of Mecca carried on outside of Palestine.[48]

For most American readers, whose knowledge of Palestine was limited to biblical references, missionary tracts, and the occasional Christian travelogue, this picture of the "Holy Land" and the British military action taking place there was culturally compatible and reinforcing of all they knew and believed of the Near East. It was also inaccurate—a combination of myth and stereotype. There was a viable local Arab culture and economy, real people living real lives. But by concentrating on biblical and crusader analogies, the press simply negated 1,300 years of Muslim civilization in the area. The overall result was that the newspapers drew a portrait of an area "perceptually depopulated" of its indigenous majority population and culture. It was the journalistic equivalent of "ethnic cleansing." The effect of this sort of reporting became all the more significant when, in November of 1917, the British issued the Balfour Declaration. For, having subtly emptied Palestine of one people, these same newspapers were now poised to confirm that land's suitability as the "national home" for another people who were themselves compatible with the West's religious image of the region.

Shifting the Emphasis to a Jewish Palestine

In the first ten months of 1917, only the *New York Times* treated Zionism as a subject of interest. However, in the last two months of that year, after the Balfour Declaration had been issued and the British were securing their hold on Palestine, most of the four major newspapers under consideration began publishing pieces on Zionist goals in Palestine with increasing frequency.[49] These articles often tied Zionist aspirations, the Allies' war efforts, American traditions, and Wilsonian idealism together against the backdrop of altruistic imperialism. This tendency would persist over time as American Zionists sought to describe their ends in terms of American traditions and foreign policy goals. For instance, quoting Rabbi Rudolph I. Coffee on November 24, the *Chicago Tribune* informed its readers that "Within a few days Jerusalem will fall into the hands of the British. Now comes the glorious news that Palestine will be given to the Jews. This is part of the plan to make the world safe for democracy."[50] The *Washington Post* of November 29 quoted Jacob de Haas, an American Zionist leader and close associate of Brandeis, explaining that "The establishment of a Jewish state under the protection of the allies, will forever defeat the Kaiser's Berlin to Baghdad scheme and eject the Turk from civilized boundries."[51] On December 12 the *Post* carried a longer piece which described the "return of the Jews to Palestine after an enforced exile of nearly 2,000 years" as "one of the wonderful romances of all history." The story also connected a Jewish Palestine to U.S. history and character, a point which suggests that Americans linked the Zionist "pioneer character" with America's own pioneer traditions: "it is believed that thousands of more American Jews will go [to Palestine]. These will be Jews who have immigrated into our own West and who are expected to carry with them into Palestine the American spirit and the characteristics of American settlers." Later this same article evoked the power of biblical analogy in its description of the return of some 9,000 Palestinian Jews who had, at the beginning of the war, fled into British Egypt. "These 9,000 children of Israel are now ready for the second exodus, 3,117 years after their first homeward migration. This time the British government will be the Moses who will . . . give to a people without a land a land without a people. All that region that is to millions of Christians a Holy Land, whose history is part of the knowledge of every cultivated mind . . . [and] is, in the year 1917, a field for the pioneer homeseeker as the primeval forests of equatorial Africa."[52]

The redefining of demographic reality is continued when we turn our attention to the *New York Times*. Here the coverage was more extensive. In 1917, the *Times* published nearly one hundred articles covering Zionist activities and the war in the region of Palestine. The picture painted by the *Times* was somewhat different from that of the other newspapers, in that the Jewish population of Palestine was given greater emphasis, even more so than the Christians. Also, as we have seen, the *New York Times* recognized the Arab nature of surrounding areas of the Near East, particularly in its coverage of the Arab rebellion in Arabia. Yet Palestine, and especially Jerusalem, were different. For example, on March 9, 1917, an editorial described Baghdad as "The city of the Caliphs,"[53] while a week later another editorial described Jerusalem as "the city of Abraham, of David, of Solomon, and of Jesus; the city too of Titus and Tancred."[54] Baghdad is conceded to the Muslims, but Jerusalem is a city of the Judeo-Christian world.

The only exception to this pattern in 1917 was an article printed in the *New York Times* on December 12 describing a speech given in Manchester England by Sir Mark Sykes. Sykes was an important adviser to the British Foreign Office and the man who had signed the Sykes-Picot Agreement dividing the Middle East between Britain and France. In this piece he explained that it was "vital for the success of the Zionist plan that it should rest upon a Jewish, Armenian, and Arab entente." Sykes warned the Zionists "to look through Arab glasses" as they sought to be "bona fide colonists" in Palestine. He drew special attention to Jerusalem, which he described as "inflammable ground" where "a careless word or gesture might set half a continent aflame. . . . Cooperation and good will from the first is necessary or ultimate disaster would overtake both Jew and Arab."[55] Unfortunately the *New York Times* reporters and editors did not investigate further the reasons for Sykes's prescient warnings, and the inherent recognition of the Arab presence in Palestine that they implied.

It was hard for the readers of the *New York Times* to "look through Arab glasses" when 95 percent of the paper's coverage concentrated on the British "crusade," the Zionist cause, or, in terms of the indigenous population, just the small percentage of the Palestine population that were Jewish. One way this last-mentioned concentration was accomplished was by reporting on the wartime suffering of the Palestinian Jews without reference to other segments of the population. Throughout the months of May and June 1917, the *Times* devoted thirteen articles to the deteriorating condition of the Jewish population. In these pieces, the Jews were alleged to be in danger of eviction, starvation, and "wholesale massacre."[56] While, as we shall shortly see, this reporting was generally exaggerated, its main fault lay in concentrating on the hardship of one segment of the population when suffering was shared by all.

During the first half of the year the *Times* coverage (some of it reprinted from another paper, the *Jewish Chronicle*) built up expectations of imminent disaster for the Jews of Palestine. This was often associated with the draconian policies of the Turks, who shifted populations about and confiscated food and animals in their war effort against the British. Then, on June 9, the paper momentarily reversed itself by reporting that Abram I. Elkus, the returning U.S. ambassador to the Ottoman Empire (who was himself Jewish), had informed "Rabbi Messinger, Second Chairman of the Swiss Zionist Society . . . that, according to his reports, no massacre [of Jews] had taken place up to the present, the rumors that massacres had accompanied the Jaffa evacuation being untrue."[57] Elkus went on to explain that wartime conditions had deteriorated for the entire population of Palestine. Turkish authorities had become increasingly arbitrary and oppressive toward everyone, particularly those whose loyalty was judged suspect. This included not only many Zionist Jews, but also elements of the Arab population. Only twice in the year's coverage did the *New York Times* allude to this fact, as when, on June 19, it reported Ambassador Elkus explaining that "The whole population of Jaffa, Moslem, Christian and Jew[,] was moved away for military reasons, then moved back. There was much incidental suffering, but no deliberate massacre."[58] Elkus's disclaimer did not prevent the *Times* from printing numerous additional later pieces which continued to give the impression that the Jews were the principal sufferers in Palestine.[59]

When it became apparent that attacks upon Jews had been exaggerated, the reporting began to focus more on the issue of hunger. Again, the Jewish population was depicted as the one in most distress. Sometimes this appeared to be confirmed by official sources. For instance, on December 10, 1917, the *New York Times* quoted the Reverend Otis A. Glazebrook, the U.S. consul in Jerusalem, as stating, "In the Holy Land the burden of misery will fall upon the Jews who predominate. They are in no danger of guns or persecution from the Turks. They are in danger only of starvation and that danger becomes greater everyday."[60]

The truth, however, was again to be understood in a more general context. There was hunger in Palestine, and the Jewish population, particularly in Jerusalem, was hard hit because traditionally they subsisted on subsidies from abroad, much of which came from countries no longer having ready and reliable ways of sending help to Palestine. But the general conditions affecting food supplies described by Glazebrook, such as "the complete and ruthless sacrifice of needs of the civilian population, to those of the army"[61] affected everyone, though one has to read carefully and analytically to understand this. Finally, it is hard to know what to make of the consul's assertion that the Jews "predominate" in the Holy Land. It was a factually incorrect statement, which should have been obvious to a consular official resident in Palestine. It is possible that Glazebrook meant to refer only to the city of Jerusalem, where there was a heavy concentration of Jews.

Taking its reportage as a whole, the *New York Times* presented Palestine as a place where a minority segment of the population was really the majority. Why did the *Times* give such play to Palestine's Jews? This was not the case with the other three papers, all of which achieved a similar effect by stressing the Christian population. The *New York Times* decision to concentrate on the Jews can, perhaps, be explained first by the fact that the paper was owned by a Jewish (though non-Zionist) family, and second by the makeup of the city in which the paper was located. New York's Jewish community was larger than those of the three other cities hosting newspapers under consideration. It was also the place of residence of many American Zionist leaders, who, anxious to disseminate information about the Jews and Palestine, doubtless made themselves available to the city's newspapers. Also, as has been noted, the *Times* reprinted stories from other papers having a particular interest in Jewish affairs, such as the *Jewish Chronicle*.

Whatever the circumstances that led to the character of the *New York Times* reportage, the result was that Palestine's Arab Muslim history, culture, and people were again overlooked. The Turks were the principal Muslims mentioned in the vast majority of stories, but they were alien outsiders and the enemy.[62] Britain's victory meant the expulsion of the Turks. No Turks, no Muslims worth mentioning. This depiction did nothing to challenge or historically update the biblical view of Palestine held by many of the paper's readership. On the contrary, the paper's coverage confirmed that view.

Thus, for the readers of all four newspapers, a Palestine under British rule with special preference given to the establishment of a "Jewish National Home" must have seemed a logical consequence of the triumph of the British "crusade." It could also be envisioned as compatible with American experience and values, and even the fulfillment of biblical prophecy. The American pioneer and the British Moses go hand in hand, securely assuring the reader of the redemption (both spiritual and material) of a place which their upbringing had led them to firmly perceive as tied to the Western world.

Newspaper Coverage of Zionist Plans for Palestine

Against this background, the *New York Times* began, as early as April 1917, reporting on Zionist plans for Palestine. Some eighteen pieces would appear by the end of the year, with thirteen of these concentrated in November and December.[63] The coverage shows how Zionist claims fit in with the style and temper of the day. Earlier, in the *Chicago Tribune*, Rabbi

Coffee had described a Jewish Palestine as "part of the plan to make the world safe for democracy." Now the *Times* reported on June 24, 1917, that a Zionist convention meeting in Baltimore announced "The [U.S.] Government will be asked to recognize the Jewish nation as one of those oppressed smaller nationalities which must have an opportunity to assert themselves after the war."[64] This followed on the *Times* giving play to British explorer Harry J. Johnson's suggestion—subsequently used in the publications of "the Provisional Executive Committee for General Zionist Affairs"—that "it will be one of the many splendid achievements of this horrible war if we not only restore Poland's nationality but the Kingdom of Israel to the Jews."[65] Anticipating what would soon be one of President Wilson's Fourteen Points (the right of self-determination), which in turn would constitute an American war aim, the Zionists and their supporters redefined the Jewish people in such a way that they, like other Western nationalities (such as the Poles), could stake a claim to a state of their own. However, neither the Zionists nor the newspapers recognized the possibility of a conflict with an identical right of self-determination for the indigenous Arab population of Palestine.[66] Just so to those readers of the newspapers who were ignorant of contemporary Palestinian realities and/or saw them in terms of biblical analogies: no conflict would have been apparent.

Subsequent *New York Times* articles covered efforts by various Zionist groups to organize support for a Jewish Palestine,[67] to raise money for both war relief in the Holy Land[68] and future use in "the creation of the Government in Palestine."[69] The *Washington Post* and the *Chicago Tribune* paralleled this reporting. On November 25, for example, the *Post* reported on a meeting of Zionist societies in Washington, D.C., celebrating the issuance of the Balfour Declaration. The article states that "the ideal of a Palestine nationalized by the Jewish race has already received the approval of Italy, France and the Holy See. . . . Zionists of Washington confidently expect an official utterance by Congress similar in purport to that of Great Britain."[70] On November 29 the same paper headlined an article "Asks D.C. Jews to Give $1,000,000," which describes "an appeal to the Jews of Washington for $1,000,000 toward the $100,000,000 fund to be raised by the Jews in the United States to establish Palestine as a Jewish state."[71] Some eight additional articles in a similar vein were published by the *Washington Post* in November and December.[72] Typical of six *Chicago Tribune* pieces on Zionist plans for Palestine was the Coffee article mentioned earlier, which, in addition to linking a Jewish Palestine with Wilsonian ideals, predicted that "in Palestine Jews can set an example of high ideals in government looking among other things to the abolition of poverty." Additional *Tribune* pieces bore such headlines as "Back to Jerusalem" and "For New Zion."[73]

Toward the end of 1917, the *New York Times* continued its reporting by covering several mass rallies held by American Zionists. Returning to Baltimore on December 16, "an historic gathering" of the Confederation of American Zionists was held, during which various resolutions were passed. One thanked the British government for issuing the Balfour Declaration and called upon "the Jews of the world to unite in the face of the eminient [*sic*] realization and the great hope for the restoration of Israel to its own land." This was then followed by another resolution which read, "the American Zionist Confederation congratulates the Arab people on the splendid achievement which they have made in the direction of an independent national life."[74] That this was reported by the *New York Times* with no sense of irony demonstrates that the paper's reporters and editors shared with their readers the same contextual blindspots that were perceptually depopulating Palestine of its indigenous people. No doubt the reporter and his editors realized that the latter resolution referred to the British promise of an independent Arab state as a consequence of the Arab revolt in alliance with the British war effort. Yet the unquestioned, and very likely unconscious, assumption was that Palestine was excluded from the area of any future Arab nation.

On December 23, at another rally covered by the *New York Times*, "thousands of New York Zionists packed Carnegie Hall" to celebrate "the British promise to restore Jerusalem and the Holy Land to the Jewish people." Among them were the Reverend Otis A. Glazebrook and Ambassador Abram I. Elkus. Both men would later become skeptical about Zionism. At the rally the war effort of the Allies and the postwar aims of the Zionists were once more tied together, as Stephen Wise, the American Zionist leader, told the crowd, "this meeting has been called in order to reaffirm the faith of every living American Jew not only in the certainty of the triumph of our arms, but in the righteousness of our aims." One of those aims, he pointed out, was represented by the Balfour Declaration. To this there was injected that vital ingredient, the requisitioned ancient past. According to another speaker at the rally the Balfour Declaration was not just "an act of politics or diplomacy, but something far deeper, a stage in the development of history which in effect added another chapter to the Bible, a modern chapter by which the Jews of today could link something of their own time to the story of the old Jewish Kingdom."[75] Thus from any number of perspectives, from the point of view of Western and American (Judeo-Christian) civilization, or from the point of view of biblical and religious tradition—all of which could be folded together as one positive, progressive, and righteous step ahead for mankind—the Balfour Declaration was something to celebrate.

Even those who did hesitate to give the declaration uncritical support were still bound up in this bipolar worldview and biblically conditioned perception of the situation. For instance, there was a *New York Times* op-ed piece of December 2, 1917, authored by Henry Morgenthau, another former U.S. ambassador to the Ottoman Empire (1913–16), who was also Jewish. This piece bears close reading, for Morgenthau had served in the Near East and knew the realities of contemporary Palestine. Yet much of what he says displays assumptions typical of Western views of the non-Western world at this time. Morgenthau begins with an acknowledgment that Jerusalem and the Holy Land had been for the last "twelve centuries" under "almost uninterrupted Mohammedan rule." Most of his audience would have equated this with Turkish rule, and not the presence of an indigenous Arab Muslim civilization. Indeed, Morgenthau himself dismisses this period as an uncivilized time when he characterizes the British victory in the region as follows: "Christians everywhere will rejoice that the Holy Land, so well known to them through both the Old and New Testaments, has been restored to the civilized world." Here he pinpoints the main source of American knowledge of Palestine, the Bible, and combines it with a standing prejudice, particularly popular as a rationalization for nineteenth-century European imperial expansion: that for the sake of civilization, the West, as the seat of progress, has not only a right, but a duty to take control, or at least influence the fate of non-Western lands. Given that "Mohammedan rule"—which he also equated with "curse of Turkish misgovernment"—was by definition not civilized, no mention had to be made of what else "twelve centuries of almost uninterrupted Mohammedan rule" might have wrought in Palestine. Had these long centuries created a viable, living Arab culture? Were not the political rights and expectations of the majority Muslims, built up over such a long time, worth consideration? All this was absent, and not because bringing them up to the audience he was addressing would have been impolitic. As we are about to see, Morgenthau did not refrain from pointing out that Palestine was of importance to more than the Jews. Rather, like most all of his contemporaries most of the time, he just disregarded the Palestinian Arabs.

Yet Morgenthau was quite aware that the Jewish claim to Palestine had to be viewed within a larger context. Thus he goes on to tell his readers:

"But not only the Jews are interested in Palestine . . . and this is what I beg my Jewish fellow religionists not to lose sight of for a moment, all Christendom too, looks upon Palestine as the Holy Land, in which every believing Christian has a deep religious interest and a right to share." Clearly, for Morgenthau as for Balfour, the Holy Land was a part of the Judeo-Christian birthright. Unlike Sir Mark Sykes, it was not "Moslem glasses" that the Zionists must look through, but rather Christian ones. On this basis he concluded that the setting up of a "limited nationalist state" would be an "error" and advocated a Palestine administered "under an international and inter-religious commission."[76] It was a suggestion that the Zionists would ignore. Later, Morgenthau would find himself in disagreement with many Zionist positions.

Jewish Opposition to Zionism

Morgenthau's ambivalent attitude toward Zionist goals reveals that not all Jews favored a Jewish-dominated Palestine. The *New York Times* was the only one of the four papers to report Jewish opposition to the Zionists. However, as it turned out, this opposition was not based on any recognition of the Palestinian Arabs, nor, with one exception given below, did the *Times* coverage of this opposition shed any greater light on Palestinian realities.

The first hint of Jewish opposition to Zionism in the *New York Times* came on May 24, 1917. The story came not from the United States but from England, and concerned English Jews. The Joint Foreign Committee of two Jewish organizations, the Board of Deputies of British Jews and the Anglo-Jewish Association, had issued a statement on Zionism which contained the following section: "the feature of the Zionist program objected to purposes to invest Jewish settlers in Palestine with special rights over others. This would prove a calamity to the whole Jewish people who hold that the principle of equal rights for all denominations is essential. The proposal is all the more inadmissable because the Jews probably will long remain in the minority in the population of Palestine, and because it might involve them in most bitter feuds with their neighbors of other races and religion."[77]

Here we see a leading group of English Jews taking note of the minority status of the Jews in Palestine, and pointing to the consequences of asserting special rights stemming from national claims. Note the objection also speaks to the issue of democratic practices and the inherent contradiction between Zionist assertiveness and democracy (as long as the Jews remained a minority in Palestine). This issue and its negative implications were never explored by the *New York Times*, nor did the paper ever broach the subject again, notwithstanding relatively extensive coverage of other Jewish doubts about the Zionist program. Also, the *New York Times* did not follow up on the story by reporting the fate of those who put forward these objections. The above statement calling into question aspects of Zionist ambitions was signed by David L. Alexander, president of the Board of Deputies of British Jews. On June 18, 1917, the London *Times* reported that he and other officers of the board had been forced to resign because the membership of that organization (including Lord Rothschild, to whom Balfour would later address his Declaration) expressed "profound disapproval of such views."[78]

The American Jewish opposition, as reported by the *New York Times*, seemed no more concerned with the demographic realities of Palestine or their implications for the practice of democracy than did Lord Rothschild. Rather, the most common anti-Zionist argument used by the Jewish opposition was that a national home for the Jews in Palestine would weaken the citizenship rights of Jews elsewhere. Rabbi Samuel Schulman, writing in a piece the *Times* picked up from another paper, the *American Hebrew*, stated that Jews, "feel and believe that their position in the Western world depends upon the maintenance of the principle that they belong to the nation in whose midst they dwell. . . . They have always rejected as an aspersion animated by anti-Semitic motives, the thought that they were aliens. The Jews in the Western lands cannot conceal from themselves the sinister possibilities that may result from the emphasis of Jewish nationality. Anti-Semites all over the world may seek maliciously to emphasize for them their hyphenated nationality."[79] This was the same argument that Lord Edwin Montagu, the highest-ranking Jewish member of the British government, had unsuccessfully employed against the Balfour Declaration.

Another interesting objection was offered by Henry Moskowitz in a long op-ed piece printed on June 10, 1917. The author asked, "what are the serious moral dangers in this nationalistic point of view from the standpoint of the Jewish soul? Here are some of them: First it is apt to breed racial egotism. . . . the establishment of the Jewish state may coarsen the quality of Hebrew spirituality and result not in a pure but in an alloyed idealism." Though this statement offered insight into the ramifications of statehood for the Jews, it did not concern itself with the democratic rights of non-Jews in Palestine. As so many non-Zionist Jews did, Moskowitz and Schulman favored cultural and religious settlement. Thus, Moskowitz found acceptable "the encouragement and financial support . . . given to Jewish colonies in Palestine" because they "help solve the problems of those Jews who have sought a refuge from persecution."[80] What these critics failed to realize was the disruptive potential of any mass influx of Western immigrants into Palestine, no matter what their motives. The consequent relegation of the non-Jewish indigenous population to the never-never land of irrelevancy, found even among the American Jewish opponents of Zionism, speaks to the pervasiveness of the bipolar worldview of the day. Helped along by historical ignorance, and subsequent "perceptual depopulation" of the Holy Land's Arab Muslims, it limited the scope of opposition to Zionism and made possible the coming transformation of Palestine.

The *New York Times* brought out its own editorial on Zionism on November 24, 1917. It emphasized that many Jews were wary of Zionism either because they were Orthodox Jews who "still cherish the belief that the return to Zion is to be preceded by the coming of Elliah *[sic]*," or because "they fear that the Zionist project might involve the possibility of a recurrence of anti-Semitism" in the Diaspora. The editors concluded that a study of "the practical working of attempts at repatriation wherever they have been made would serve as a safeguard against errors which might be committed under the guidance of yearning and idealism."[81] What errors did the *New York Times* editors have in mind? Certainly there is no evidence pointing to any concern over the possible violation of the rights of the indigenous majority population. In nearly one hundred articles the Palestinian right of self-determination had never been raised. Instead, by concentrating on the Zionist movement, the paper had simultaneously emphasized the possibility and legitimacy of repopulation through "repatriation" even while belatedly suggesting that the process needed study to avoid the unspecified "errors" of "idealism."

The only other of the four newspapers to editorially call into question Zionist plans for Palestine was the *Los Angeles Times*. The editors of this paper brought out two editorials about Palestine and the Zionists. The first, entitled "What of Jerusalem?" appeared on the 27th of November and reflected the editors' fears that "an independent and unguarded Hebrew nation . . . occupying Palestine would not last long. It would soon be the prey of greedy neighbors as in ancient days. The United States should not be asked to alone play big brother to the resurrected Jewish nation. . . . it appears to the [L.A.] *Times* that at present we have too much on our hands to embark in the colonization of Palestine and rebuilding and repeopling of Jerusalem."[82] This apprehension may have been generated by the fact that in 1917–18 the British had periodically, though not very seriously, suggested that the United States accept a mandate over Near Eastern territory. Knowledge of this effort may have led the *Los Angeles Times* editors into believing that the United States could end up with responsibility for a Jewish Palestine. Here the editors' isolationist leanings seemed to have momentarily overcome their interest in reviving biblical Israel, at least under the official auspices of the United States. Even so, it is important to note that the paper's editors had no principled objections to the "colonization," "rebuilding," and "repeopling" of Palestine. Such language could only be used by people working from within a bipolar worldview that assumed the altruistic nature of imperialism.

In a second editorial, published on December 24, 1917, titled "Will the Jews Return?" the fears of the *Los Angeles Times* editors of any official American responsibility for the "colonization" of Palestine seemed to have been allayed. Here they asked the question "what of Jerusalem? The question that gave much concern to David, the psalm-singer of Israel, is today uppermost in the minds of the Christian world. Will the Jews return to the land of their fathers? Only time will tell. . . . The Jewish state in Palestine may become one of the notable examples of democracy in the world of popular governments."[83]

It is apparent that, by late 1917, there were misgivings about Zionism.[84] What is important to note, however, is that most of it was expressed in as ethnocentric language as was Zionism itself. Most of the Jews in America knew no more of the demographic and cultural realities of Palestine than did their Christian fellows. The over one thousand years of Arab cultural, religious, and political existence in Palestine were largely unknown. And at those rare times when such facts did surface, as in Henry Morgenthau's observations, they were quickly set aside as part of an uncivilized hiatus. The Zionist leadership, on the other hand, was in contact with Jewish communities in Palestine and may well have had a clearer and more accurate picture of Holy Land demographics. However, they did not make a point of it. And when, as in the case of the British Joint Foreign Committee, other Jews pointed out that Zionist ambitions pursued in the presence of a non-Jewish Arab majority were bound to bring "bitter feuds," the message was immediately stifled. In any case, most of those who did object to Zionist aspirations in Palestine did not do so out of concern for the rights of indigenous non-Jewish peoples. The "perceptual depopulation" of Arab Palestine, operating within the context of a colonialist bipolar worldview, allowed objections to the "repeopling" of Palestine to focus almost exclusively on possible negative consequences for the Jews themselves, and then primarily for those living in the Diaspora.

Consequences

In 1917 Palestine was a land filled with hundreds of thousands of Muslim men, women, and children. West of the Jordan River the land was dotted by hundreds of viable, productive villages, towns, and cities.[85] The existence of this society, in an area of long-standing interest to many Americans, was an observable fact. Indeed, there were scores of American Protestant missionaries who had lived for a century in the greater Syria area of which Palestine was a part. These missionaries communicated regularly with their leadership in the United States, and that leadership was, in turn, influential with both the public and the government. Nonetheless, in the eyes of most of the American public and press, this Palestinian reality did not exist. This paradox was possible because the facts, though observed, were misinterpreted or dismissed as irrelevant. We are here confronted with the phenomenon of selective perception, by which we focus our attention on that which supports our cherished beliefs and interests. That which does not is disregarded or devalued to the point where it can be ignored. Arab society in Palestine contradicted the Holy Land *Weltanschauung* of the American people and press in 1917. It therefore had to remain unseen or denigrated, because to recognize it as real, vital, and legitimate would have upset a religiously sanctified perception of the area that drew almost exclusively from the Bible, and to a lesser extent from the Crusades. Although at least 1,300 years out of date and distorted by historical ignorance, the biblical and Crusader visions that abounded in the pages of U.S. newspapers were, in terms of ideas and perceptions, what General Allenby's troops were in terms of occupation forces. One held the ground in Palestine, the other reinforced an imaginary Palestine that "held ground" in the American psyche.

By the end of 1917 Palestine was in British hands. Seen by most as the "land of the Bible," Zion now presented a problem. The question was being publicly asked, What would be done with this Holy Land? From what has been described above, it follows logically that its future could only be one that was consistent with its image as an extension of the Judeo-Christian West. Also, with Palestine "perceptually depopulated," the landscape was assumed to be available for settlement. Repopulating it was to be made all the easier by the fact that Western attitudes in 1917 were still very much influenced by nineteenth-century colonial thinking.

Thus, Palestine became as much "a field for the pioneer homeseeker as the primeval forests of equatorial Africa."

The Zionists had the virtue of perceiving Palestine as their ancient homeland and being perceived by many Americans, their president, and press, to say nothing of the British, as most compatible with the Holy Land *Weltanschauung*. Being simultaneously of the West and biblically identified with Palestine, they were certainly in the right place at the right time. Thus, the notion that the British would now give "a people without a land, a land without a people" made perfect sense to Americans in 1917, because it was seen as religiously and historically logical. So it was that American perceptions of the Holy Land and Zionist visions of Palestine uniquely meshed.

The Balfour Declaration was obviously a product of its time. Its legacy would, however, remain ongoing. In the 1920s the American Zionists would build on the foundation now laid, and develop a campaign to mold both American popular and government opinion so as to increase support for their goals. To do so, all of the attitudes described above—the bipolar worldview, belief in an altruistic imperialism, and adherence to a biblical characterization of Palestine—would have to be maintained. Alongside them would be elaborated additional themes already suggested in the press, such as the Zionist as a reincarnation of the American pioneer. By the time America settled back into its preferred posture of isolationism following World War I, the stage was already set to argue that a Jewish Palestine should be considered an exception—a special part of the world with which Americans could and should identify.

3

Early Perceptions of Mandate Palestine

The 1920s began with a great and lasting confusion over the legal basis of the postwar mandates. The confusion lay in the belief that British control of Palestine (and French control of Syria) was "legal" because it was the product of an award or grant from the international community as represented by the League of Nations. That is, that the "international community" had called upon the British to take up a mandate in Palestine and create a national home for the Jews. This latter objective was also believed to have international endorsement because the Balfour Declaration was written into the prologue of the mandate document for Palestine. The notion that all of this had origins with the League could be based on the fact that the mandate system was laid out in Article 22 of the League Covenant, which formed part of the Treaty of Versailles. Thus, the British often referred to their actions in Palestine on behalf of the Zionists as part of a solemn obligation given to it by the international community.

This version of the story, which came to be widely accepted in the 1920s and thereafter, is in fact misleading or at best incomplete. The mandates for Palestine, and those in other parts of the world distributed to the victors after World War I, did not originate with the League or with that vague entity, the international community. They originated with the victors themselves, who then used the League to lend legitimacy to and, after the fact, ratify their actions.

The Mandate System and the Spread of Empire

From April 19 to 26, 1920, the British and French met at the Italian seaside resort of San Remo to work out the outlines of a postwar settlement in the Middle East. It was at this meeting that they carved up much of the the defeated Ottoman Empire, and assigned themselves the spoils in the form of mandates. Some have argued that this was, in fact, a League of Nations meeting.[1] However, the Allies themselves had created the League just a few months before, in January of 1920, and the organization was, in terms of postwar settlements, in no position to do more than reflect British and French desires. Even so, it would be over two years (July 24, 1922) before the League got around to officially ratifying the British mandate for Palestine. Upon doing so it created the basis for the assertion that the mandate, and the Balfour Declaration which was written into it, were both "enshrined in international law."[2]

American Zionist reaction to the San Remo Agreements, wherein Britain gave herself the Palestine mandate, was overwhelmingly positive. Both San Remo and the Zionist reaction were covered in the press, especially the *New York Times*. For instance, on May 12, 1920, the *New York Times* described a rally and march of some forty thousand people in New York City. They carried "banners with inscriptions of gratitude toward the San Remo Conference for awarding the Palestine Mandate to Great Britain."[3] The notion of an "award" from an international conference, the real nature of which (a gathering of the victors) was not described in the story, lent legitimacy and respectability to the mandate even before the League of Nations came into the equation. As the *Los Angeles Times* put it later, citing British colonel Ronald Storrs, the action taken at San Remo presented the Palestine mandate as "the high and noble task placed on our shoulders by the voice of nations."[4] The jump was thus effortlessly made from divison of the spoils of war to "awards" made by the "voice of nations."

According to agreements made between President Wilson and the British and French at the Versailles Peace Conference in 1919, mandates would eventually be sanctioned and supervised by the League of Nations. Thus in Article 22 of the League Covenant the purpose of the mandates was defined as follows:

1. To those colonies and territories which as a consequence of the late war have ceased to be under the sovereignty of the states which formerly governed them and which are inhabited by peoples not yet able to stand by themselves under the strenuous conditions of the modern world, there should be applied the principle that the well-being and development of such peoples form a sacred trust of civilization and that securities for the performance of this trust should be embodied in the Covenant.

2. Certain communities formerly belonging to the Turkish empire have reached a stage of development where their existence as independent nations can be provisionally recognized subject to the rendering of administrative advice and assistance by a Mandatory until

such time as they are able to stand alone. The wishes of these communities must be a principal consideration in the selection of the Mandatory.

The British and French did not take this wording seriously. After all, if they had, the French would not have been able to move into Syria at all, for the ignored King-Crane Commission report had shown that, outside of coastal Lebanon, no one in that region wanted anything to do with a French mandate. Just so the people of Palestine: they had registered their preference for unification with an independent Syrian state rather than a British mandate and had overwhelmingly rejected the whole idea of a Jewish National Home.[5]

Nor did the British take seriously the idea of having to answer to the League of Nations for its conduct in a mandate territory such as Palestine. Lord Balfour made this very clear in a strikingly honest speech given before the League Council on May 18, 1922. The speech was occasioned by the fact that the League had been slow to ratify the mandates, and so Balfour was seeking to push the process forward, while at the same time reminding the League members not to take their authority over the mandates too seriously. "Remember," he told the council, "a mandate is a self-imposed limitation by the conquerors on the sovereignty which they obtained over conquered territories. It is imposed by the allies and associated powers themselves in the interests of what they conceived to be the general welfare of mankind." In other words, if there is any international law playing out here, it is the "law" of conquest. Furthermore, Balfour proceeded to make it clear that, whatever the convenant's noble words about the "well being and development" of the mandate peoples being a "sacred trust of civilization," it did not apply to Palestine. Referring to the development of a Jewish National Home, Lord Balfour told the council, "the general policy has already been decided, and is outside any discussion which could take place around this table. . . . Nobody need be under the least fear, and nobody, let me add, need entertain the least hope that those broad lines of policy are going to suffer any alteration."[6]

The real authority for the Palestine mandate did not lie with the League of Nations, or even in the "awards" made at San Remo. It rested in the simple fact that Britain had conquered Palestine and would do with it what it would, albeit under the guise of a mandate. The League of Nations was a fact of life that Balfour and others were willing to pay lip service to in the form of yearly reports to its Mandates Commission, but that was about it. As time went by, Britain would run Palestine like a Crown Colony.

The Full-Belly Approach Comes to Palestine

One of the themes that linked the Jewish National Home, the Palestine mandate, and idealistic international accords like the League covenant was altruistic imperialism. That is, the belief that both the Zionists who went to Palestine and the indigenous population would benefit from the British guided mandate. And, if the local people benefited enough economically, they would then be willing to share the country with the incoming European Jews. This is what is sometimes referred to as the "full-belly theory" of colonialism. As Winston Churchill told the Palestinians while visiting Jerusalem in April of 1921, "It is manifestly right that the scattered Jews should have . . . a national home in which they might be reunited, and where else but in Palestine, with which the Jews for three thousand years have been intimately and profoundly associated? We think it is good for the world, good for the Jews and good for the British Empire. And it is also good for the Arabs dwelling in Palestine, and we intend it to be so. . . . They shall share in the benefits and progress of Zionism."[7]

Despite their awareness of the of steadfast Arab opposition to Zionism, Balfour, Lloyd George, and Churchill seem to have held on to the hope, at least in these very early years of the mandate, that they could turn Palestine into a place of happy cohabitation. This can be seen in the final portions of Balfour's May 18 speech before the League Council. He told the council that, despite their having no meaningful say in the formulation and execution of the Palestine mandate, it was nonetheless important that they proceed to ratify it because "the task thrown upon the mandatory in Palestine is one that . . . requires for its adequate development the obtaining of large pecuniary resources. Unless we are able . . . to develop the economic capacities of Palestine to enable it to support a much larger population in much greater comfort than is at present possible, then our hopes as to the future of the country are no doubt doomed to disappointment. . . . Anything which postpones or even appears to postpone the final and definitive settlement of our problem [the ratification of the mandate] discourages the lenders and makes it more difficult to obtain their much needed assistance."[8]

The American Zionists and press also saw the Palestine mandate and the Balfour Declaration in this positive light. However, by 1920, out of our four newspapers analyzed, only the *New York Times* was giving much coverage to Palestine. The *Times* assured its readers in April of 1920 that "the building of a new Zion" would not undermine the Arabs' "property and legal rights."[9] On the contrary, the Zionist project would, as Nathan Straus, a philanthropic supporter of Jewish colonization, explained, "rehabilitate" the Holy Land after "hundreds of years [of] a criminally indifferent government."[10] In these early years of the mandate, the picture painted of the anticipated "new Zion" was that of a "humming mart of modern trade."[11] Agriculture too would be modernized, bringing into "cultivation vast areas of soil which are at present barren wastes."[12] More ominously the *Times* reported on a World Zionist Organization meeting in London, in July of 1920, where a resolution was adopted stating a major aim of the organization was "that all land in Palestine be declared the property of the Jewish people and that the control of this property be gradually assumed by the Palestinian state. . . . To permit the rapid possession of Palestine lands, the [Jewish] National Fund shall devise means whereby private capital can be utilized for the purchase of land under conditions which will assure subsequent transference of such lands into national possession."[13] How this was to be made compatible with the assertion that the Arabs of Palestine were sure to "share in the benefits and progress of Zionism" was not explained to the readers of the *New York Times*.

The Palestinian Arabs had immediately grasped the contradictions between the myth of altruistic imperialism and the realities of Zionist ends. The result was resistance that was well reported in the *New York Times*. As early as April 1920 Palestinian Arab leaders were warning British authorities of trouble if the Balfour Declaration was actually implemented.[14] Then, on April 8, 1920, the *Times* reported on "riots" in Jerusalem, commenting that "anti-Semitic feeling has developed acutely recently among the Arabs." In this piece the Zionist response was reported to be "we won the country by the sword and we will keep it by the sword."[15] The year 1921 saw rioting in Jaffa, and violence often made the headlines in American reporting on Palestine thereafter.[16] In truth, a low-level war had commenced between Arabs and Zionists that would go on indefinitely. The British response to this early violence was reported in the *New York Times* of April 17, 1920. Here the British government was said to have instructed General Allenby, then in charge in British Palestine, to "do everything possible to prevent trouble, but to ignore Arab proposals."[17] This policy would last until the latter part of the 1930s.

Early Press Perceptions

As described earlier, the West viewed Palestine as a Holy Land properly belonging to the peoples of the Judeo-Christian world. Such a viewpoint reduced the Muslim majority of that land to an unimportant status through a process of perceptual depopulation. On those relatively rare occasions when "the natives" were noted, it was assumed that altruistic imperialism in the form of the mandate and Zionism was to their benefit. Given such assumptions, a sympathetic understanding of Palestinian resistance was beyond the American people and press. Take, for instance, the *New York Times* editorial comment on Palestine of February 5, 1921, which asserted, "The mandatory [authority] is responsible for placing the country under such political, administrative and economic conditions as will secure the establishment of a Jewish national home and the development of self-governing institutions."[18] The inherent contradiction that this statement entailed prompted a follow-up editorial the next day to the effect that the Arabs need not worry, for whatever the mandate says about a Jewish National Home, its intent was "not a Jewish state."[19] Somehow, denying the open secret, repeated by Zionists in the *Times* itself,[20] that Zionism ultimately aimed for a state, made Zionism seem to be of little threat to the Palestinians. Likewise, the *Washington Post* just could not understand why the peoples of the former Ottoman Empire were so resistant to the newly established mandate system. On February 11, 1921, the *Post* editors observed that "it was supposed that they [the Arabs] would welcome the substitution of the enlightened rule of civilized countries like France and Great Britain . . . for the tyrannous and inefficient rule of the Sultan. But the expected enthusiasm failed to materialize, and the provinces of the former Turkish empire . . . showed that they preferred self-government with all its faults to good government under a foreign power."[21] In a bipolar world where mandates were an expression of altruistic imperialism, this choice seemed to make no sense.

This prevailing worldview led to unbalanced reporting in the American press, most of which was to be found in the *New York Times*. The idyllic "upbuilding" of Palestine by the Zionists and British was described in great detail despite the fact that the owner of the *New York Times*, Adolph Ochs, was a Jew who did not favor the creation of a Jewish state in Palestine.[22] What we may conclude from this is that the predominance of pro-Zionist pieces in the *New York Times* was not an editorial decision, but rather a reflection of the New York area's positive interest in Zionist activities. It also reflected a shared belief in altruistic imperialism on the part of both readers and reporters.

Thus, between 1921 and 1924 (and beyond) a continuing stream of articles described Zionist activities and their developmental prospects.[23] For instance, on February 17, 1921, the *Times* put out a piece entitled "Jews in Palestine Tillers of the Soil," which included the assertion that "nearly all the work on the land is being done by Jews."[24] On May 11, 1921, a day after the Jaffa riots, the *Times* ran an interview with Samuel Elfenbein, Zionist entrepreneur, who claimed to have "made a close study of the business prospects" of Palestine. "There is opportunity . . . for any one with capital and patience to build up big enterprises," he told the paper, and he was confident "that the political and racial troubles in the country will soon be composed enough to allow great development."[25] At the end of the year the same theme prevailed. On December 25, 1921, the *Times* quoted Professor Otto Warburg of the Kaiser Wilhelm Institute in Berlin, who was described as a Zionist "agricultural expert" (he was actually a physiologist), as predicting "the rapid development of the Holy Land into a source of fruit supply for all Mediterranean countries." Palestine is, he said, the "California of the East."[26]

In these years the comparison of Palestine to the United States developed into a popular and persistent tactic on the part of those Zionists seeking to build American support for their cause. It can properly be seen as a precursor to today's often cited claim that "Israel is the only democracy in the Middle East." In the 1920s this supposed affinity between Americans and the Zionists took the form of an analogy with the American pioneer experience. Accordingly, Zionism was transforming the Holy Land just as early English settlement and the subsequent western expansion had transformed America. Take for example the series of articles written by Bernard Rosenblatt, a leading spokesman for the Zionist Organization of America (ZOA), and published by the *New York Times* in June of 1922. In his article of June 11, subtitled "Progress of Jewish Settlement in Palestine That Continues Great Tradition," he tells his readers, "These immigrants to Palestine are indeed the Jewish Puritans." Their settlements are "the Jamestown and the Plymouth of the new House of Israel." The settlers are akin to "followers of Daniel Boone who opened the West for American settlers." They are "Jewish Pilgrim fathers . . . building the new Judea even as the Puritans built New England" while "facing the dangers of Indian warfare."[27] And just as in the case of the Pilgrims and the Puritans, "the Jews are bringing prosperity and happiness in Palestine."[28]

In a follow-up piece on June 25 entitled "Boom Town in Palestine,"

Rosenblatt, writing about Tel Aviv, said that "It can well be compared to one of our booming Western towns." He goes on to compare Tel Aviv to Los Angeles and describes it as a "melting pot" for Jews from around the world. Then he passes on to a comparison of Tel Aviv with its neighboring Arab town of Jaffa. "From Tel Aviv to the [Arab] port of Jaffa one passes from the twentieth century into the second century."[29]

To complement the Rosenblatt articles, the *Times* ran, in 1922, some eighty-eight additional pieces that favorably described Zionist and British activities in Palestine. Among these we find articles on public health,[30] the business climate,[31] and the successful American Zionist effort at fund-raising.[32] In 1923 and 1924, which were relatively quiet years in Palestine, coverage fell off a bit, but the pattern remained the same. Numerically, the Zionists and their cause got "good press."[33]

Critics and Doubters

Against this optimistic backdrop there were occasional critics and doubt-ers whose opinions did find their way into the press reports. The *Times* had a habit of checking the passenger lists of incoming ocean liners and then doing dockside interviews with people of note. In August of 1920 they met and interviewed John P. Peters, "rector emeritus of St. Michael's Episcopal Church" in New York City. He was just coming home from a trip to Palestine. To the question of what was the present situation in the Holy Land, he replied, "The great difficulty the British government has to contend with in Palestine is the bitter feelings on the part of the Moslems and the Gentiles toward the Jews. They believe that the latter are coming into Palestine to seize their property. They ask how Americans would feel if they saw a horde of foreigners coming in to grab their country."[34]

Then, in 1921, the *New York Times* sent its own "special correspon-dent" on a tour of Palestine. This was Talcott Williams, the former di-rector of the Columbia School of Journalism. Williams had a particular interest in the area, for he was born in Lebanon to missionary parents and spoke fluent Arabic. In his first piece, published on April 13, 1921, he repeated what Peters had related a year earlier. "The political horizon in Palestine is clouded," Williams reported, "by an agitation of Moslems and Christians against Zionists, who they believe are striving to obtain control of the country and drive the Palestinians out of business." However, those Jews who "speak Arabic and know the customs of the country" and have come "individually to invest capital in business" will find the "Moslems are friendly."[35]

But Zionism was not about individual Jews coming to "invest capital," and the Arabs knew that. In a later piece, Williams quoted Musa Kazim Pasha al-Husayni, a former mayor of Jerusalem. "We do not mind the Jews who have lived with us for many years," he said, "but we object to the so-called Zionists who shout 'Palestine for the Jews.' . . . If that is justified then the Arabs have the right to go to Spain and demand it as a national home because their ancestors lived there for 900 years."[36] Williams went on to report favorably on the "American Zionist medical relief" and Zionist agricultural efforts. He also interviewed Nahum Sokolow, chairman of "the Zionist Commission" in Palestine, who told him that "all that is needed to insure success is a continuous supply of dollars from the United States to keep the work of development going. . . . When the country is full of Jews from Europe and America—a million or two—it may be necessary to extend the colonization scheme across the Jordan."[37]

How were newspaper editors and their readers to make sense of these occasional contrasting views? The general acceptance of the paradigm of Palestine as Holy Land, now under the influence of altruistic imperialism, was bound to dictate their understanding of the situation. Arab concerns were reduced to native ignorance or idiosyncrasy. Thus, when in July of 1922 the Arabs held protest strikes against the League of Nations' ratification of the British mandate for Palestine, the *Times* report attributed this "inflamed" state to the fact that the Arabs were "an impulsive race."[38] The *Los Angeles Times* went further and, in an editorial on the ratification, implied that the Arabs did not know a good thing when they got it. Speaking of the mandate, the *L.A. Times* asserted that "in the case of Palestine nothing but good is likely to result," for it means "a program of plain development for the country for the benefit of its inhabitants. And if the future settlers come chiefly from the race that originally possessed it, why, there is nothing under the mandate to prevent it. . . . Zion rejoices and nobody can find an exploitable grievance."[39]

The 1922 Joint Congressional Resolution

A case study of the strength of the paradigm described here can be found in the House of Representatives' hearings held on the 1922 Joint Congressional Resolution in support of the Balfour Declaration. The events that led to this resolution began on March 30, 1922, when a delegation of Massachusetts Zionists paid a visit to their senator, Henry Cabot Lodge, to urge him to introduce a resolution in the Senate in support of the Balfour Declaration.[40] Lodge, who had made his reputation resisting United

States "entanglements" in European affairs (including the ratification of the Versailles Treaty), was, however, coming up for reelection. He therefore agreed to the Zionist request, commenting that "I feel that the effort of the Jewish people to establish a national home in Palestine is not only natural, but in all ways to be desired."[41] Almost simultaneously, a delegation of New York State Zionists approached their representative in Congress, Hamilton Fish, with the same request, and he too agreed.

Both men consulted Secretary of State Charles Hughes, who, on April 11, wrote to Lodge that he had "no objection" to such a resolution, and even went so far as to suggest wording for the text.[42] Why was Hughes so forthcoming? Perhaps because as an appointed officer of an elected president, he was as desirous as Lodge to accommodate an organized group of voters. Whatever the case, Hughes's helpful reply was almost certainly made without prior consultation with the State Department's Division of Near Eastern Affairs (NEA). As we shall see, the personnel in this section of the State Department, led by Allen Dulles, opposed U.S. support of Zionism, arguing instead for a neutral stance on the Jewish movement.[43] Dulles and his companions were career civil servants and thus not subject to the interest group pressures applied to those in elected and appointed offices. They were, moreover, tied to a traditional definition of U.S. interests in the Middle East, which included such things as the missionary endeavor and trade, but not Zionism. Indeed, tying the country to the Zionist cause could only alienate the Arab population, with whom an expansion of economic relations was sought, and get the U.S. "entangled" in the affairs of a British sphere of influence. If Hughes was concerned about such entanglements, the only evidence of it at this time was his instructions to Lodge and Fish to change the resolution wording from the United States "supports" a Jewish National Home in Palestine, to the United States "favors" such a home.[44] The secretary's cooperation with Lodge and Fish seemed to signal State Department acquiescence in their efforts.[45]

Before the resolution went to Congress for a vote, the House Committee on Foreign Affairs held hearings on the issue (Lodge never allowed such hearings in the Senate). These hearings, orchestrated by Hamilton Fish, who was himself a Zionist, were held against the backdrop of an organized Zionist effort to get their ZOA members to promote the resolutions as "a local issue with Representatives and Senators who sought election."[46] The hearings were held between April 18 and 21, 1922. Fish brought in such Zionist leaders as ZOA president Louis Lipsky to testify. A number of pro-Palestinian American witnesses, among them academics such as the Yale professor Edward Bliss Reed (the grandson of Daniel Bliss), also appeared. These latter witnesses were probably called on the recommendation of the missionary establishment, which by now was not so sanguine about Zionism.

Also included in the list of those who appeared were Arab Americans who were now organizing themselves to debate the issue of Palestine with the Zionists. This is a little-known piece of history that deserves more attention from historians of the Arab-Israeli conflict. Notable here was Fuad Shatara, a Palestinian-born American citizen then practicing medicine in New York. He came before the committee representing an organization called the Palestine National League. In his testimony Shatara explained the Palestinian position:

> The Arab people of Palestine ask, first, that a national government shall be created that will be responsible to a parliament elected by those inhabitants of Palestine that live there—Christians, Mohammedans, and Jews. Second, the abolition of the present policy in Palestine to regulate the immigration, which is to be controlled by this national government according to the capacity of the country to support new immigrants. Those people [the Zionists and the British] say "We are the judges of the capacity. . . ." [But] it is for us [the Palestinians] to say who we shall admit and refuse from coming into our country.

Shatara went on to call for an investigation of the situation in Palestine by a "neutral commission" and that Congress suspend judgment on the matter until it saw the report of such a commission. Essentially, Shatara was asking for an updated repeat of the largely forgotten King-Crane Commission. "We are willing to abide by the report of a neutral commission into the affairs of Palestine prior to settling this question," he told the committee.[47]

It was to no avail. Representative Fish was determined to push the resolution through, and the members of the Foreign Affairs Committee were incredulous of the information and positions taken by those who spoke against the Zionists. Indeed, the tone taken by Hamilton Fish toward Shatara and other Arab Americans during the hearings was often that of a prosecuting attorney. Others on the committee viewed the matter through a number of distorting stereotypes. Representative W. Bourke Cockran of New York likened Jewish immigration into Palestine to the white man's arrival in the New World,[48] and Representative Henry Allen Cooper of Wisconsin refused to believe there was a significant socialist element among the Zionists in Palestine (a subject we shall consider shortly) because, he asserted, the Jew was "proverbially a believer in private property."[49] The attitude of these men reflected the prejudicial view held by the Congress as a whole. Cindy Lydon, in a piece entitled "American Images of the Arabs," tells us that "a survey of Congressional opinion reveals that virtually no favorable characterizations of Arabs found their way into debates on Middle Eastern issues during the lengthy period from 1919–1931." Most of these debates had to do with Palestine, and in them "the Arab was depicted as backward, poor and ignorant," while Zionist colonialization held out the promise of turning "a ravaged and spoiled land" once more into a "land of milk and honey." Furthermore, Congress considered that aiding the Zionist movement was "in line with the principles of self-determination," that is, self-detemination for the "Jewish nation," and not for the unfit "backward" Arabs.[50]

In other words, the bipolar worldview and its corollary of altruistic imperialism held sway in Congress as it did in the rest of the country. Though it must have been a shock to the Arab Americans who naively felt that they could count on the universal application of such American principles as support for self-determination and democracy, the resolution easily weathered the congressional hearing. Both the House and Senate readily passed the joint resolution supporting the Balfour Declaration on September 11, 1922. President Harding signed it on September 21. The president felt that returning the "Hebrew people . . . to their historic national home" would allow them to "enter on a new and yet greater phase of their contribution to the advance of humanity."[51]

By 1922, that contribution was being assumed to have a character compatible with American values. As we have seen with Bernard Rosenblatt, the image of Zionism evolving in the American mind was now a recasting of the American frontier experience. Hamilton Fish, celebrating the victory of his resolution at a January 1923 dinner given in his honor by the American Zionist leadership, carried the theme even further. In a short speech which suggested not only the American sentiment on Zionism, but also the picture held by many Americans of the Muslim world, Fish avowed the open secret that what the Zionist movement really aimed at was a Jewish state in Palestine. Then he told his hosts, "I see a vision that if such a state is created . . . there will be a great republic, built on democratic principles standing between the two great Mohammedan worlds— that of Africa and Asia—standing between those warlike races as a guarantee to the peace of the world. . . . They will fashion their government after the ideals of ours and believe in our flag . . . because it represents freedom, liberty and justice and that is what we want to see eventually in Palestine."[52]

The Socialist Nature of Zionism in Palestine

It is testimony to the strength of this Westernized and also very American-ized vision of Zionism imbedded within the paradigm of the bipolar worldview, that it masked facts that, if faced with open eyes, would prob-ably have ended all American support for the Balfour Declaration and the Jewish National Home. We can make this assertion based on the fact that, while Hamilton Fish, Bernard Rosenblatt, and other Zionists were pro-jecting American values and traditions into Zionism, most of the Zionists actually resident in Palestine were singing the praises of the young Soviet Union and following a decidedly socialist path.

There can be no doubt that Zionism in Palestine from the 1920s on-ward was dominated by socialists. As Walter Laqueur tells us "labor Zion-ism emerged as [the movement's] strongest political force . . . for it shaped the character of the Zionist movement and subsequently the state of Is-rael."[53] The leader of this dominating socialist movement was none other than David Ben Gurion, who declared in 1921 that "we are following a new path which contradicts developments in the whole world except Rus-sia."[54] Thus, as Hamilton Fish was telling Americans that Zionists in Pal-estine would "fashion their government after the ideals of ours and believe in our flag," Ben Gurion was declaring that it was Palestine's destiny to be "developed as a socialist Jewish state."[55]

The evolving socialist nature of Zionism in Palestine was ultimately accepted and actively supported by most of the leaders of the World Zion-ist Organization. Men like Chaim Weizmann who were not themselves socialists nonetheless became convinced that only by following a socialist line of economic development could all available resources be directed toward the rapid absorption of a maximum number of Jewish colonists.[56]

In the early 1920s Weizmann observed that middle- and upper-class Jews from Europe or the United States were not moving to Palestine in significant numbers. Only the Jewish working class of Europe had the desire to immigrate in numbers high enough to "upbuild" Palestine and make it Jewish. Those relatively few Jews with money to invest who did immigrate and establish businesses behaved like good capitalists and hired the cheapest labor they could find. This turned out to be the local Arab population and not their fellow Jews.[57] In other words, the capitalist im-perative to maximize profits stood in opposition to the Zionist priority of providing work to the maximum number of colonists. Further, because the working-class immigrants were largely without resources, the WZO had to subsidize them by job creation and artificially high European-level wages in Palestine. This was necessary because without the maintenance of a European living standard, emigration would soon outstrip immigration. To create and maintain a congenial economy and the required level of subsidization would require not only a steady inflow of cash, but also socialist-style control of resources and profit.

American Zionist leaders were well aware of this turn of events. Louis Brandeis, leader of the Zionist Organization of America until 1921, fought against the move toward socialism, putting forth instead a vision of Zionism as a form of American Progressivism.[58] Indeed, he was eventually ousted from the leadership of the ZOA in part because of his inability to reconcile to the WZO policies. Yet the socialist nature of Palestinian Zionism never became common knowledge in the United States. The press hardly mentioned it. For instance, the *New York Times* published roughly 450 articles on Palestine and Zionism in the 1920s, and only 12 mentioned socialist activities in the Jewish colonies.[59] The ZOA leaders, who were the main source of information for the press, kept quiet about the whole subject except to deny its importance every time it did happen to come to public light. Typical of their public position on this matter was a letter to the *Times* by Emanuel Neumann, national director of the United Palestine Appeal (one of the fund-raising organizations seeking money to subsidize socialist development), in which he explained "it is not true that the labor organizations in Palestine are communistic. The communists are a mere handful, for the most part paid Soviet agents[,] and have not made any impression on the large number of organized workers."[60] Technically Neumann was correct. There was a difference between communists and socialists among the Zionists in Palestine. The socialists were the majority and the communists "a mere handful." However, within the context of a United States made paranoid by the Red Scare, it is doubtful if the distinction would have been appreciated by the American public had the facts been fully known.

The State Department was also receiving information on socialist activities among the Zionists. The American consulate in Jerusalem had noted the presence of "Bolshevik agents" and blamed them for the problems that were now developing between Arabs and Jews.[61] It should be noted that the Palestinian Arabs were also calling attention to Bolshevism among the arriving Zionists. The Executive Committee of the Arab Palestine Congress sent a message to the U.S. secretary of state, dated May 8,

1921, that stated, "We have repeatedly notified the governments of the Allies that the Jewish immigrants are introducing and spreading in Palestine the spirit and principles of Bolshevism. . . . We urgently demand again that the Jewish immigration should be stopped so that bloodshed and devastation in the country should come to an end."[62] This appeal went unanswered. Despite the fact that the United States was in mortal fear of both socialism and communism, the State Department could not get any more exercised over these allegations than could the press. In the department, as elsewhere, there was a general feeling that the "Bolsheviks" were small in number and the British could certainly take care of them.

One other reason that so little attention was paid to the socialist nature of evolving Zionism in Palestine was the stereotyped image of the Jew in the American mind at this time. Oscar Handlin, in an article entitled "American Views of the Jew at the Opening of the Twentieth Century," tells us that the Jew was seen as an "entrepreneurial, money-making personality."[63] This helps explain the disbelief, noted above, of Fuad Shatara's testimony before Congress that socialism was a popular ideology among the Zionists in Palestine. At that time Representative Henry Allen Cooper of Wisconsin had responded, "Do you think the Jew . . . proverbially a believer in private property, would circulate any law that would destroy private property?"

The constant drumbeat of progress and development pictured in the press and put forth by the Zionist leadership played to this theme. "There is room for capital and men in Palestine," Arthur Ruppin, head of the Zionist Department of Colonization in Palestine, told the *New York Times* in 1922. "Take an instance which will appeal particularly to the American—namely real estate. The American has the reputation of being the best developer of land values in the world. In Palestine there is room for real estate experts. Land can be bought either to be developed into urban quarters or garden cities. In both cases investment will pay."[64]

Ruppin put forth this bit of capitalist enticement even though he well knew that the WZO had set up the Jewish National Fund to buy and collectively hold all the land of Palestine as state land so as to ensure its status as "the inalienable property of the Jewish people."[65] Indeed, private speculation in and ownership of land was looked down upon by the WZO and Zionists in Palestine because it only drove up prices of land sought by the Jewish National Fund.[66] Ruppin's sales pitch about "real estate experts" and "investments" that "will pay" was simply an example of a Zionist leader tailoring his message to the audience—in this case Zionism as capitalism for the American community, from which WZO sought and received millions of dollars.

Thus, Americans paid little attention to the existence of socialism in Palestine. Superficial news coverage, concerted image building, and the existence of a traditional stereotype of the Jews combined to undermine the significance of Palestine's "Labour Zionism." For the Zionists it was a most fortunate combination of circumstances. Given the fact that in America the 1920s opened with the infamous Red Scare and witnessed growing fear of left-wing ideology, the truth about the socialist nature of Zionism in Palestine would likely have been fatal to ZOA efforts.

The Position of the State Department on Zionism

We must include a look at the State Department in this survey of attitudes toward mandate Palestine in the formative first half of the 1920s. The State Department of this period has been seen as hostile to Zionism and thus is not viewed with favor by American Zionists and their supporters. Frank E. Manuel, in an early study of what he titled *The Realities of American-Palestine Relations,* notes that, in the 1920s, the State Department saw the American Zionists as "a nuisance." He goes on to observe that "the Department of State and the Congress, of course, never thought alike on Palestinian affairs under any administration, because they moved in different orbits."[67] Peter Grose in his work *Israel in the Mind of America* makes the same observation. "Indeed, from 1917 all the way to 1948, United States policy toward Palestine was hung up on a contradiction. One set of statements would be forthcoming from Presidents and Congressmen . . . supportive of Zionism. Then another set of official 'policy' statements would come from the State Department presenting more guarded attitudes toward Jewish aspirations."[68] For pro-Zionist commentators the reason for this dichotomy is clear. It was because the department was seeded with those who were at best anti-Zionists, as Manuel and Grose portray them, or with anti-Semites, as Naomi Cohen, in her book *The Year after the Riots,* would have us believe.[69]

There can be no doubt that NEA was unenthusiastic about the Balfour Declaration. However, there is no reason to believe that this position was driven by a dislike for Zionism as an ideology or, worse, by anti-Semitic feelings. There were, in fact, traditional policy reasons to explain the positions taken by Allen Dulles and his NEA fellows. In a memo of May 26, 1922, concerning British behavior in mandate Palestine, Dulles gave the standard list of interests that had shaped American policy in the Middle

East since the nineteenth century. "The attitude of the Mandatory power towards American interests in Palestine, our philanthropic [missionary] and commercial interests as well as the capitulatory and other rights . . . is a question of real concern." These traditional categories were all compatible with the prevailing ideology of a bipolar worldview and altruistic imperialism. They also covered important specific interests, such as the strong assertion by the State Department that the United States had a right to compete for Middle East oil. However, the addition of new categories to the list of interests, such as the Jewish National Home, was approached with great caution bred of tradition—the traditional fear of entanglement in European political affairs. And that is just where Dulles and his companions thought official government support for Zionism would lead. From NEA's point of view, the issue of a Jewish National Home in Palestine was part of the internal affairs of a British mandate territory. And that being the case, Dulles observed that "the Department has no desire to interfere in matters which primarily concern the relationship between the mandatory power and the natives of Palestine."[70]

Therefore, when it came to Zionism, the position NEA decided to advocate was one of neutrality. As Dulles asserted on May 22, 1922, in a memo to Leland Harrison, the assistant secretary of state, he felt "strongly that the Department should avoid any action which would indicate official support for any one of the various theses regarding Palestine, either Zionist, [Jewish] anti-Zionist, or the Arabs."[71] As we shall later see, NEA adhered faithfully to this position throughout most of the interwar period. The result was a reluctance to put pressure on the British to do the things that the American Zionists desired. A good example of this can be found in a 1923 incident involving the issue of Jewish immigration into Palestine.

The question of Jewish immigration to Palestine came before the department in late October of 1923. At that time the Chief Rabbi of Kansas City, Simon Glazer, had an interview with President Calvin Coolidge in which he discussed the Zionist project and apparently asked the president to use the influence of the U.S. government with Britain to "facilitate a large Jewish immigration" into Palestine. Glazer followed up the interview with several letters to the White House in which he summarized his talk with Coolidge and repeated his request.[72] He felt that the United States had the right to exercise this pressure because Palestine was not a British colony but rather a mandate territory, in which others too had a vested interest. That included the United States, whose concern for Palestine, Glazer explained, "extends to the limit of the influence of the

Congress-Resolution favoring Palestine as a homeland for the Jewish people."[73]

The job of formulating an answer to Glazer fell to C. B. Slemp, the president's secretary. Slemp recognized that the reply would have to be carefully crafted, for it would "probably . . . be given the widest possible publicity by the people interested in this matter."[74] Thus he sought the advice of Secretary of State Hughes. Hughes had seen nothing objectionable about the congressional joint resolution that was, in any case, a domestic gesture of support for a position already adopted by the British in Palestine. Glazer's request, on the other hand, sought to get the United States involved in pressuring the British to alter their Palestine immigration policy. That was something the secretary of state was not willing to do. Hughes, therefore, took the opportunity in his reply to Slemp's inquiry to formulate what amounted to a brief position paper on the subject of Jewish immigration into the Holy Land. He told Slemp that British policy was not "a matter that directly concerns American interests, provided of course there is . . . no discrimination against American nationals." He also offered the observation that "since we ourselves take the most stringent measures to control immigration, I do not feel that we could properly approach the British government with a view to any change in their present immigration regulations in Palestine." Finally, he noted that "for your confidential information," the issue of Jewish immigration was causing the British "serious political difficulties." Palestine was a small country with limited resources and thus, "from the reports available to the Department," there had already been admitted "as large a number of persons as . . . public order and the economic situation of the country permitted."[75] He then offered Slemp some suggested wording for a reply that would gently, but firmly, rebuff Glazer's request.

In the 1920s the State Department did not believe that Jewish immigration into Palestine touched on American interests and therefore sought to have the United States maintain a neutral stance towards it. One can compare this attitude to the keen interest taken by the press in the activities of those same Jewish immigrants and their organizations. What Glazer and other Zionist leaders may have sensed was that rising popular interest might be used to get around State Department neutrality. If enough American voters could be made to appear consistently interested in the Zionist transformation of the Holy Land, could those they voted for stay disinterested? The result of growing interest might eventually cause the project of a Jewish National Home, including the immigration issue, to become an American diplomatic interest whether the State Department approved or not. The State Department personnel in the 1920s never grasped the possibility of such a redefinition of national interests through the workings of the press and new special interest groups such as the Zionists.

What Did Interest the State Department in Palestine?

If the State Department was not anxious to endorse Zionism, that did not mean it was not interested in Palestine. Indeed it was, but only within the traditional categories of American interest elaborated by Allen Dulles. After World War I it was the category of "commercial interests" that most often drew the department's attention to the Holy Land. And what commercial opportunities might there be in Palestine? Trade before the war had largely been limited to exporting Singer sewing machines and importing licorice.[76] However, all that had apparently changed when, after the war, exploitable deposits of oil had been confirmed in many areas of the Middle East, and were suspected in Palestine. All members of the new League of Nations were supposed to have equal access to the natural resources of mandate territories, but of course the United States was not a member of the League. Thus, the State Department had to find some other way to ensure U.S. commercial access to Palestine and its alleged oil resources.

The press made an effort to explain this situation to the American people. For example, the *Chicago Tribune* told its readers in an editorial on February 23, 1921, that "the principal point at issue between the United States and Great Britain . . . was the development of oil resources in the Near East."[77] The *Washington Post* put forth the same opinion on February 24 and explained that "the provisions of the [League] covenant relating to mandates were so ambiguous that the British government found an opportunity to discriminate against American citizens in the worldwide struggle for oil."[78]

To improve the situation the State Department proceeded to negotiate bilateral treaties with England and France to define American rights and privileges within the new mandate territories. A central goal of these treaties was to promote an "open door" for American business. With reference to Palestine and the question of oil, the *New York Times* explained to its readers on May 10, 1922, that "a virtual agreement has been reached between the United States and Great Britain" that would "amply protect the rights and interests of American citizens in the mandated territory" by allowing Americans to "participate on an equal footing with the nationals of Great Britain . . . in the exploitation of the natural resources of Palestine

and in its commerce and industry."[79] This judgment was, however, premature. The agreement of which the *New York Times* spoke, the Anglo-
American Convention on Palestine, would not be signed and ratified until
1925. And even thereafter, the State Department would never be quite
satisfied that Britain was really allowing Americans "equal footing" in
terms of economic access.

The suspicion that Britain sought to treat Palestine like a Crown
Colony, and thus monopolize economic "exploitation," started early in
the State Department. An initial test of American "economic rights" in
Palestine involved Standard Oil's access to pre-war concessionary grants
made to it by the former Ottoman government. These concessions had
been given for the purpose of determining, by way of a geological survey,
whether commercial amounts of oil did in fact exist in Palestine. The State
Department took on the role of advocate for Standard Oil with the British
Foreign Office in an effort to give the Open Door theory some real substance. However, the department met considerable resistance not only
from the mandatory government in Palestine, but also from the Zionists.

On August 12, 1921, L. I. Thomas, director of Standard Oil Company
of New York (hereinafter referred to as SO), wrote to Secretary of State
Hughes requesting State Department assistance. He explained that "notwithstanding repeated protests . . . the British Government has refused to
permit [SO] any prospecting or research work [in Palestine].[80] The State
Department agreed to assist, and written representations were made to the
British Foreign Office on September 15. This effort brought quick results,
with Lord Curzon, the foreign secretary, writing to George Harvey, the
U.S. ambassador, on October 10 that "informal permission will be accorded Standard Oil Company . . . to conduct researches within the limits
of the areas over which the company is known to claim concessionary
rights . . . on the strict understanding . . . that no permission can be granted
for the exploitation of these areas until the treaty of peace with Turkey
enters into force and until the terms of the Mandate for Palestine are
finally settled, and on condition that the company will undertake to furnish a full and complete report on result of their investigations."[81]

At this point SO balked, and for an interesting reason. They asserted
that their claims were "legally obtained from the Turkish government
prior to the war" and therefore they saw no reason to recognize the right
of Great Britain to condition their right of exploitation to the settlement of
treaties and mandates. In other words, SO was questioning "the present
administrators of Palestine whether known as the Palestine or as the British Government, as having the authority to prescribe terms." And indeed,

the company was "loath to believe that our Government recognizes any right in the British Government to interfere with or delay the development of claims legally obtained."[82] The State Department took no exception to the SO position and instructed the embassy in London to continue to negotiate with the British and to urge on them an "accommodating spirit."[83]

In the meantime the State Department was keeping Addison Southard, U.S. consul in Jerusalem, fully advised. And the consul in turn had explained to Washington the complicated nature of the competition for mineral rights in Palestine. SO had competitors in Shell Oil as well as a Zionist company known as the Dead Sea Undertaking Company.[84] There was also the fact that the British government itself was in the oil business as a controlling partner of the Anglo-Persian Oil Company and had significant interests in the Turkish Petroleum Company.

The question of the exploitation of any commercial oil on the SO sites seems to have been moot because the American company could not force Britain to relinquish its ultimate control of natural resources in mandate Palestine. But the British did not, at this point, so much desire to shut SO out of Palestine as to use the company to its own ends. So the British authorities insisted that a complete copy of the report on any findings would have to be turned over to the government in Palestine. This was necessary, according to the Foreign Office, because "the government of Palestine is not at present in a financial position to create a Geological Survey Department."[85] However, according to Southard, this request came from Winston Churchill, then head of the Colonial Office, at the urging of the Zionists. The American consul speculated that if companies investigating mineral resources in Palestine had to make their findings known, then the Zionist concerns, which still hoped to gain concessions claimed by SO and others, could have the expensive early investigative procedures performed for them, by their own competitors.[86] In the end SO did reluctantly accept the conditions laid down by the British. Perhaps they believed that once they had the data they sought they could renegotiate. In any case, on January 18, 1922, Thomas wrote to Hughes indicating SO's acceptance of "the permission stated by the British Government . . . subject to the conditions set forth in the Foreign Office communication."[87]

One would have thought that this would end the matter. However, this was not the case. Now SO's troubles shifted from London to Jerusalem. Officials in the mandate government questioned the number of sites the SO concessions covered, and the State Department had to go back to the

British government in London to clarify the matter—this time winning a judgment in SO's favor.[88] Then Southard reported to Washington that "the Director of the local Department of Commerce and Industry . . . [a] very zealous Zionist and naturally not in favor of mineral explorations by Standard Oil or any other interest not working under Zionist auspices . . . has persisted in quibbling in various ways as to what areas they should explore."[89] Obviously this local official was not aware of the alleged plan of Churchill and the Zionists to eventually take advantage of SO's exploratory work. However, at this point Southard lost all patience and advised the SO geological survey team that, the matter of sites having been clearly defined by London, they should simply ignore the local director of commerce and "start with the work."[90] Following this advice, the SO engineers finally began their fieldwork.

There is an epilogue to this story. SO finished its geological survey by December 1922, yet we find, in October 1923, the British government complaining to the State Department that they had yet to receive SO's promised report.[91] At State Department urging SO finally gave over the report to the British in February 1924 on the understanding that it was "for the confidential information of the Palestine Government only."[92] SO had stalled on the matter quite purposely. In a letter to the State Department, Thomas said the company's reluctance was because "it does not seem proper for an American company to be forced to give the result of their labors to a foreign government, especially as the British Government . . . holds a controlling interest in the Anglo-Persian Oil Co. Ltd. which is our competitor in nearby areas."[93] Thomas's protest rings hollow when one considers the fact that the results of SO's survey showed that there was no exploitable oil in Palestine. Was there something else behind the company's stalling? The answer to this question is to be found in a "memorandum of a conversation with Mr. L. I. Thomas and Judge Speer, of the Standard Oil Company of New York, with regard to geological investigations in Palestine." It was written by Allen Dulles, head of NEA, on November 28, 1923. In the memorandum Dulles recounted that "I gathered from Mr. Thomas that they [SO] had agreed to turn in their Palestine holdings to the Turkish Petroleum Company and did not desire that company to learn at the present moment that the . . . investigations had led them to believe that their Palestine claims were of little value."[94] Was SO seeking to "turn in" their Palestine concessions for a price and thus found it expedient to keep secret the fact that what they were selling was worthless? From SO's point of view it might have seemed a just revenge, for Turkish Petroleum was a British-owned company.

Despite the discovery that Palestine had no exploitable oil reserves, the SO episode represented the type of activity in support of which the State Department was willing to act. Commercial access in the Middle East for U.S. companies was a traditional category of national interest, and oil was certainly an important aspect of that interest. Importantly, the case also suggests that in some significant areas, the economic activities of the Zionists were not in fact, nor were perceived by the State Department to be, synonymous with the economic interests of the United States. Indeed, in the case of SO, the Zionists were seen as a roadblock to the exercise of the economic "rights" of an important U.S. concern. Clearly, as long as it was constrained within its traditional ways of thinking about national interests, the State Department had little cause to foresee any merging of U.S. and Zionist interests.

However, the details of this episode did not make it into the American press, for it would seem that neither Standard Oil nor the State Department sought any publicity over the matter. Thus, the economic news coming from Palestine was less about Zionist roadblocks to American business than the alleged opportunities for investment and profit offered to Americans by Zionist colonization.

Conclusion

As we move into the second half of the 1920s, the position taken by the State Department that Zionism was not to be included in the list of American national interests faced greater and greater opposition. It was a position that seemed to contradict an evolving popular perception of Zionism as a worthwhile venture within the framework of altruistic imperialism. And it also ran counter to the growing conviction that Zionism reflected American values.

As we have seen, this popular perception of Zionism was in many ways distorted. The Balfour Declaration was written into the British mandate by the British and Zionists themselves, but somehow, by the early 1920s, both the declaration and the mandate were popularly perceived as flowing from an agreement taken by the international community. The Zionists themselves were seen in the United States as latter-day American-style pioneers, when in reality most of their number on the ground in Palestine saw themselves as socialist pioneers. They were supposedly "upbuilding" Palestine for the benefit of not only immigrating Jews, but the natives as well, when in fact they were creating an ethnically exclusive society. Nonetheless, given the American way of seeing the Holy Land, Palestinian Arab resistance seemed wrongheaded.

In the latter half of the decade these misconceptions would only grow stronger and more ingrained. And as they did, the State Department's position would become less and less compatible with popular opinion. Yet, over time, it was popular perceptions that would have a political impact in this area. The diplomats seemed only to talk to themselves, while the Zionists increasingly talked to Congress and the press. In the end, NEA was heading for the same realm of irrelevancy as the Palestinian Arabs.

4

The Calm before the Storm

At mid decade, the American Zionists had "captured" the American press. That is, it was the American Zionist "spin" on Palestine that most often appeared in the newspapers. Zionist success in the field of public opinion was aided by the fact that their message made sense within the context of a Western bipolar worldview that portrayed the Holy Land as an extension of the Judeo-Christian West and promoted altruistic imperialism. Within this context, Zionism was accepted as a civilizing agent in the redemption of Palestine.

The Zionists were further helped in winning over the American public by the sporadic and unorganized nature of the opposition. There was only occasional and brief public debate. The American missionary establishment, which had so much invested—both materially and emotionally—in the Middle East, did not mount an effective challenge to Zionism. After World War I the Protestant missionaries faced a dilemma in Palestine. Their position there was facilitated by the imperial rule of Great Britain. Yet, in many of its policies, Great Britain favored Zionism. It can be surmised that this had a muting effect on those Protestant missionaries who were having second thoughts about Zionism, but did not wish to undermine the British position in the Holy Land. On the other hand, a good number of Protestants, both in the United States and Britain, supported Zionism as a step in the direction of the fulfillment of biblical prophecy.[1]

The State Department stayed completely out of the public eye on the issue of Palestine. This was largely a function of the department's self-image and culture. State Department personnel did not see their role as a public one. Nor did they believe the public at large had any role in shaping foreign policy. In any case, not seeing Zionism to be among U.S. national interests in the Middle East, the department took a neutral stance in regard to it.

In the Jewish community, there was some resistance to Zionism from Jews who feared that it would increase anti-Semitism and negatively impact Jewish citizenship rights around the world. But this stand did not speak to the immediate needs of the Jews of central and eastern Europe, who were Zionism's chief source of immigrants to Palestine. Nor were anti-Zionist Jews nearly as well organized as the Zionists.

In the 1920s, the only group which sought to publicly challenge the Zionists were Arab Americans. For instance, as early as 1921 the Palestine National League, which represented many of those Arab Americans active on this issue, published a book entitled *The Case against Zionism*. Drawing upon the writings of both Arab Americans and American Jewish leaders and scholars opposed to Zionism, the book not only made the case against a Jewish National Home in Palestine, but also laid out the sort of political future progressive Palestinian Arabs sought to build. That future was strongly influenced by Woodrow Wilson's advocacy of self-determination. "The will of the people [should be] declared in a free manner. . . . a national government responsible to a parliament [should be] elected by those Palestinians who lived in the country before the war—Moslems, Christians and Jews." While the Palestine National League was capable of articulating this point of view, it was not successful in reaching the American public. Arab American numbers were very small and league membership attracted only a fraction of that community. Thus, except in the ethnic Arab press in places such as Detroit and New York, their efforts and opinions received only rare attention.[2]

Progress Means Peace

Under these circumstances the picture in the popular American mind in the mid 1920s was of Palestine being colonized by American-style, Zionist pioneers. We have seen that this was the picture put forth by Brandeis in the early part of the decade, and it was one that persisted. For instance, the naturalist and explorer Carveth Wells, who worked out of the American Museum of Natural History, returned from Palestine in January of 1926 and told the *New York Times* "In Palestine I found villages of Zionists— Jews with bobbed hair and New York clothes, saloons, shoe-shining stands and something of a Wild West appearance, with machine guns mounted in concrete blockhouses to keep away the Arabs."[3] Through their developmental efforts, these American-style Zionists and their fellows were bringing the Holy Land into the modern age. The Palestinian Arabs, like the American Indians, could only benefit if they did not resist. But whether the natives resisted or not, this process of "upbuilding" would, like progress itself, inevitably triumph.

This picture comes through strongly in the thirty-four *New York Times* articles on Palestine published in 1925, and represents a pattern followed for the rest of the decade.[4] Under titles such as "Building Boom in the Holy Land"[5] and "New City for Palestine,"[6] a picture of modernization and improvement was maintained with which an American reader could readily identify. "The colonies which have been started by the Zionists in the fertile districts are all in flourishing condition," wrote Talcott Williams, once more touring Palestine for the *New York Times*. "Standing on the hilltop between Haifa and Nazareth one beholds a magnificent sight with the new houses erected by the Zionists, roofed with red tiles, grouped together on the community plan." This was "comfort produced by the labor of their [the Zionist settlers'] own hands."[7] It was a description that nicely conformed to the American work ethic.

If the American reader of 1925 would have found nothing offensive about Williams's praise of "colonies" planted by Europeans in the Middle East, so they were unlikely to find anything amiss in the negative stereotyping of the indigenous population. Thus, Williams, who was otherwise an astute and analytical observer, notes the prevalence of malaria (which the British, Jewish, and Arab health officials were then combating) and proceeds to explain that "the Arabs do not know when they have malaria because it is no novelty for them to have a tired feeling. They are always ready to lie down and rest beside their camels and goats."[8] This image of the primitive was often reinforced by contrasting age-old native methods with some new modern enterprise or technology introduced from the West. Thus, in a piece entitled "New Olive Trade in Palestine," the Arabs are described in their "mud huts" pressing oil with the help of a "blind camel turning a grindstone." The "blind camel" method was then shown against the "new electrical plant" built for the same purpose by "foreign capitalists."[9]

These images were easily accepted because they fit into the general view that altruistic imperialism was rescuing the Holy Land from primitive backwardness. Approaching the *New York Times* stories with this assumption, the American reader was unlikely to conclude that the Palestinians were due equal, much less preferential, consideration relative to the colonizing Zionists. Thus readers would have found quite reasonable the opinion offered to the *Times* by William Rappard, a member of the League of Nations Permanent Mandates Commission. "Zionism is one of the most extraordinary political phenomena that I have ever studied," he said. "Palestine is an intellectual fairyland because the contrasts are so astounding. The Arabs are in the majority, but they have nothing to give the world comparable to the Jews either in energy or intellect."[10]

In contrast to this picture, the *Times* did print, in 1925, two (out of thirty-four) pieces offering some insight into the Arab point of view. These came in the form of interviews with Habib Lotfallah, a "representative of the King of the Hedjaz," upon his visit to the United States. Here Lotfallah laid out Arab grievances. The British had broken their promise to support the creation of a united Arab state in the Middle East in exchange for wartime aid against the Turks and Germans. As a result Arabs, including Palestinians who should be part of such a state, were instead ruled by colonial powers under the guise of mandates. Lotfallah's perspective was not anti-Jewish. Commenting on Zionism, he asserted that "the Zionists represent a small part of the Jewish race, the Jews represent a small part of the Semitic race, and the Semitic race is comprised of Jews, Christians and Mohammedans." However, "European diplomats seemed bound to segregate the various peoples" and the Balfour Declaration was "part of that program." He predicted that "the setting up of a Zionist state will create trouble for the Jews themselves."[11]

The *Times* interviewer, Howard Mingos, reported Lotfallah's opinions as credible in part because he judged the ambassador "so much a cosmopolite that he would not be taken for an Arab. Here he might be identified as a New York businessman."[12] Though Lotfallah might not have appeared out of place in Manhattan, his arguments were markedly out of step with American popular perceptions of the Holy Land.

The American Zionists never let such publicly expressed opinions pass without a response. They quickly labeled Lotfallah's views as "political propaganda" and asserted that the prediction of "trouble" for the Jews in Palestine was "absurd." Absurd because, according to Colonel Frederick H. Kisch of the Zionist Executive, "the presence in Palestine of an increasing number of Jews determined to build up the agriculture and industrial life of the country means progress, which in turn means peace."[13]

Calm and Reconciliation

Indeed, at mid decade the picture painted of Palestine in the American press was one of calm and reconciliation.[14] An op-ed piece by a regular contributor to the *New York Times* whose pen name was "Xenophen" (an ancient Athenian social commentator) gave a sense of the prevailing optimistic outlook. "While the Jews and Arabs are by no means fully reconciled, the poisonous venom that permeated the relationship of these two racial groups has disappeared." The writer then asserted that "British occupation of Palestine" could be "hailed by the world as a crusade in the cause of civilization."[15] Chaim Weizmann, president of the World Zionist Organization, and a man the *New York Times* characterized as "leading . . . the colonizers of Palestine," agreed. In November of 1926 he told a gathering of Zionists in New York City that "the Arab problem . . . today has lost its acuteness and our relations with the Arab people are on a solid foundation."[16] While this claim was an exaggeration, it did reflect a lull in an ongoing pattern of confrontation.

Why did it appear that Arab-Jewish tensions had abated by 1926? Several suggestions were put forth at the time. For instance, some observers saw as significant the fact that Britain's first colonial high commissioner in Palestine, Sir Herbert Samuel, had recently been replaced by Viscount Herbert Plumer, a soldier with long field experience. This was the case with Fannie Fern Andrews, who, when addressing the League of Women Voters' "School of Politics," held at Radcliffe College in early 1926, asserted that the appointment of "a military man" as chief colonial administrator in Palestine had "the psychological effect of relieving the tension" between Arabs and Zionists.[17] And according to a *New York Times* report in April 1926, "businessmen in Jerusalem and Haifa, both Jews and Gentiles . . . said that while the government remained in the hands of the British they did not fear trouble with the Arabs or Bedouins who were more afraid of Lord Plumer then they had been of [the former commissioner,] Herbert Samuel."[18] The British themselves seemed to have believed that fear was at least part of the reason for the prevailing relative calm. As the deputy inspector in charge of the Palestine Gendarmerie told the *New York Times*, "the principal factor that has kept our Arabs quiet . . . is that they have seen how their co-religionists have been treated in [French controlled] Syria. . . . On the Syrian side villages and towns have been destroyed and fired and the fertile land has been laid waste. [Also] They [the Arabs of Palestine] are getting to understand the newly arrived Zionists have . . . raised the standard of living [and] this has benefited the native laborer because he still lives on the same scale as his ancestors have done for centuries."[19]

Thus, the popular view, compatible with the bipolar worldview and the notion of altruistic imperialism, was that British firmness, combined with Zionism's having "raised the standard of living" for the natives, had brought peace and progress for everyone. This was a result ideally postulated for the colonial exercises of the day. As Rabbi deSola Pool, of the Spanish and Portuguese Synagogue of New York City, put it upon his return from Palestine in September of 1926, there now existed "complete public security," which constituted the best evidence of the good relations which exist among all elements of the population. "Christian, Moslem, and Jew have settled down to work which creates real material values . . . and no less real spiritual values of cooperation and friendship."[20]

There certainly was firmness and fear in Palestine, but "cooperation and friendship" would prove more elusive. As to the increasing Arab standard of living, recent scholarship has demonstrated that the Jewish economy the Zionists were evolving in Palestine was designed to be ethnically exclusive and wherever possible to not include the Arabs at all. As far as the Zionist leadership was concerned, Arabs were employed only as cheap labor on jobs no Jews would do. Even this was only a temporary expedient. In circumstances which allowed their replacement by immigrating Jews, pressure was put on Jewish employers to fire their Arab workers.[21]

Evaluating the Image

Nonetheless, economics did play a role in producing a brief relative quiet just past the mid-decade mark. The nature of that role, however, had nothing to do with interethnic prosperity. In fact, it was a retreat from prosperity that facilitated relative calm. From 1926 into 1928 the Jewish economy in Palestine suffered a sharp economic downturn. This had the effect of lessening the pace of Zionist activity (for instance, housing and other construction were particularly depressed at this time), and temporarily caused Jewish emigration out of Palestine to exceed immigration into the country. This gave the Palestinian Arabs a false sense that the whole Zionist experiment was on the verge of collapse. As the Jerusalem newspaper *Mirat al-Sharq* put it, here was "proof of the assertion that Palestine could never contain a national home for the Jews. . . . The number of Jews leaving Palestine is large [and] larger numbers will leave during the coming years."[22]

The cause of the economic troubles was explained by the American vice consul in Jerusalem, Clayton Aldridge, part of whose job it was to follow economic developments. On November 5, 1926, he sent to the State Department a detailed analysis of the situation entitled "Present Difficulties Confronting the Jewish National Home."[23] Aldridge explained to the State Department that the economic troubles were "a direct result of the recent financial crisis in Poland. . . . 57% of Palestine immigrants during the first six months of 1926 came from Poland."[24] He then pointed out that many of the Polish immigrants "had investments in Poland or in Polish currency, many had property or business interests in Poland . . . on which they were dependent for support, many were more or less dependent on relatives in Poland." As a result, the financial crisis in Poland in 1926 undercut the income of these colonists and this in turn undercut "credit for industry and building [in Palestine]. . . . The building trades in Tel Aviv were suddenly crippled and hundreds were thrown out of employment." As a consequence, "the past three months [August, September, and October 1926] have witnessed the unusual spectacle of an exodus of colonists from the country greater in number than the corresponding influx of immigrants." It was a situation "which appears temporarily at least to have offered a serious setback to the progress of the Jewish National Home."[25]

This view of the situation was never to appear in the U.S. press. The economic troubles in Palestine were hardly mentioned in the pages of the *Chicago Tribune, Los Angeles Times,* or *Washington Post.* With the *New York Times,* where coverage was more extensive, the story came through in a confusing fashion. Thus, while the paper noted "a slump in business in Palestine because of lack of capital,"[26] it often contradicted that picture with other accounts of ongoing economic development. For instance, in September 1926, in the midst of the crisis, a *New York Times* editorial described "a twelve-story office building . . . going up in Jerusalem. The city has a real estate boom. Shops, factories and dwelling houses are being built by the hundred. . . . Where the patient ass used to plod along on the dirt trails there are now motor vehicles whirling over paved streets."[27] Seventeen days later the *New York Times* was describing this "real estate boom" in very different terms. "While there was an industrial depression . . . and some unemployment, which was chiefly in the building trades . . . the agricultural outlook was very good."[28]

It is useless to look for consistency in the *Times* reporting of the economic downturn. It is simply not there. All one can say is that the balance of reporting runs in the direction of muting the crisis. Besides doing so by virtue of contradictory stories, there was also a tendency to concentrate on what was planned for the future rather than what was going on in the present. Thus articles appeared on plans for public works that would spur the Jewish economy. Bernard Rosenblatt, now president of the Jewish National Fund, told the *New York Times* in May of 1927 that despite some economic trouble "Palestine is making remarkable progress. There are three outstanding enterprises that will soon transform the Promised Land into a Land of Promise. 1. The Rutenberg concession [designed to generate electricity] has finally secured the initial $5 million and work on the larger Jordan dam will begin in a month. . . . 2. Private capital has been enlisted in the Dead Sea project [for mineral extraction]. . . . 3. But greatest of all is the Haifa Bay project . . . in connection with the construction of the harbor at Haifa."[29] In other articles as well, *New York Times* reporting on Palestine dealt with the great amounts of money being raised in the United States for investment in the country's Jewish economy.[30] The implication here was that with money constantly pouring in, the economy must be growing.

None of this hedging on the seriousness of the crisis could overcome the private anxiety felt by Zionist leaders over the emigration statistics. In a September 26, 1926, interview with Aldridge, Colonel Kisch of the Zionist Executive tried to put the best face forward on this phenomenon, albeit with a Social Darwinist slant. "I found . . . that not a few Jews were leaving the country. Who are they? In most cases the weaker elements . . . those who have not been able to adapt themselves to the difficult conditions . . . and for whom the strain of a lowered standard of living has been too great. Such an exodus of the less fitted is a normal phenomenon in connection with every process of colonization."[31]

Displacing the Arab Laborer

The "weaker elements" of the Jewish population might have been leaving Palestine, but unemployment was to continue at embarrassingly high rates for some time to come. This persistent fact did, eventually, undercut the lull in Arab-Jewish tensions. Why should unemployment in the ethnically defined Jewish economy of Palestine bring increasing friction with the Arabs? The reason lay in the capitalist behavior of some Jewish entrepreneurs who were, at this time, more interested in profit than in Zionist ideology.

On December 18, 1927, the *New York Times* reported that due to the economic downturn in Palestine, "there are frequent clashes between Jewish and Arab workers over the few jobs available."[32] Actually, the problems were more complex. Zionist labor groups were pressuring Jewish employers to replace Arab workers with unemployed Jewish labor. Their agitation was particularly aimed at those Jewish-owned agricultural enterprises which had chosen to rely on cheaper Arab labor. As Chaim Weizmann explained in his autobiography, "the [Jewish agricultural] colonies were more in the nature of businesses. . . . The settlers dealt in oranges as they had dealt in other commodities back in Russia. Most of the labor was Arab, and the Jews were overseers. There was no pioneering spirit."[33] In other words, some Jewish agricultural concerns in 1920s Pal-

estine, as yet unassimilated into the evolving socialist and ethnically exclusive Jewish economy, ran on a standard capitalist model. Hire the lowest-
cost labor available. And since most Jewish immigrants tended to shun
menial agricultural labor or demanded higher, European-level salaries,
Arab labor got these jobs.

But now, in the latter half of the decade, with Jewish unemployment
high and emigration outpacing immigration, every job was important to
the Zionist leadership. Thus, as the *New York Times* reported in late
1927, "in several cases where Jewish colonists have employed Arabs instead of Jewish laborers the latter have attacked their native competitors,
who have had to be protected by the police."[34] By early 1928 the *Times*
was reporting "serious clashes between Jewish and Arab workers" at orange groves such as those at Petakh Tivah, the result of which was the
firing of the Arabs and their replacement by hundreds of unemployed
Jews.[35] The *Times* now had a "special correspondent," Joseph M. Levy,
resident in Palestine, and he attributed this transition from Arab to Jewish
labor to Jewish ethnic solidarity. The Jewish landowners "having come to
the country with the desire to . . . build up the land by providing work for
the immigrant naturally gave them preference over the Arabs in spite of
the fact that the wages they demanded were considerably higher."[36]

The truth was not quite as simple as Levy portrayed it. Considerable
pressure was brought to bear on the Jewish landowners in question to
effect this transition. The pressure was part of an increasingly aggressive
campaign appropriately deemed "the conquest of labor."[37] In an interesting twist, the Jewish-on-Arab violence that came along with this struggle
for jobs was laid at the feet of a small number of "communist agitators"
by the *New York Times*.[38] This was an interpretation that fit well into the
"Red Scare" assumptions held by Americans in the 1920s about their own
labor unrest. While such press reports made it seem that only a few "communists" were responsible for Jewish-Arab labor conflict, the violence
was in truth triggered by the tactics of Palestine's mainstream Zionist labor organizations. However, the socialist orientation of these groups had
less to do with their behavior than the ethnocentric aspects of Zionist
ideology.

Debating the Paradigm: The Carnegie Report of 1926

The economic troubles that began in 1926 may have helped prompt second thoughts about Zionism in some influential quarters—particularly
those quarters which took the civilizing aspect of the bipolar worldview

seriously. Among such observers questions were raised over whether Zionism would or could fulfill its role as a vehicle for development benefiting colonists and natives alike. This is one way of reading a report, dealing in part with Palestine, issued on behalf of the Carnegie Endowment for International Peace in late November of 1926. Its author was Henry Pritchett, a trustee of the endowment. The *New York Times,* noting the prestigious source of the report, gave it front-page coverage under a headline reading "Pritchett Reports Zionism Will Fail."[39]

The Carnegie report concluded that the Zionist effort to colonize Palestine was both "unfortunate and visionary." Its continuance was bound to "bring more bitterness and more unhappiness both for the Jew and the Arab." While Zionism was the product of "well meaning men," it was also an "artificial" movement whose leaders no longer "appreciate . . . the interests of the existing native population." Pritchett questioned Palestine's capacity to support both its indigenous population and massive infusions of European settlers. He argued that "it is impossible to settle a million people in Palestine without, to a great extent, displacing the present Arab population." To carry on such a program would be unfortunate all around. Why so? Not only because that was not the end altruistic imperialism was supposed to have, but also because, in the process of displacing the Palestinians, the Jews themselves would become corrupted. "If Palestine could be cleared of the Arabs and populated with Jews exclusively and thus become a pure Jewish state, no thoughtful man could doubt that this would be an unfortunate situation for those Jews who live in Palestine. The segregation of any national group by itself has seldom failed to develop a personality and national character that was aggressive, egotistic, and without capacity for cooperation with the rest of the world. No one can doubt that these qualities would develop themselves in a Jewish state."[40]

The challenge of the Carnegie report was a powerful one. First of all, it was issued by an institution with credibility well beyond that of the occasional visiting Arab dignitary or the returning tourist. Secondly, the conclusions Pritchett's report drew challenged Zionist ends within the framework of the bipolar worldview that gave the movement at least part of its credence. Clearly, altruistic imperialism would not succeed if Zionism was to bring only "bitterness" and the inevitable displacement of the Palestinians. Of course not many Americans would have actually been concerned with Palestine's Arabs, or even been particularly aware of them. However, the stark forecast of such a high-profile foundation was enough to worry the American Zionist establishment.

As was their habit, Zionist leaders responded to the Carnegie critique with a prolonged and intense counterattack. The first responses were reported in the *New York Times* on November 30, 1926, only a day after Pritchett's report had itself been published. Leading the rebuttal was Chaim Weizmann. He described Pritchett's observations as "the usual stock-in-trade of anti-Zionist agitators." He claimed that Dr. Pritchett, who was a well-trained academic researcher and had traveled in the Near East, was completely misinformed. "The Jewish colonization project is safeguarding every right of the native population," and thus fear of displacing the Palestinians was "groundless," the Zionist leader told the *Times*. Weizmann did not explain how the Zionist movement safeguarded Arab rights. Rather, he claimed that Jewish-Arab relations were so improved as to make Palestine "the only peaceful spot in a part of a world full of unrest." Weizmann then asserted that "it has been admitted by those responsible for the security and order of Palestine that Jewish work . . . has acted as one of the most potent stabilizing forces for peace of the country."[41]

The same *New York Times* report quoted Rabbi Stephen Wise, the New York–based American Zionist leader, as saying, "surely Dr. Pritchett must have seen with what scrupulous care the Jewish settlers have regard for the interests of the Arab population. Does not Dr. Pritchett know that a referendum today of the Arab population of Palestine would result in a great majority in favor of Jewish settlement in Palestine?" Other American Zionist spokesmen were quoted as asserting that Pritchett was working under a "delusion" and only showing how "woefully ignorant" he was of Palestinian affairs."[42]

The Zionist leaders kept up their efforts to discredit the Carnegie report for another week, repeatedly labeling it "superficial" and nothing but a "theological treatise." The notion that there was little Arab-Jewish tension remained a constant theme. Stephen Wise told the *Times* on December 6 that "We have peace with the Arabs save among the renegade Mohammedans, and in the group of absentee landlords in Egypt and Syria, whose bitterness against us arises, not out of our oppression of the Arabs, which they know does not exist, but because . . . they know we are liberating the serfs of Palestine. We are helping to free the Arabs, to lift them to new levels of life."[43] Such an assertion certainly fit neatly into the press-supported picture of steady modernization in Palestine. As such it would have seemed more in tune with popular views than the Carnegie critique. Both Weizmann's and Wise's claims, of course, did not reflect actual Zionist labor practices, or the problem of the dispossession of Arab peasants from land purchased by Zionist organizations.[44] However, these practices had not gotten wide press and therefore had not factored into the American image of Zionism.

Therefore, it is all the more surprising that, despite the positive press image presented of Zionism, the *New York Times* editors took seriously Pritchett's charges. A November 30 *Times* editorial observed that "Dr. Pritchett's unfavorable verdict on the movement to set up a Jewish National Homeland in Palestine . . . compels attention," for he can be "presumed to view the problem objectively." The *Times* editorial then called for a debate on the "concrete problems" the report had raised. "Are there in Palestine the possibilities of a sound economic foundation for large-scale Jewish settlement? Is it a fact that the Jewish agricultural colonies have been kept alive by artificial stimulation? Even if the economic foundations are there, can a large Jewish population be developed without displacing the native Arabs?"[45]

It is possible that personal reservations about Zionism held by Adolph Ochs, the owner of the *New York Times,* influenced the paper's editorial department on this occasion. However, both the owner and editors seemed not to have realized that the bulk of their own paper's coverage, which had created a strong picture of Zionism as a beneficent modernizing and civilizing movement, had already helped undercut the possibility of any real debate. Thus by 1926, the Carnegie report, and the *Times* editorial itself, were too discordant with the popular image of Zionism to make much of an impact.

Henry Pritchett did not help matters when he chose to retreat in the face of Zionist criticism. On December 5 he told the *New York Times* that "he did not intend to enter into any debate on the subject."[46] By the end of 1926 this challenge to Zionism was largely over. And throughout 1927, American Zionists were again asserting, and the press again reporting, that, as Nathan Straus put it, "the Holy Land is being rebuilt. The friction between Arabs and Jews is constantly decreasing."[47]

Economic Crisis Brings British-Zionist Friction

If the American Zionists sought to deny Jewish-Arab conflict in the face of economic crisis, they had no such reticence when it came to friction with the British. Palestine's economic problems were often publicly linked to perceived shortcomings of British support for the Zionist cause.

Great Britain, of course, was supposed to be Zionism's partner in the redemption of Palestine through the auspices of the Jewish National

Home. This was certainly the popular image built up by the press in its coverage of the Balfour Declaration. However, the depth of the economic crisis in the latter years of the 1920s created a kind of moment of truth. It was a moment when the real level of devotion of one's partner could be put to the test. For the American Zionists, and many Zionists in Palestine as well, the British would fail this test.

The proof of the failure came in 1927. In July of that year a British government report on the economic situation in Palestine was submitted to the League of Nations Permanent Mandates Commission. It described "the financial situation of the Jewish population" as "unsatisfactory," and concluded that "Jewish enterprise has not yet succeeded and cannot immediately succeed in increasing the country's production to a level which would maintain its increasing population."[48]

On receipt of the report the Mandates Commission asked the British government what it was doing about this situation, given the fact that, under the Palestine mandate, the British were supposed to be promoting the Jewish National Home. The British reply was remarkably noncommittal. "The [British] government states that its policy aims to place all inhabitants, irrespective of race or religion[,] on a footing of equality. The acts of good government themselves create conditions favorable to the development of Jewish settlement in Palestine."[49]

Even in the best of times, evenhandedness was not what the Zionists expected from their British allies. And given the economic situation, the British stance brought sharp criticism, particularly from American Zionists. One of those voicing the loudest criticism was Stephen Wise, who, during the Fifteenth Zionist Congress at Basel, Switzerland (September 1927), pointed out that a mere "opening of the door of Palestine for Jewish activity is not a sufficient facilitation for the creation of the Jewish National Home."[50] Rather, he suggested, it was necessary for the British to adapt their policies in Palestine in order to rescue the Jewish economy. For instance, immigration policies should be liberalized so as to attract a greater number of Jewish "capitalists"—that is, people with at least $2,500 of investment capital.[51] There should also be a British guarantee that employment and profits from planned industrial development "be safeguarded for Palestine and its people" (by which Wise meant Jewish colonists).[52]

The American Zionist criticism of Great Britain, along with a corresponding demand that the World Zionist Organization be more assertive in its dealings with the British, developed into an attack on Chaim Weizmann. Weizmann had built Zionist strategy around cooperation with Britain and her imperial ambitions in the Middle East. On this occasion Weizmann successfully defended his cooperative approach, and Wise quit the Basel congress early as a result.[53] The argument between Wise and Weizmann reflected deeper ongoing philosophical and economic differences between American and European branches of the movement over the proper strategy for Zionist development in Palestine. These differences went back to the Brandeis-Weizmann dispute in the early 1920s and were now accentuated by the economic crisis that seemed to imperil the whole Zionist undertaking.[54]

Although Weizmann and the American Zionists were able to patch up their differences, the estrangement between the British and the Zionists only became sharper. As we shall see, this had much to do with the growing difference in how each side defined Palestine's ultimate status. The Zionist goal was a sovereign Jewish state, and for the Zionists, the British were important as facilitators of this end. That is how Zionists understood the British commitment made in the Balfour Declaration. In this context, a British policy of evenhandedness toward Arabs and Jews constituted an unacceptably "passive attitude toward Palestine Jewry."[55] And as Wise's attitude demonstrated, there were many Zionists who were quite capable of quickly turning on their erstwhile British benefactors if they were perceived to be too "passive." The British, on the other hand, did not seem to understand the basis of Zionist suspicion. They believed that the Balfour Declaration mandated the creation of a Jewish National Home within a Palestine that was ultimately a permanent part of the British Empire.

These different perceptions created serious problems. In the long run, they would not only divide the Zionists from the British, but also complicate U.S.-British relations when it came to Palestine. Why were the British not coming to the rescue of the Zionists in the forthright fashion Stephen Wise expected? Why were they instead seeking, at least in their reply to the League of Nations Mandates Commission, "to place all inhabitants" of Palestine "on an equal footing"? The answer lay with the evolving nature of British Middle East policy.

By the late 1920s there were still British politicians, some of whom were members of Parliament, who maintained an active interest in the promotion of the Jewish National Home. However, officials in the Colonial Office and the mandate government itself now saw Palestine as a de facto Crown Colony. Because they saw the area as a Crown Colony, the local British officials were not anxious to unduly antagonize the majority Arab population for the sake of Zionist ambitions the ends of which, after all, clashed with the evolving British point of view. Palestine could not be both a British Crown Colony and an independent Jewish state.[56]

A hint of this dilemma comes through in an August 1928 *New York Times* interview with Colonel Josiah Wedgewood, a British MP sympathetic to Zionism. In the interview Wedgewood urged the British government to forthrightly proclaim that its aim was the creation, within one generation, of a "Jewish dominion within the British Empire." Doing so, he felt, would "end immediately the present policy of indifference and resentment . . . which marks the attitude of [British] Palestine officialdom to the Jews."[57] In a follow-up piece published in early September, Wedgewood suggested that if the British brought the Zionists into the Palestine government to a greater degree, "the Jews would feel more sensibly their responsibility toward the state and their weaker neighbors [the Palestinian Arabs]."[58] Wedgewood was trying to merge the diverging British and Zionist ambitions for Palestine. In truth, it was like trying to square a circle. Everyone now had a different picture of the Holy Land's political fate.

The State Department Worries about the "Open Door"

Back in the United States, there was yet another point of view, that of the State Department. The Division of Near Eastern Affairs had been watching developments in Palestine through the consulate in Jerusalem. The economic crisis in the Jewish economy had been noted and followed. So had the evolving British attitude. As will become apparent, the American diplomats had decided that they no more approved of the British Crown Colony position than did the Zionists, though for very different reasons.

One of the ways that both the British and the Zionists hoped to alleviate the economic troubles in the Jewish economy in Palestine was through the promotion of large development projects. We have seen that American Zionists placed much emphasis on these as they sought to minimize reports of high unemployment. Bernard Rosenblatt had particularly promoted such projects as the construction of Haifa harbor.

There were others, however, who did not look upon such undertakings with the same unreserved optimism. The Palestinian Arabs, who by now clearly understood that their role in the evolving Jewish economy was to be restricted to temporary cheap labor, feared that the Zionists would pressure the British authorities to exclude them from all or most of the jobs generated by such undertakings.[59]

The State Department, watching economic developments in Palestine, also suspected that there would be discriminatory practices in these projects, though it was not the exclusion of the Arabs that worried them. As the *New York Times* had explained earlier in the decade, the State Department had expended considerable effort in trying to make sure that Americans could "participate on an equal footing . . . in the exploitation of the natural resources of Palestine and in its commerce and industry."[60] This was America's "Open Door" strategy, which sought to maintain the right of commercial access to the territories of the world's dominant empires. In the case of Palestine, the Open Door strategy had sensitized the American consular staff in Jerusalem to issues such as the bidding procedures on large and lucrative undertakings. In the reports of the American consul, Oscar Heizer, the Haifa harbor project came in for particular scrutiny in this regard.

In July of 1928 Heizer alerted the State Department that the British government had set aside $5 million for the construction of a new harbor at Haifa. This was a project the *New York Times* had predicted would transform Haifa into "the most important commercial center not only of Palestine but of the entire Near East."[61] Noting that contracts would soon be open for bids and "American contractors may wish to make tenders for the work," Heizer informed the State Department that he had asked the local British authorities for the specifications necessary to prepare bids.[62] To his surprise, Heizer never heard back from the mandate bureaucrats, and this made him suspicious. American relations with Palestine were now regulated by a bilateral agreement, the Anglo-American Convention on Palestine, and this (at least in theory) gave the United States the same access to Palestine's markets as the British themselves.

Suspecting that the British authorities might not have as serious an attitude to U.S. treaty rights as they should, Heizer went to see Palestine's director of public works, one F. Pudsey. Sure enough, Pudsey told the consul that an English engineering firm had already been approved for work on the initial stages of the harbor, after a bidding process involving only British firms. Heizer told the State Department that London had "notified eleven specially selected English firms providing them with the approved specifications."[63] The British had arbitrarily cut the rest of the world out of this lucrative deal and in so doing had upset more than just the Americans. Questions were subsequently raised by the Italian and French governments, which also had firms interested in competing for the work.[64]

Heizer's news caused consternation at the State Department. Alanson Houghton, the U.S. ambassador in London, was instructed to "orally" discuss the matter with the Foreign Office.[65] The British reply to Houghton's inquiries was initially "evasive and unsatisfactory." However, in order to avoid what was promising to develop into a diplomatic scandal over the bidding process, the government in London suspended the contract with the British engineering company and transferred responsibility for selecting contractors to the authorities in Palestine.[66] The result was the breaking up of the work into smaller contracts which, in the judgment of the State Department's Division of Near Eastern Affairs, would be unlikely to attract American firms, because "the amount [of money] involved in each case would hardly be sufficient to be of interest."[67] No further protests were made by the State Department over this issue.

The whole affair did, however, generate one final word on the evolving British attitude toward Palestine. Heizer had left the Jerusalem consulate in late 1928, and his place was taken by Paul Knabenshue. On June 12, 1929, the new American consul had an "informal conversation" with the British high commissioner, who was by this time Sir John Chancellor. In the course of the conversation Knabenshue remarked that the British government seemed to "adopt a line of action . . . which might seem in harmony neither with the spirit of the mandate nor the provisions of the American-British Mandate Convention." Knabenshue was here referring to the British attempt to monopolize the business generated by the Haifa harbor project.[68]

Chancellor's reply was that the decision to let contracts through the Palestine mandate authorities had nothing to do with an attempt to keep out non-British bidders. Rather, the decision reflected an effort to respond to "the question of local labor which had been raised by the Jews."[69] In other words, keeping contracts local would assure the creation of work for unemployed Jewish colonists. As we have seen, the British were under intense Zionist criticism for not doing more in the face of their economic crisis. This was one way the British could respond to that criticism.

This made sense to Knabenshue, but he decided to explore his original observation a bit further. "I said that from remarks dropped here and there by various British officials . . . it would seem that many of them held the view that insomuch as they were administering the country here, they saw no reason why they should not reap the benefit of the contracts and concessions." To this the high commissioner replied, "Yes . . . considering that we conquered the country at the expense of many of our lives and are administering it also at considerable expense to ourselves." Knabenshue

then politely reminded Chancellor that "while this would be a very reasonable view . . . in the ordinary course of events, unfortunately, the terms
of the mandate . . . waived this advantage in equity and gave equal opportunity to the states which were members of the League of Nations and to
the United States by treaty." The high commissioner did not choose to
argue the case further, and the interview turned to different matters.[70]

What the American consul might not have realized was that the British
had never taken the League mandate seriously. As Balfour had honestly
pointed out in 1922, the mandate was a voluntarily assumed restraint on
British "sovereignty" over Palestine. The British had conquered Palestine
and thereby had, in their own eyes, the right to incorporate it into their
empire. Therefore it was not Britain that was in Palestine by grace of the
League mandate. Rather, it was the League of Nations (via the mandate)
that was in Palestine by grace of the British government. And thus how the
mandate was to be interpreted, and how far it was to be enforced, was to
be determined by London. This attitude also affected British perceptions
of the Anglo-American Convention on Palestine, and, as Stephen Wise no
doubt suspected, Zionist aspirations in Palestine as well.

Though Knabenshue may not have placed all of this in its historical
context, he drew the correct implications from his interview with the high
commissioner. His report to the State Department after interviewing
Chancellor ended this way: "I am forced to the conclusion that our British
friends are finding it difficult to view Palestine . . . as anything but a British
crown colony. One cannot but gain the impression that not only the British administrative officials in Palestine itself, but also the British government as well, resent any interference in the administration of Palestine,
either on the part of other foreign governments, irrespective of the terms
of the mandate and their treaty rights, or even the Mandate Commission
itself."[71] He might also have added the Zionist movement to this list.

Thus, as they approached the end of the decade, the focus of the British,
the Zionists, and the American State Department were all different. The
British were focused on integrating Palestine into the British Empire. To
this end her policies had become, at least in her own eyes, more "even-
handed" as to Arabs and Jews. They also sought to reserve much of the
colony's "contracts and concessions" for British or local firms. The Zionists generally were focused on overcoming the economic crisis and revers-
ing the emigration-immigration ratio. Their goal was to maximize immigration and, when a Jewish majority was achieved, discover the virtues of
democracy and self-determination. Ultimately, they aimed for an independent Jewish state. The U.S. State Department's focus was on the Open

Door. However, while the U.S. government could protest Britain's violation of American treaty rights in terms of economic access, there was not much the State Department could do in practice.

Meanwhile, the nature of American popular opinion was increasingly shaped not by State Department interpretations of events, but rather by those of the American Zionists. This was because it was the Zionists who reached out to the public and in so doing influenced most of the press reporting on Palestine. In the press, the American Zionists focused on keeping up the image of progress and development in Palestine and thereby minimizing any negative publicity generated by the economic crisis of 1926–28.

Against this Zionist campaign the cause of the Palestinians could not compete. On rare occasions an article would appear in the *New York Times* describing the demands made by Arab Americans that Palestine be granted "a constitution along democratic and liberal lines."[72] But these occurances, even when combined with critiques of Zionism as offered by the Carnegie report, could make no lasting impact. Why should they, when the public had for years been repeatedly told that Palestine was at peace and modernizing through the auspices of altruistic imperialism? Within that "normal," ideologically comfortable view the Palestinians could be dismissed as, at best, passive receivers of the blessings of modernity, or at worst, obstacles along the road to progress. However, that most Americans had no real context within which to understand or take seriously Palestine's Arabs, and that the Zionists encouraged this "perceptual depopulation" of the Holy Land, did not mean that the Arabs were not, in fact, there.

Who Should Own the Wailing Wall?

As 1928 drew to a close, an ominous incident occurred that would remind all who cared to pay attention that the Palestinian Arabs, with a focus on their own rights and needs, were still a factor in the Holy Land. Indeed, this incident, which took place at the Wailing Wall in September, reflected the religious tensions that would help bring about the Arab rebellion of the following year. The incident was also important because it provided the Zionists with another example of that British "evenhandedness" they so much disliked. In turn, it provided the British with a strong indication that the Zionists had no intention of acquiescing in treatment that was anything but preferential. Finally, a comparison of American newspaper coverage of this affair with the official report of the American consul in

Jerusalem shows how pro-Zionist assumptions were powerful enough to selectively shape the portrayal of the facts, and place both the Arabs and the British in a bad light when they seemed to stand against the Jews in Palestine.

On September 28, 1928, J. Thayer Gilman, now the vice consul at the U.S. consulate in Jerusalem, telegrammed the State Department to report a disturbance at the Wailing Wall. The event had occurred on the morning of the 24th. Gilman would lay out the incident in detail, beginning with an explanation that, while the Wailing Wall was legally "Moslem religious property," it was also "considered by orthodox Jewry as one of its holiest places." Therefore, the fact that the Wall was not Jewish property was, for many Jews, a cause of "deep chagrin and disappointment."[73]

The Muslim religious authorities who oversaw the site had a long-standing policy of allowing Jews to worship at the Wailing Wall. But given the contentious nature of the times, and their awareness that Orthodox Jews felt the Wall should belong to them, the Muslims guarded their claim closely. They saw the Wall as part of the Mosque of Omar (Dome of the Rock), whence Muhammad was believed to have ascended to heaven. Therefore, according to Gilman, the Muslim authorities were "very careful not to permit the introduction of any innovations or fixtures [by Jewish worshippers] which might create a precedent that might later become firmly established and form the basis of a claim to the privilege of conducting services or even erecting a synagogue on the site as a matter of right."[74] A short piece in the *Washington Post* affirmed as much when it reported that "a Moslem delegation informed the [the British High] Commissioner . . . that they consider the wall a part of the Mosque of Omar and never would permit ownership by Jews. . . . They asked that . . . [the Jews] be given no 'rights beyond those enjoyed under the Ottoman regime.'"[75] It was this Muslim insistence that customary practice determine Jewish worship at the Wailing Wall that was the backdrop of the September 1928 incident.

On the evening of September 23, described in Gilman's report as "the eve of the Day of Atonement, generally considered to be the holiest day of the Jewish religious calendar," a complaint was filed with the local British authorities in Jerusalem by the Abu Madian Waqf association. This was the Muslim organization that took care of the immediate area adjoining the Wailing Wall. It seems that the Orthodox Jews who had come to worship that evening had affixed a dividing screen, meant to separate male and female worshippers, to the narrow pavement in front of the Wailing Wall. This upset the Muslims for two reasons. First, they viewed the screen as an innovation departing from customary practice. And second, place-ment of the screen appeared to be a provocative act because it prevented free access along the pathway used by local Muslim residents when going from one end of their neighborhood to the other.

In response to the complaint, the British deputy district commissioner visited the area during the evening of the 23rd, arriving during the Jewish religious service. According to Gilman's report, the official decided that the screen should be removed "before the service of the following day" and so instructed the "beadle," the Jewish religious official on site. How-ever, as it turned out, the "beadle" ignored the directive.

The next day, September 24, the Muslims made a second complaint. At this point an officer of the British Palestine police, Lieutenant Duff, ac-companied by several constables, was sent to the Wailing Wall with orders to remove the screen. According to Gilman, "members of the [Jewish] congregation present were asked to take away the screen but they refused to do so, completely ignoring the presence of the police as they were at that moment in the midst of the high prayer. . . . The police therefore undertook to remove the screen themselves, whereupon the worshippers . . . endeav-ored by force to prevent the screen being taken away. In the ensuing scuffle a number of worshippers were hurt and the screen torn."[76]

The Muslim authorities saw this as the necessary preservation of cus-tomary practice and thereby the upholding of their rights. The British interpreted their actions as the necessary maintenance of balance between the two religious communities. The Jews, however, both religious and secular, reacted as if their entire community had been insulted. Within days large protests and strikes erupted. The Zionists made a demand that the whole issue of ownership of the Wall be reviewed. Gilman's conclud-ing assessment of all this reads as follows: "While the disturbances at the Wailing Wall last Monday morning undoubtedly proved a severe shock to the religious sensibilities of the most orthodox of the Jewish sects, it can not help but be felt that the majority of the exaggerated demonstrations which followed were timely propaganda for the acquisition of the site."[77] Certainly the Muslims agreed, and became even more suspicious of Jewish intentions. This heightened defensiveness set the scene for the 1929 rebel-lion.

How did the press cover the story? Once more, the *New York Times* was the only paper to provide extensive coverage. The story was filed with the *Times* by Joseph M. Levy, who was now that paper's permanent stringer in Palestine. Levy had actually filed the story on October 4, but for reasons that remain unknown, the *Times* editors failed to run it until the 28th, more than a month after the episode.[78] In any event, a comparison of Levy's rendition of events with that of Gilman is an object lesson in the problems of interpretation. The different emphases and use of facts reveal the high degree of variance which existed between official views and those served to the public via the press. Levy told the story this way:

> The turbulent history of Palestine . . . appears to be still lingering in present times under a most modern administration, that of the British mandate authorities, as was evident during recent clashes between Jews, Arabs and British police officials over the sacred right of Jewish worshippers to do penance on Atonement Day along the Wailing Wall, one of the last remaining citadels of prayer in the Holy City. . . . While more than 1000 Jews were in the midst of their most sacred prayer . . . a British police officer came up and gave orders to remove the partition separating the men from the women. This partition . . . was placed there in accordance with orthodox ritual. What actually antagonized the Jewish population of Palestine was the fact that this partition had been put up there before the High Holy Days [perhaps here Levy is referring to the evening of the 23rd] and remained there without any disturbance until the morning of the Day of Atonement when it was removed by force by the order of the Deputy Commissioner. . . . After pleading for more than ten minutes with the police officers to be permitted to at least finish the prayer, the guardians of the law proceeded with the removal of the partition. . . . a struggle ensued during which several men and women were injured by police using their whips and clubs.[79]

Levy does go on to explain that the screen had been removed following a complaint on the part of the Muslim religious authorities, but offers his judgment (a not unusual practice for journalists of the day) that even if the partition represented "an infraction of the status quo . . . no reasonable excuse can be found for the disrespect displayed by the interruption of the sacred prayer on the holiest day of the year."[80]

Obviously we have two very different stories here. If we work on the assumption that Gilman's laying out of the facts (leaving aside his interpretation of them) was accurate and complete, and that Levy could have carried out an investigation that would have revealed to him those same facts, one can only conclude that Levy's rendition is distorted. An example here would be Gilman's explanation that the issue at hand was the screen while Levy reported that the issue was the "sacred right of Jewish wor-shippers to do penance . . . along the Wailing Wall." It is impossible to say whether Levy reported it this way on purpose or, caught up in the Jewish indignation of the moment, only bothered to learn the Zionist version of events, which he then passed on uncritically. The latter is more likely, for Levy was not a Zionist extremist. He was a member of a moderate circle of Jews who, under the influence of Judah Magnes, supported compro-mise and accommodation with the Arabs.[81]

Whatever the truth, it was Levy's version, or one similar to it, that was reported in the American press. Take, for instance, the short piece that appeared in the *Los Angeles Times* on September 26. "While hundreds were engaged in prayer a troop of Anglo-Arab police appeared and or-dered the removal of a screen set up . . . according to religious law. On the people refusing the police belabored the devout and dragged several along the ground. . . . Meanwhile excitement spread among the Jews. . . . The chief rabbis were informed by the acting High Commissioner that the incident was caused by a demand of Amin Husseini, chairman of the Su-preme Moslem Council and extreme Arab leader, concerning the position of the screen."[82] Both press versions depict the Muslims as unreasonable. This fit well with the prevailing bipolar worldview, which assumed Islam to be a fanatical religion, hostile to the Judeo-Christian faiths. Both the *New York Times* and the *Los Angeles Times* stories also called into ques-tion Britain's continued fidelity to the Balfour Declaration and, by impli-cation, her position as a partner of Zionism within the context of altruistic imperialism. It would not be the last time the British reputation suffered in this regard in the American press.

Conclusion

In the United States the 1920s was an era of Zionist image building. The motifs of civilization, progress, modernity, peace, stability—"upbuild-ing," to use the Zionist term—were becoming firmly associated in the American mind with the Jewish National Home. This process of image building occurred against a backdrop of the West's general bipolar world-view. It was an outlook that approved of imperialist ventures as long as they were rationalized as altruistic, as part of the movement of civilization West to East. Within this worldview Zionism was the chosen vehicle of redemption for a Holy Land that was religiously dear to the West.

The major tool used in the image-making process was the press, particularly the *New York Times*. The press played this role in part because its major sources of information were pro-Zionist. There were the energetic and attentive American Zionist leaders such as Stephen Wise. There were the *Times* reporters such as Talcott Williams and Joseph Levy. There was even a Zionist news agency, the Jewish Telegraphic Agency, that fed reports on Palestine and Zionist affairs to U.S. papers across the country. All of these sources supplied news and analyses sympathetic to the Zionist point of view. However, it is important to understand that that point of view would not have prevailed so readily and completely if it had not fit so well the bipolar worldview and its pro-imperialist corollaries. That it did so made it almost inevitable that the press would publish a far greater number of pro-Zionist pieces than those that called the movement into question. It also made it inevitable that when contradictory material did appear in the press, it would have little impact upon the popular mind. Such material was too out of sync with prevailing opinions and perceptions. Thus, neither reports of labor strife, nor religious rivalry at the Wailing Wall, nor the gloomy predictions of the Carnegie report could have lasting effect.

The same situation accounts for the fate of ongoing efforts by Arab Americans (they will reappear in 1929) to put the Arab point of view before the American public. Those involved with the American missionary movement had, in the 1920s, either fallen silent on the issue of Zionism or become supporters of the movement. And then there was the State Department, which, at least in theory, was in a good position to challenge the Zionist picture of events in Palestine. The State Department had firsthand information which often contradicted or called into question Zionist reports and analyses. And the department staff were respectable men whose views could have demanded attention. However, the State Department chose not to publicly challenge the Zionist message. This was in large part because the department's culture precluded any active role in shaping popular views. In their self-imposed, ivory-tower isolation, the personnel of the Division of Near Eastern Affairs focused narrowly on economic issues and arcane aspects of the Anglo-American Convention on Palestine that were of little interest to most Americans. These subjects certainly had none of the popular romance of the vast colonizing venture that was Zionism.

This was how things stood as we approach the watershed year of 1929. In that year the Arabs of Palestine would rise up in rebellion. Many lives would be lost, including those of numerous U.S. citizens. The image of

88 | America's Palestine

Jewish-Arab tranquillity so carefully cultivated by American Zionists as one of the consequences of their modernizing efforts in Palestine was quickly shattered. How would the American press and public react to such an obvious flaw in the Zionist picture? Would it lead to an unraveling of that picture and the withdrawal of popular American approval of the Jewish National Home? Or would the matrix of Zionist images hold fast and determine the American interpretation of events? It is to these questions that we must now turn.

5

Storm

The 1929 Rebellion

The year 1929 was destined to be a very troubled one for Palestine. However, at least from the point of view of the American press and public, it did not start off that way.

Continuity: Peace and Prosperity

In the first half of 1929 the press continued to present images of Zionist progress in Palestine. Articles appeared, particularly in the *New York Times,* that described expanding Zionist agricultural enterprises,[1] banking activity, and factory production.[2] This development promoted demand for foreign imports, including American automobiles,[3] and a tourist trade which saw 63,319 visitors come to Palestine in 1928. Seven out of ten were Americans.[4] As Felix M. Warburg, an American Jewish banker and philanthropist who served as vice president of the Palestine Economic Corporation, told Jewish investors in June 1929 upon his return from the Holy Land, "the people do not want charity, but business. . . . both dividends and gratitude will come to you if you stand by your people."[5] His message had long ago brought forth American largesse. By the latter half of the decade some $49 million of private American investment and aid had poured into Palestine.[6] All this activity allowed Joseph M. Levy to file a report with the *New York Times* in January of 1929 that announced "paved roads expedite travel, shops modernized."[7] In economic terms, it seemed that Palestine was getting better and better.

A message of Western-style social development also continued. Hadassah, the American women's Zionist organization, was sponsoring the construction of hospitals and health clinics throughout Palestine. These were funded by annual American contributions of up to $600,000.[8] The Hadassah effort was reported as no less than revolutionary—"the uprooting and discarding of age-old superstitions." As Jane Grant reported in the *New York Times* in April 1929, "If a juxtaposition of the twentieth and tenth centuries could be conceived some idea might be gleaned of the herculean labors Hadassah has had to perform."[9] Hadassah's efforts became a symbol for both Zionists and the American press of how the evolving Jewish National Home was bringing the Holy Land out of a primitive state and into the modern world.[10] This was what altruistic imperialism was supposedly all about.

For the Zionists the combination of economic activity and good works such as those of Hadassah combined to produce an enterprise of worldwide significance. Nahum Sokolow told a group of Zionist leaders assembled at New York's Waldorf Hotel in March 1929 that "out of Palestine a fresh spiritual life will develop to remodel the conscience of humanity. In Palestine we have a glorious mission for the whole world."[11] However, from other quarters, the picture of Zionism spearheading altruistic imperialism was called into serious question. A 1937 report by the American consulate at Jerusalem entitled "Population Trends in Palestine since the War" made clear that Zionism had not offered any widespread benefits to the non-Jewish population. The report pointed out that most Arabs were not treated at Jewish hospitals or clinics (for instance, in the year of the report, only 102 had been seen in such settings). Zionist educational efforts were for exclusive use of Jewish children. "It is the Palestine government and private [non-Zionist] organizations," the report concludes, which are responsible almost entirely for health and education of the Arab masses."[12] The facts laid out in this report went unreported and largely unknown in America during the interwar period.

The truth is that the Palestinian Arabs, along with their culture and hopes for the future, continued to be largely ignored or dismissed. Of the fifty-one *New York Times* articles on Palestine that appeared in the first seven months of 1929, only two dealt with the Arabs in more than passing fashion. One of these, coming in April, contrasted the modern medicine of the Zionists with Arab attitudes which were alleged to be "steeped in a belief in myth and magic . . . all kinds of ancient rites, conjurings, smearings, amulet wearing and weird incantations."[13] The other, ultimately more important, article appeared in January. Though only a paragraph long and buried in the back pages of the newspaper, it noted that "When Sir John Chancellor, the new High Commissioner for Palestine, visits London next Summer he will consult . . . on the demands for the establishment of a Palestine parliament recently submitted to him by a delegation of anti-Zionist Arabs."[14]

This topic would be followed up later in the year with a longer piece filed for the *New York Times* by Joseph M. Levy. Levy's handling of the story is an example of an approach often taken by Western observers on those rare occasions when the outlook of indigenous peoples was addressed. Even while taking note of Palestinian desires for representative government, the reporter does so in the form of a critique.

In his story Levy told of Palestinian disappointment at the high commissioner's comments made before the League of Nations Mandates Commission in July. Chancellor had told the commission that "Palestine is as yet not ripe for self-government," thus rejecting the Palestinian Arab request for a parliament. Levy agreed with this decision and remarked that "the High Commissioner proved himself an excellent strategist and a wise administrator." He goes on to explain that "the Arab Nationalists of the Holy Land have long been clamoring for representative self-government. . . . They look at their neighbors, Transjordan, Iraq, Syria and Egypt and feel that they too are entitled to something similar in the way of an assembly. They apparently forget or ignore the shortcomings of each of these governments, and fail to realize that not one of them has been successful."[15] Each of the countries noted in Levy's article was under colonial occupation, a status which, if considered from the Arab perspective, necessarily skewed the efforts of the experimental "assemblies" he described as "not successful."

From the Western perspective, however, Arab abilities to maintain a democratic style of self-government ran against the established way of seeing the Middle East. The alleged lack of those abilities was in fact one of the justifications for the mandate system. As it was once put in the *New York Times,* "the notion that the Arabs of Palestine would or could form an independent state is fit for Bedlam only."[16] By taking this sort of approach, the press translated the Arab discourse into a form accordant with the Western way of seeing Palestine. At the same time the Arab point of view was delegitimized.

Thus the press reports consolidated the process of "perceptually depopulating" the Holy Land of its indigenous inhabitants. Unless the colonized put themselves in active opposition to the developmental enterprises of the colonizer, they were (in terms of Western perceptions) fated to obscurity. They were, by definition, that which was being replaced.[17] The historian Melvin Urofsky put this well when describing Zionist attitudes toward the Palestinians. "The Jews . . . really had given very little thought to the Palestinian Arabs," looking upon them as did "most occidentals," as "poor, benighted natives."[18]

Discontinuity: The Rebellion of 1929

In August of 1929 the "poor, benighted natives" put themselves in violent opposition to the colonizer. Once more the Wailing Wall was the initial site of conflict. Tensions had been building over the status of that shared sacred site since the problems of the previous year. As the summer of 1929 approached, construction that enhanced the Muslim presence in the neighborhood adjacent to the Wall provoked fears in the Jewish community that this would lead to further restrictions to Jewish worship at the Wall. Inflammatory newspaper articles on the issue of the Wall's status began to appear in both the Arab and Hebrew presses. A "Pro-Western Wall Committee" was established by the hard-line Jewish Revisionist Party, which set about organizing anti-Muslim demonstrations in Jerusalem. The Muslims in turn felt threatened and provoked by these moves and organized protest actions of their own. The scene was thus set for an explosion, and it came after the mid-day Muslim prayers on Friday, August 23, when Muslim rioters invaded the Jewish quarters of Jerusalem. Soon this disturbance transformed itself into a nationwide Arab uprising lasting into early September. During the uprising, 133 Jews were killed and another 339 wounded, while 117 Arabs died and 232 were wounded.[19]

Because little attention had been paid to Arab concerns, and emphasis placed on alleged improvement in Jewish-Arab relations, the rebellion in Palestine took Americans completely by surprise. As late as June 12 Felix Warburg was telling the *New York Times* that "all seems to be at peace in that little country."[20] How would the shock of such widespread violence, wholly out of step with the standard Zionist picture, be interpreted by the American press and public? One might expect that such an unpredicted development would call into doubt the theory that Zionist colonization created peace through economic progress. However, this was not the case, for the theory had within it a subset of axioms which postulated the "natives" as barbarians, religious fanatics, and irredeemably anti-Western. We have seen part of this picture presented in the press during General Allenby's fight for Jerusalem in December 1917. It is to these axioms that the Zionists, and the American press, turned to explain the Arab rebellion of 1929.

Newspaper Coverage of the Rebellion

A sense of this interpretation can be had from the front-page headlines appearing in the *Chicago Tribune, Washington Post,* and *Los Angeles Times,* as well as the *New York Times.* All four newspapers gave the rebellion extensive coverage. The *Chicago Tribune* of August 25 read "Jews Attacked by Moslems at Wailing Wall." That of August 26: "12 Americans Die in Holy Land Riot," and that of August 31: "British Smash Arab Raids on Jewish Towns." The *Washington Post* of August 28 read "British Shoot Warring Arabs in Haifa Riots." On August 30 it was "Arab Butchery of Jews Bared in Creed Riots," and on August 31, "22 Massacred as Arabs Raze City with Fire." The *Los Angeles Times* of August 24 read "Blood Flows in Holy City"; August 28, "Arabs Kill Americans"; September 2, "Arab Mobs Run Wild"; and September 3, "Arabs Raid Colonies." The *New York Times* headline of August 25 read "47 Dead in Jerusalem Riot—Attacks by Arabs Spread." August 26 had "12 Americans Killed by Arabs in Hebron," and September 3, "British Seize 1,000 Arabs Gathering for an Attack."

These headlines were at best inaccurate and incomplete. Arab violence did result in bloodshed and the victims were often men, women, and children who had given no obvious offense. Sometimes the victims were Americans. But with rare exception the stories that accompanied the headlines failed to contextualize the violence in any way that could represent the broader political, economic, and cultural issues that had driven the Palestinians to admittedly bloody action. This incompleteness was itself a form of interpretation that allowed for a picture of Arab behavior that conformed to the established Western, bipolar way of seeing the Holy Land.

The rare exception came in the reporting of Vincent Sheean. Sheean, who reported for the North American Newspaper Alliance, was one of the very few reporters who tried to give a balanced picture of events, assigning part of the blame for the violence on the Zionists. On August 26, 1929, the *Los Angeles Times* printed one of his dispatches describing the outbreak of Arab violence as a response to Revisionist Zionist demonstrations of August 14 and 15. He described these demonstrations, which took place during a Muslim holiday, this way: "A fearful responsibility rests on the Zionist Fascisti who precipitated the present crisis . . . [by] assembling in Jerusalem [on August 14] from all parts of the country for a nationalist demonstration of the most dangerous and provocative character in the heart of the sacred Moslem district. . . . The area was crowded with brawny young Fascists from the colonies. . . . They were spoiling for a fight. . . . The next day [August 15] they marched . . . and made a formal nationalist demonstration . . . before the house of the Grand Mufti. Moslem feelings then rose to the highest pitch."[21]

With the exception of Sheean, there was no concerted effort on the part of the American press to understand the Zionist role in bringing about the troubles of 1929. Thus, in the search for what motivated the violence, most of the stories that accompanied the headlines concentrated on religious animosities over the shared sacred site of the Wailing Wall. Relying once more on Zionist sources (the Jewish Telegraphic Agency was widely utilized at this time) the press drew the following sort of conclusions. On August 18 the *New York Times* described the violence as being "apparently unprovoked assaults" by Arabs[22] which it later attributed to "aroused Moslem fanatics" whose attention had been focused by an opportunistic leadership on the Wailing Wall.[23] The *Los Angeles Times* in an August 24 piece entitled "Source of Trouble" stated, "The trouble is said to have arisen out of an attack by the Arabs on the Jews . . . at the Wailing Wall,"[24] and on August 30 printed a front-page political cartoon depicting a Jewish worshipper at the Wall overshadowed by the figure of a giant Arab about to strike him with a sword.[25] The *Chicago Tribune* described the violence as "race riots" occurring because of Muslim "objection over aspects of Jewish ritual at the Wailing Wall."[26] Finally, the *Washington Post* concluded on August 24 that "Arab assaults on Jews" were caused by "the Wailing Wall controversy."[27] This preoccupation with the Wailing Wall reflected the Western assumption that religion, not economics or resistance to colonialism, was the prime motivator of the Muslim population. And the sanguinary nature of the revolt confirmed the assumption that Islam was, as one American congressman put it at this time, a violent religion of "frenzy and fanaticism" practiced by "bigoted Arabs."[28] Thus the uprising was made to fit the Western way of seeing the Muslim world and precluded the need to seek further causes for the troubles.

There was also plenty of editorial comment, some of which did, sometimes, suggest a broader context for the violence. However, such suggestions had little correlation to the headlines and stories that shaped popular perceptions of events. On the other hand, editorial comment was almost always reflective of the bipolar perception that divided the world between civilized West and uncivilized East.

The editorials transformed the rebellion of the Palestinians into a symbolic struggle between these two poles. For instance, the editors of the *Chicago Tribune*, while suggesting that "observing the growth of Zionist colonies the Arab must feel that in due time he will be secluded from what is to him as much as the Hebrew a Holy Land,"[29] also asserted that "the influence of the Jewish leadership [in Palestine] has been enlightened and humane and it must be recognized as an important force in the extension of civilization. . . . in such a controversy the interest of western civilization . . . must rest with the Jews." The editorial then added that "our [the United States'] own immediate interest is in the protection of the Jews, some of them American . . . and all of them in race and religion related to a valued element of our own country."[30] The *Tribune* editors later applauded the fact that "the British government is sending soldiers, battleships, and marines . . . and a permanent force large enough to keep the Arabs in check."[31] The *New York Times* commented that "Whatever may be said of the wisdom of the aspirations and activities of the Zionist organization" the Jews residing in Palestine have "undeniable rights" given them by both the League Mandate and Great Britain.[32] The present Arab challenge to these rights was "a recrudescence of horror. We had come to think such reports of rapine and massacre impossible. . . . A complacent civilization finds it all a rude and painful blow."[33] The paper speculated that the situation in Palestine might trigger other demonstrations by Muslims across the world, an event that would be "dangerous to European interests" and awaken the "old dread of Europe that the Moslems may unite again . . . and overthrow white dominion."[34] The *Times* chastised Great Britain because it "did not take the precautions which its responsibilities demand. . . . The weariness of the British taxpayer does not remove the British Government's obligations as the Mandatory Power in Palestine."[35] The *Los Angeles Times* praised the rapid use of force by the British to suppress "religious war in Palestine" which was in danger of "inspiring the natives of every country under British rule to attempt a similar revolt."[36] The *Los Angeles Times* editors then observed that "it would be ideal were the wild Arabs of the desert to open their hearts to moral suasion" but "unhappily sweet reasonableness does not seem to be the strongest point of the Bedouin sheik. What he does thoroughly understand and appreciate, however, is the song of the bullet and the crash of the high explosive shell."[37] The paper noted that "the Zionization of Palestine probably will not be accomplished without further difficulty of the same sort."[38] Finally the *Washington Post* focused on the loss of American life. "The country is shocked at the news that 12 American Jewish boys have been killed and 30 wounded in the attacks the Arabs have suddenly unloosed." The *Post* attributed this to "a fanatical outbreak of holy-war fervor originating in incidents at the century-old [*sic*] Wailing Wall."[39] The paper warned that "the fury of the Palestine outbreaks gives a more menacing aspect to the situation, by indicating the workings of a vast conspiracy that may envelop in flames all Moslem countries under British influence or dominion."[40] Under the circumstances the *Post* urged the British on to maximum effort in Palestine: "nothing short of a complete eradication of this fanatical movement against the Jewish race will be worthy of present-day civilization." To which it added that "the dispatch of an American warship . . . prepared to send bluejackets and marines to Jerusalem in case of need might have a beneficial moral effect."[41]

The overall effect of the press coverage of the 1929 rebellion was to meld press and Zionist views and present a picture of Arab aggression that was unprovoked, motivated by religious fanaticism, and threatening the beneficent expansion of civilization. Here Zionism functioned, as the *Chicago Tribune* put it, as an "extension of civilization." And since Americans had a "sympathetic interest in the advancement of civilization" it followed that the United States should "support the establishment upon just conditions of Jewish industry and culture in Palestine."[42] Indeed, as we shall see, this is exactly the outcome Zionist public relations efforts were aimed at—the view that the Jewish National Home be seen as an implicit aspect of American national interests in the Holy Land.

State Department Reactions to the Rebellion

No doubt most State Department personnel shared the bipolar worldview of the general public. The United States had rationalized its own colonial occupation of such places as the Philippine Islands (to say nothing of the conquest of the American West) in terms of altruistic imperialism. Thus, State Department officials had little doubt that British rule in Palestine would serve to advance civilization. Yet as we have seen, the diplomats were not swept along by the American Zionist campaign. Hemmed in by their traditional definition of national interests in the Near East, and seeing it as their duty to protect the United States from unnecessary foreign entanglements, the State Department took a hands-off, neutral position on the issue of the Jewish National Home.

In the first half of 1929 the State Department, like the press, had paid little attention to the underlying tensions between Arabs and Jews in Palestine. The cable traffic between the department and its Jerusalem consulate focused on economic issues and fretted over Britain's inclination to administer Palestine as if it were a Crown Colony. These matters were considered important because they impacted on how well the Anglo-

American Convention on Palestine, the treaty that governed U.S.-British relations in the country, was implemented. This, in turn, translated into the extent to which American business had access to the area.

All such matters, however, were temporarily put aside when, on August 23, 1929, the State Department received a cable from its consul general in Jerusalem, Paul Knabenshue, announcing "renewed Wailing Wall incidents have given rise to conflicts throughout Old and New Jerusalem between Arabs and Jews. A number of casualties both sides reported. The authorities are doing everything possible to control the situation. Several [British military] aeroplanes were circling low over the city this afternoon."[43]

The State Department immediately opened a file on the new situation, entitling it "Conflicts between Arabs and Jews over Wailing Wall in Palestine." One might initially conclude from this title that the department, like the press, would make little or no effort to analyze the situation as anything but a religious conflict over a shared sacred site. However, over time, Consul Paul Knabenshue would seek to offer a more extensive and probing analysis.

Knabenshue suggested that the violent Arab uprising was an almost inevitable result of the manner in which the Balfour Declaration was interpreted and implemented by the British, and actively argued that there should be a change in how the British administered the mandate in Palestine. In the end, his argument amounted to the proposition that the Palestinian position was actually more compatible with American ideals of altruistic imperialism than was Zionism. The key factor for Knabenshue was the Palestinian demand for a "representative assembly." The consul general's cables on this subject, while staying within the framework of the bipolar worldview, became a source of pressure on the State Department to understand and react to the Palestine situation in a way sympathetic to Arab demands.

The Knabenshue Analysis

Knabenshue began his analysis for the State Department with the contention that the Zionists were at least partially to blame for the 1929 outbreak of violence (or what American Jews of that year began to call "an Arab pogrom").[44] He based this on the belief that Revisionist Zionists had, through demonstrations and parades at the Wailing Wall and in neighborhoods of Muslim Jerusalem, behaved in such a way as to provoke the Arab uprising.[45] More important, however, the consul general identified what he considered broader contextual roots of the conflict. Thus, "while the controversy over the Wailing Wall undoubtedly furnished the spark which caused the recent explosion . . . the attendant incidents were, however, merely phases of the present dangerous situation. . . . The basic cause of the serious troubles . . . arises out of the Balfour Declaration."[46]

Knabenshue noted that the Balfour Declaration had two clauses, the first promising a Jewish National Home and the second promising not to violate the "civil and religious rights of the non-Jewish communities." In his opinion, the articles of the mandate that were used to implement the Balfour Declaration "artificially stimulated" immigration and officially facilitated land transfers. These acts had, according to Knabenshue, led to an "interpretation of the [first part of the] Declaration" in a manner that "violate[d] the second part of the Declaration and in so doing are in violation of paragraph four of Article 22 of the [League of Nations] Covenant, and hence, as might be said from an American point of view, are 'unconstitutional.'"[47]

Back in 1922, after earlier Arab disturbances, the British tried to clarify the situation by interpreting the first clause of the Balfour Declaration through a White Paper. According to Knabenshue, it stipulated that "Palestine is not to be converted into *the* National Home of the Jews, but merely a Jewish home may be established in Palestine."[48] Nonetheless, the Zionists had continued openly pressing for greater immigration and land transfers, which put, in the long run, effective pressure on the government in London. Thus the consul general pointed out that "to any student of the situation," including the Palestinian Arab leadership, "it is quite evident that the Zionist's ambition was, and still is, to convert Palestine into . . . a Jewish state and by economic pressure to force out the Arabs, or reduce them to impotency, until Palestine should become as Jewish as England is English."[49] Later, he further explained that Revisionist Zionists were "indiscreet and openly proclaim this policy, but the more moderate element are for the moment endeavoring to conceal this secret but nonetheless definite ambition."[50] All of this had led to constant rising tension between Arab and Jew in Palestine, the latest manifestation of which was the 1929 violence.

Knabenshue had a two-part solution to this problem. First he suggested "the formation of a legislative assembly with proportionate representation, the mandatory authority to have the power to propose legislation to the assembly and to enact it into law by ordinance if the assembly should refuse to pass it."[51] And second, a "new constitution [for] the country" that would "provide that there can be no legislation or governmental or other activity against Jews as Jews. . . . In Palestine it should be clearly understood that they have equal rights with the rest of the population."[52] These reforms would establish "that the Jews can settle in Palestine as of right and not on sufferance"[53] while also providing a legislative avenue to satisfying the "simple and quite understandable" demands of the Arabs for government "represented according to population . . . immigration control . . . [and] control of land sales."[54]

To the consul general this seemed a good compromise which would allow the Jews a place in Palestine while eliminating the worst of Arab fears. It also seemed to make good sense from the American perspective on altruistic imperialism. A supervised representative democracy with constitutional guarantees was the answer. If such changes did not come, Knabenshue speculated, "we are going to have a bloody uprising in Palestine which is going to be infinitely worse than heretofore, and which will . . . lead to a serious international situation."[55]

Paul Knabenshue, on the spot in Jerusalem, not only was an eyewitness to the Arab rebellion, but also had a non-Zionist understanding of what preceded it. Yet he also argued for the right of Jews to be in Palestine. His attitude, however, was certainly shaped by the bipolar worldview of his day. His solution to the problem in Palestine was premised on the assumption that good government was Western-style government, and that the British were called upon by the mandate to supervise the establishment of a representative regime. For Knabenshue, the problem was not colonialism as such, but rather the particular way mandate-style colonialism had been carried out in Palestine. Here, the process had not been used to tutor the natives in self-rule.

One can question how well Knabenshue's reforms would have worked in practice. The Zionists were not interested in democracy in the absence of a Jewish majority. They had no intention of trading their desire for a future Jewish state for constitutional guarantees under a representative government with an Arab majority. Stephen Wise's comment, quoted in chapter 2, clarified the Zionist view on this matter. He noted that the British mandate had freed the Zionists from the prospect of rule under "Arab suzerainty, an indignity and dishonor which Jews could not have tolerated." And indeed, Knabenshue's opinions caused the American Zionist establishment to turn quite hostile toward him, eventually mounting an effort to have him replaced.[56]

A second problem with the consul general's reformist ideas was that, though they pointed the way to a democratic solution, they were not really compatible with the popular American way of seeing the Holy Land.

Popular opinion saw the Zionist movement as an agent of a superior civilizational force. It embodied progress and development. Such movements do not subordinate themselves, even with constitutional guarantees, to a "more ignorant" non-Western native majority. Thus, even if the State Department had chosen to take up and popularize Knabenshue's solution, it would have clashed with the accepted American frame of reference for the problem in Palestine.

Nonetheless, the consul general had hope that, as a consequence of the Shaw Commission sent by the British government to investigate the 1929 violence, there would be a move in the direction he outlined. Based on this expectation he urged the State Department to "prevent any one speaking on behalf of the United States Government making a statement at this juncture which it might be difficult to retract should subsequent events make desirable a different attitude."[57] In other words, Paul Knabenshue was telling his superiors to prevent the U.S. government from committing itself to the Zionist cause because the Shaw Commission might recommend concessions to the Arabs of a democratic nature. However, as we shall see, Knabenshue's superiors had no intention of supporting his position.

Zionist Pressures

Paul Knabenshue was not the only one giving the State Department suggestions on how to respond to the Arab rebellion. A second source of pressure came from the American Zionists. Through petitions and a campaign to influence public opinion the Zionist Organization of America attempted to move the government toward seeing the Jewish National Home as an integral aspect of American national interests. To this end they put forth three main arguments, all of which would parallel positions popularized in the press. These arguments had the virtue of being compatible with the bipolar worldview as applied to Palestine, while at the same time readily associating the Zionist effort with more specific American interests and responsibilities.

The argument with the most specific impact was that American lives had been threatened and lost and thus the government should act. In the press coverage of the many rallies, marches, and protest meetings held across the country, this message was clearly stated.[58] The sentiments expressed below are typical in the 160 letters and petitions from senators, congressmen, and Jewish and non-Jewish organizations to be found in the State Department files.[59] For example, Representative Emanuel Celler of

New York in a telegram dated August 25 noted the death of American students at Hebron and the large number of American citizens resident in Tel Aviv and Haifa where fighting had broken out. He then asserted that "the State Department cannot view with complacency these Arab raids upon American interests. The cruiser Raleigh now in European waters should be immediately dispatched to the scene of disorder and the strongest representations should be made to the British Colonial Government."[60] Representative Jeremiah O'Connell of Rhode Island told Secretary of State Stimson on August 28 that "a high duty devolves upon the United States of America to lead the way in seeking an amelioration of the present deplorable situation in Palestine. . . . The protection of the rights of our own nationals should be asserted with all the strength and vigor of this powerful nation."[61] And Rabbi Louis Gross, the editor of the *Brooklyn Examiner*—"published for Brooklyn Jewry which is the largest Jewish community in the world"—told President Hoover in a telegram of August 24 that "the recent massacres of Jews in Palestine" were "scenes of horror enacted which menace the life and limb of American citizens." Therefore Hoover should use his "powerful moral influence . . . to avert further calamity and desecration in the Holy Land."[62]

A second and related argument was that a large American financial investment was threatened by the violence.[63] For instance, in Celler's communication on August 25 he noted not only the need to "prevent further loss of life" but also the need to prevent the loss of the "property of American Jewry which has been pouring millions of dollars in Palestine."[64] Isadore Morrison, acting national chairman of the Zionist fund-raising organization United Palestine Appeal, in a telegram to the State Department on August 26 reminded the secretary of state that during the past decade American Jews had "sent to Palestine upwards of twenty five million dollars."[65] And William Spiegelman, editor of the Jewish Telegraphic Agency, in a telegram sent to Secretary of State Stimson, suggested that the United States might consider taking over the Palestine mandate because of its "special significance to the American public since funds of American citizens have been and are expected to be the largest factor for the reconstruction and rehabilitation of the Holy Land."[66]

The third main argument was that there were not only American lives and property at risk, but also the advancement of Western civilization. Thus Morrison in his telegram to the State Department added the notion that all those millions invested in Palestine had brought the country "Western culture, industries and commerce."[67] William Spiegelman, in his communication with Stimson, told the secretary of state that out of the crisis "the Jewish National Home in Palestine will emerge with greater strength for the further spreading of Western civilization" and asked him for a statement about what the U.S. government was going to do to help.[68] Senator Robert F. Wagner, a member of the Foreign Relations Committee, took to the radio in New York City to build public support for U.S. action in Palestine. Speaking on ABC Radio on September 1 he delivered an address reported upon the next day in the *New York Times*. Wagner declared that the "accumulated decay of 2,000 years had been supplanted by Western civilization and standards" thanks to "the personal sacrifice of thousands of the best of the Jewish race." He then asked, "is all this to be swept away. . . ? Is the noble Jewish dream to be turned into a nightmare by the cowardly dagger of the assassin? The conscience of mankind cries to High Heaven that these shall not come to pass." He reminded his audience that "the United States Government by appropriate resolution [the 1922 congressional resolution approving the Balfour Declaration] expressed its satisfaction" with the Zionist effort, thus implying a certain American responsibility to support it.[69]

It should be noted that not all American Jews supported the position of Senator Wagner. The 1929 Arab rebellion did cause some soul-searching. Emanuel Neumann, who was by this time the educational director of the Zionist Organization of America, feared the possible loss of popular support due to "a reaction especially on the part of liberals who will say that the Zionist experiment in Palestine cannot be continued at the point of a bayonet."[70] However, while there may have been some of this feeling, no evidence of it is found in any of the four newspapers under consideration. As with the Carnegie report in 1926, any second thoughts about Zionism in 1929 were without lasting impact.

Counterpressure from Arab Americans

As we have seen, there was a group of Arab Americans who sought to put the Arab point of view before the American people and government. Earlier, they had organized themselves into the Palestine National League. Fuad Shatara, who had represented this group at the congressional hearings of 1922, was now the league president. In 1929 this organization sought to put the Arab rebellion in context and explain to the American people that the bloodshed was a response to British and Zionist policies over the past decade. In this endeavor the league allied itself with two other Arab American groups, the New Syria Party, headed by Abbas Abushakra, and the Young Men's Moslem Association, led by Abd M.

Kateeb. Also active in this effort was the well-known Arab American writer Ameen Rihani.

These activities first drew the attention of the press on August 29, 1929, when the *New York Times* reported that "a group of Arabian citizens and sympathizers living in or near New York met yesterday afternoon [August 28] to protest against the unfairness [of press reports] dealing with the present Palestine rioting." The trouble was "political and economic," Mr. Abushakra told the *Times* reporter. The Zionists had been "given a permanent home at the expense of the majority." The meeting forwarded explanatory cables to "several clerical and secular leaders denying the allegation that the attacks of the Arabs on the Jews were motivated by religion." One of these, sent to the Mandates Commission of the League of Nations at Geneva, explained that the "present deplorable events in Palestine are the outcome of the Balfour Declaration. The Wailing Wall is merely an incident" flowing from conditions created by Zionist settlement. To President Hoover, Secretary of State Stimson, and Senator William Borah, they cabled, "We regret present situation in Palestine. Zionism is responsible for these conditions. Application of Balfour Declaration under British mandate deprives Arabs of all their rights. Abrogation of declaration is only means to insure permanent peace. Arabs the world over look to American sense of freedom and justice to uphold Arabs in their struggle for national independence." Other telegrams were sent to Pope Pius XI, Prime Minister Ramsay MacDonald in England, and King Feisal of Iraq and other Arab leaders.[71]

Then, on September 9, 1929, representatives of the three Arab American groups met in Washington, D.C., with both Secretary of State Stimson and the British ambassador, Sir Esme Howard. Led by Ameen Rihani, the group included Peter S. George, Elias Joseph, George Sadak, Frank Sakran, and Ally Joudy. They told Stimson that while they "deplore the acts of violence" and "mourn the dead of both Arabs and Jews," events had to be understood within context.

For ten years the Arabs of Palestine have in vain protested and petitioned both to the British Government and the League of Nations. . . . Their demands for a national representative government . . . have all met with a deaf ear. . . . For ten years the Arabs have struggled and they have persisted and they have been patient. And all this time a small Jewish minority from Central and Eastern Europe, supported by funds from America and by the fiat of British power, have been making encroachments upon the rights of the overwhelming Arab majority. . . . Here is the fundamental cause of the present uprising. Religion has nothing to do with it. Racial feeling has nothing to do with it. It is a conflict between the Arab nationalism of the native majority and the Zionism of a small minority of foreign Jews.[72]

They then presented to the secretary of state demands similar to those mentioned in the above telegrams.

Stimson's reply to the group was remarkable for its simpleminded nature. He was receiving pressure from American Zionists to condemn the Arabs, and perhaps his political instincts dictated that he not address the substance of the Arab American argument. In any case, Stimson told Rihani and his colleagues that "the cause of civilization, the cause of better understanding among peoples of different races and religions is never served by violence and recrimination." What the United States wanted to see in Palestine was "peace and cooperation." He then concluded this way: "if your delegation can play a part in emphasizing the qualities of moderation and thoughtfulness which are so needed in any approach to the present problem of Palestine, you will have served an eminently useful and eminently American purpose."[73]

The U.S. Government Position

As Stimson's reply suggests, the arguments of the Arab Americans were brushed aside. The Zionists, however, could not be so easily dismissed. This was because their three arguments, referencing American lives threatened, treasure lost, and civilization menaced, were more consistent with the concerns being voiced by popular opinion, particularly as expressed in the press. Those arguments, loudly and consistently expressed throughout late August and September 1929, created pressure significant enough to make both President Hoover and Secretary of State Stimson take pains to explain and defend their official position of non-intervention. For instance, President Hoover responded positively to a request for a statement to the Jewish protest meeting of twenty thousand held at Madison Square Garden on August 29. In it he stated that he believed that the recent tragedy in the Holy Land would result in "greater security and greater safeguard for the future, under which the steady rehabilitation of Palestine as a true homeland will be even more assured." The Zionists responded to the president in a way that mixed their own cause with American and civilizational themes. At the August 29 gathering they announced that "we hail these [Hoover's] words as expressing the mind of America and the resolve of the civilized world that the great work of reconstruction which has been so well begun in Palestine must not retreat before the onslaught of fanaticism and savagery."[74]

On the other hand, the executive branch of the government resisted Zionist demands which conflicted with its position of non-intervention. For example, when Hoover received a Zionist delegation at the White House on August 27 he told them that he was "deeply concerned for the safety of all American citizens in Palestine" but that he felt "the British Government had taken strong and extensive measures for the restoration of order."[75] Hoover also voiced his concern over the anti-British nature of American Jewish protests (an extension of the critical approach taken by American Zionists during the recent economic crisis in Palestine). He indicated that he was determined to resist calls for U.S. intervention and he did not want to embarrass the British in any way.[76] Secretary of State Stimson took a similar line. In his stock replies to the myriad letters and petitions the State Department received, he assured the Zionists and their supporters that the department had strongly urged the British to act vigorously in Palestine and had reminded that government of their obligation to protect American lives and property, finishing the reply with assurances that the British were indeed doing just that. When approached directly by American Zionists seeking more aggressive American support, he rebuffed them.[77]

However, the State Department also resisted Paul Knabenshue's efforts to promote a reinterpretation of the mandate in a way that would limit the definition of the Jewish National Home while promoting a democratic and constitutional form of government. When, in 1930, the consul general suggested to Stewart Spencer Davis, the acting high commissioner in Palestine, how this might be accomplished, he was pointedly reprimanded by the State Department. He was told to "avoid being drawn into any discussions of the situation and scrupulously refrain from expressing an opinion to anyone whomsoever as to the possible position which this government might take" on any reinterpretation of the mandate.[78]

The way the State Department handled the 1929 situation, resisting the entreaties of American Zionists, Arab American anti-Zionists, and its own consul general in Jerusalem, argues for a motive of avoiding "entanglements" rather than anti-Semitism or even ideologically driven anti-Zionism. On the one hand the State Department was accepting of altruistic imperialism in the form of British-controlled Palestine. This brought no great risk of entanglements, and U.S. interests were, at least in theory, protected by treaty. On the other hand, the American Zionist vision of

altruistic imperialism in Palestine demanded active U.S.-government support. To the State Department policy makers, that equaled entanglements,
and therefore they sought to make a distinction between national interests
and the Jewish National Home. Thus, they qualified their pro-imperialist
perspective on Palestine in a manner that the popular point of view, as
expressed in the press, did not.

Yet at least in the 1920s, the State Department never went beyond
taking a non-interventionist, neutral stand on this matter. To be sure, there
was much grumbling against Zionism in the form of internal memos of the
Division of Near Eastern Affairs.[79] However, these complaints did not
translate into active opposition to the Jewish National Home either with
other branches of the U.S. government or with Britain. For instance, there
is no evidence of NEA seeking to shape or change public opinion on the
issue of Zionism. And the documents suggest that the division offered its
opinion to Congress (where it might have exercised some influence if it
had wished) only when asked. Therefore, while Zionism was certainly not
favored by the State Department, it was not actively campaigned against
either. The State Department simply took the position that it was not a
U.S. national interest.

Conclusion

Although the 1929 Arab rebellion contradicted the "progress means
peace" theory of Zionist colonization, it did not result in any critical re-
examination of the Zionist venture in the popular press. And despite the
fears of Zionist leaders that the 1929 rebellion would alienate liberal support, there was (judging from the press) no significant change in American
attitudes toward the Jewish National Home.[80] Why was Zionism able to
withstand having a major aspect of its own public relations message
proven incorrect? Perhaps it was because the bipolar worldview that governed the overall Western way of seeing the Holy Land was, through centuries of religious and imperialist teachings, too deeply imbedded to be
challenged by occasional contradictions. It was taken for granted that the
non-Western natives—in this case, as the Los Angles Times characterized
them, the "wild Arabs of the desert"—were barbarians prone to fanatical
violence. And this meant a general acceptance of the fact that "the
Zionization of Palestine probably will not be accomplished without further difficulty [rebellion] of this sort."[81]

This point of view governed the press reaction to the 1929 rebellion,
essentially melding it to the Zionist interpretation of events. Zionist

sources proved to be the major ones for press pieces, and the stories they told followed consistently from the premises of the prevailing bipolar worldview. Other points of view, such as those of Arab American activists, were too discordant to be taken seriously.

The prevailing pro-Zionist discourse, as it manifested itself in the newspapers, as well as telegrams, petitions, and resolutions sent to the president, Congress, and the State Department, created a source of pressure on the government to identify the Zionist program as worthy of official support—specifically, to identify the Jewish National Home with U.S. national interests in Palestine. As we have seen, the State Department, bound to resist "foreign entanglements" beyond recognized American spheres of influence, insisted on official neutrality toward Zionism. This produced a de facto competition between the State Department and the Zionist Organization of America over defining what really should constitute national interests in the Holy Land.

However, from a public relations standpoint, only one side in this contest was active. The American Zionists had long been promoting their views. The State Department, on the other hand, operated in a much more insular fashion. It never publicly debated the Zionists, and beyond the confines of the State Department and executive branch of government, the diplomats rarely offered their critique even in private. Therefore, the fact that the State Department resisted including the Jewish National Home in its interpretation of American national interests should not be mistaken as an offensive or attack posture. Rather, the department's position can be best regarded as defensive—seeking to hold off the pressure of the Zionists.[82] The long-term inadequacy of this defensive posture would begin to show in the 1930s. In that decade the Zionists would begin to wear down State Department resistance.

6

The 1930s

New Storm and Subtle Changes

The 1929 Arab rebellion did not lead to a resolution of the problems besetting Palestine. For example, Jewish immigration administered by the British mandate authorities continued as a major source of friction. Indeed, as virulent anti-Semitism increased in Europe in the 1930s, the British came under ever greater pressure to maintain or increase legal immigration quotas, and illegal immigration became more prevalent.[1]

As more immigrants came into the Holy Land, land sales to Jews alienated more of the country from Arab control. Though the total acreage involved was not great, the psychological impact of the process was strong on the Arab population. This was because land acquired by the Zionist organization through the auspices of the Jewish National Fund was deemed to be for "the sole use of the Jewish people" and resulted in an increase in the number of evictions of Palestinian peasants. This problem did not go unrecognized. The British investigatory commissions looking into the causes of the 1929 rebellion concluded that what was needed was "a reduction in Jewish immigration" and a "tighter control of land purchases by Jews."[2]

Renewed Rebellion

For the Palestinian Arabs, there seemed to be something of a domino effect in operation. As racist Europeans oppressed the Jews, discriminatory Western immigration laws channeled them to Palestine, where they became part of a colonial process that displaced Arabs. As Jamal al Husseini, a member of a leading Palestinian family, told the *New York Times* in June of 1936, "we are sorry for the Jews in Europe, but we can't see why we should be the victims of their colonial expansion."[3]

The situation made it increasingly clear that the British were now caught in a trap of their own making. The Balfour Declaration had promised a Jewish National Home in Palestine while at the same time promising not to "prejudice the civil and religious rights of the existing non-Jewish communities." It was an illusionary balancing act that was only feasible in the imaginations of imperial politicians—a fact the British government would finally admit to in 1937. In the resulting Jewish-Arab competition, it was bound to be the party which could exercise the greatest pressure on Great Britain that would prevail. This party clearly was the Zionists, for they possessed a cultural and religious affinity with the British, had an alleged strategic value to the empire, understood the ins and outs of English parliamentary politics, and, last but not least, had had their representatives in place in London since before World War I. The Arabs could bring pressure to bear on the ground in Palestine, but the ultimate decisions were made by politicians in Britain.

The inability (at least until the approach of World War II) of the British leadership to chart a course independent of Zionist pressure was clearly demonstrated in 1930s. At the beginning of the decade, in 1930, under pressure from the World Zionist Organization, the British government repudiated the Passfield White Paper (issued after an investigation of the 1929 rebellion) calling for concessions to the Arabs of Palestine. This reversal exacerbated the situation for both Arabs and British imperial administrators in the Holy Land. Then, in late 1935 the British high commissioner in Palestine, Sir Arthur Wauchope, seeking to lessen tensions, championed the idea of a legislative council "designed to secure the advice and assistance of the people of Palestine in carrying on the government of the country."[4] On the face of it, this was a good idea, reflecting the accepted principle of eventual self-determination for mandate territories. But it also raised the spectre of majority rule at a time when the Jews were still a minority of the population. Thus, unless the suggested council was completely powerless, it represented a great threat to the Zionists, so they automatically opposed the project.[5]

On the other hand, the legislative council proposal raised the hopes of the Arabs, for Wauchope had initially indicated to them that the council would have some say on the issues of immigration and land sales. But then Zionist pressure was brought to bear in Great Britain. Chaim Weizmann traveled from Palestine to London in February 1936 to campaign against the proposal.[6] He was so effective that both the House of Commons and the House of Lords registered opposition to the project as "totally unfair to the Jews."[7] Backtracking in the face of this domestic political uproar, Prime Minister Ramsay MacDonald told Wauchope to exclude immigration and land sales from the purview of the proposed council. This in turn upset the Arabs, who felt "they had been betrayed" yet again.[8]

Soon thereafter, in mid April 1936, violence broke out, initially in Jaffa, and then throughout all of Palestine. Quickly the local Arab factions formed a united front and instituted a nationwide general strike that was to last until the government met its demands for cessation of Jewish immigration and land sales to Jews. The violence rapidly escalated, and by the end of May the *Chicago Tribune* could report that "there is a growing conviction among many observers today that Palestine is undergoing a major, well organized rebellion rather than simple anti-Jewish disorders."[9]

How the Newspapers Saw It

Nonetheless, most American "observers" continued to perceive events in Palestine through the classical framework of the bipolar worldview. Indeed, that worldview supplied the interpretive context for all coverage of the 1936–39 rebellion. Thus, the renewed violence in 1936 often retriggered the old laments of 1929. Rebelling Arabs were labeled "bandits," "brigands," and "terrorists" by the *New York Times, Chicago Tribune, Los Angeles Times*, and *Washington Post*.[10] Their resistance to British and Zionist colonialism was attributed to "the blind forces of nationalism and religious fanaticism" by the *Post*,[11] anti-Semitism and "racial enmity" by the *L.A. Times*,[12] and "racial" animosity by the *Tribune*.[13] The *New York Times* frequently referred in its stories to an atmosphere of "chaos, panic, arson and terrorism" due to Arab "civil disobediance."[14]

Letters and Op-ed Pieces

Those op-ed pieces and letters appearing in the *New York Times* reminded readers that the Zionist colonies in Palestine stood amid "a sea of the native population of Arabia . . . [as] an outpost of Europe." These were the words of the paper's "special correspondent," who wrote op-ed pieces under the pen name of Augur (a reference to a diviner of ancient Roman times). "The success of the Palestine enterprise," he continued, "is a success for Europe. It helps maintain the prestige of the white race in the East."[15]

Others took a different, but still essentially pro-imperialist approach. For instance, a "Christian delegation representing the Pro-Palestine Federation of America" (a pro-Zionist Christian organization) observed, in 1936, that much of the "white race" was under "the dark spectre of bigotry and prejudice" (that is, anti-Semitic persecution in Europe). This called for "the Anglo-Saxon community of nations . . . to blaze a trail for the dawn of a new era of freedom, justice and human enlightenment." The best way to do this, according to the Pro-Palestine Federation, was through the "restoration of the land of Israel to the children of Israel." Such an action would serve as "a guiding star in this great struggle for a better world and a better humanity."[16]

Individuals wrote to the *New York Times* to point out that Palestine was "a neglected land" now being "reclaimed from the desert" by the Zionists.[17] This was a process once more endangered by "a veritable reign of terror . . . caused by Arabs."[18] American politicians such as Emanuel Celler, and the long-standing supporter of Jewish colonization Nathan Straus, agreed. They drove the point home in a radio broadcast reported by the *New York Times* on June 8, 1936, during which the two men compared Arab behavior in Palestine to Indian attacks on American colonial settlers.[19]

Editorial Positions

Editorial views reiterated the same points, demonstrating the consistency of the bipolar worldview across the country and over time. In an editorial published at an early stage in the Palestine rebellion, on April 21, 1936, the *New York Times* sought to answer the question, Why was there an uprising in Palestine? The answer offered was, because "Moslem religious fanaticism is easily stirred against the unbeliever," and also "the inertia and conservatism of an economically backward people intensify their natural resentment against the thrust of expanding, energetic newcomers." The "newcomers," the Zionists, continued to represent modernity. "The Jewish immigrants have developed scientific agriculture, harnessed water power and established industries able to utilize the natural resources of the country."[20]

A *Washington Post* editorial published a month later also spoke of this transformation, all the more notable for having been maintained in the face of worldwide depression. The paper then repeated the notion that transforming Palestine into a Western place must benefit the indigenous peoples. "Almost alone of any country in the world the Holy Land has been enjoying a large measure of prosperity. Industry and agriculture have flourished there as never before. . . . In this prosperity, the result in very large measure of Jewish capital, labor and skill, Arabs have shared with Jews. . . . The modernization of Palestine has greatly improved the lot of the Arab fellahin and the Arab worker by making that land a more healthful, cleaner, happier place to live in, by permitting them to enjoy a higher standard of living than was possible in the past." If this supposedly altruistic imperialism brought such benefits, then why would the Palestinian Arabs throw it all aside and rebel? It seemed to the *Post* editors that the answer must lie in the ignorance of the Arabs and the selfish scheming of their leaders. Thus, they concluded that Palestine's Arab leaders stirred rebellion because Zionist modernization of the economy meant "a potential if not actual weakening of their economic power and the possibility that their political power as feudal overlords will disappear. No wonder, then, that they have invoked to their aid the blind forces of nationalism and religious fanaticism."[21]

General Coverage

General coverage in all four newspapers reinforced these well-established assumptions. For instance, Joseph M. Levy, still the *New York Times* correspondent in Jerusalem, told the paper's readers at the end of May 1936 that "anyone acquainted with the Moslem Arab mentality is aware that it is no easy task to arouse the Arab to rebellion. But once the Arab's religious fanaticism is aroused he becomes wild and almost uncontrollable."[22] A month later Levy was explaining, "the Arab, son of the desert, believes he has become a hero in defying the . . . British Empire." As a consequence, "the whole country is infested by brigands who place no value on human life."[23]

Defying the British Empire, as well as Zionism, was seen as defiance of modernity. For example, on June 30 this aspect of altruistic imperialism was pictorially melded with the suppression of Arab resistance. On that day the *New York Times* published a photo entitled "British Soldiers Blow Up Part of Jaffa, in Palestine" along with the explanation that "An engineering unit sent to the Holy Land to assist in restoring order was used on June 18 to help in the work of modernization."[24] Part of the old city of Jaffa had previously been described by Joseph M. Levy in the *Times* as "a nest of agitation, bomb throwing and shooting."[25] By the end of June a company of Royal Engineers arrived and, supposedly to clear away "centuries old, congested, unsanitary buildings," started dynamiting the offending parts of Jaffa. This paved the way for the "construction of two roads for the benefit both of that quarter and the town as a whole."[26]

The *Washington Post* coverage, also using an East-versus-West perspective, described "Hate Sweep[ing] the Levant."[27] The paper reported that "Rioting Arabs" have "burned an orange grove owned by Felix Warburg of the United States."[28]

Los Angeles Times coverage depicted the Arab rebellion as "new anti-Semitic disorders" through which "rioting Arabs . . . spread terror and destruction through the Holy Land."[29] The paper emphasized the danger to "600 American citizens" located in Jerusalem and covered the efforts of Leland B. Morris, the American consul, to "advise them what to do in case of outbreaks."[30] An *L.A. Times* political cartoon appearing on May 20 depicted a large, profiled face of an Arab with a great black beard and a headband on which was inscribed "racial enmity." The face appears to be pursuing a frightened, diminutive figure labeled "Palestine." The cartoon is captioned, "By the Beard of the Dark Prophet"—an obvious reference to Muhammad and Islam.[31]

Finally, the *Chicago Tribune* characterized the Arab rebellion as a "New Race Clash"[32] and pointed out that at least some of the places under attack had been "financed in the U.S."[33] The *Tribune* had a special correspondent, Alex Small, traveling in the Middle East at this time, and he emphasized that the achievements of Jews in Palestine were largely due to outside financial aid. "Palestine is a remittance country" he wrote.[34] And it was these remittances that allowed places such as Tel Aviv to "grow like a Florida boom town."[35]

The Crusader Theme Reemphasized

In the midst of the violence the crusader aspect of the bipolar worldview was reemphasized. The occasion for this was the May 14, 1936, death of Edmund Allenby. All four papers commented on the death of the man who had led the British army in the capture of Jerusalem during World War I. On May 15, 1936, the *L.A. Times* ran an article, "Holy Land's Captor Dies," in which it noted that "the restoration of the Holy Land to Christianity was the culmination of the most brilliant of Allenby's many military drives of dazzling swiftness."[36] The paper followed up with an editorial the next day memorializing Allenby. In it the editors declared that "though many of the once stirring events of [World War I] are destined . . . to pass into oblivion, there is one that is indelibly written in the history of the race. December 9, 1917 . . . a date that will be held in eternal memory. That day saw the victorious troops of Christianity enter the gates of Jerusalem and restore to the Chosen People the Holy City of Zion."[37]

The *Chicago Tribune* ran the story of Allenby's death on May 15 and commented that he had "delivered the Holy Land from seven centuries of Moslem domination . . . [in] one of the most brilliant victories of the world war. The military success gripped all Christendom."[38] The *Washington Post* editorial on Allenby's death stated that "the capture of Jerusalem and the smashing of Turkish power in Syria and Palestine, gave him a place in history with Richard Coeur de Lion, Godfrey de Bouillon and others who had sought to place the cross above the crescent in the Holy Land."[39] Finally, in what could have been read by Muslims as an insult to the prophet Muhammad, a *New York Times* editorial of May 15 suggested that Allenby would be "remembered in the Near East as God's prophet . . . and in the history of the human race his name will be permanently written as . . . the Deliverer of the Holy Land."[40] Elsewhere the *Times* described him as "the last Crusader."[41]

The Actions of the ZOA

But Allenby was not the "last Crusader." It would have been much more appropriate for the *New York Times* to have titled him the first of the modern crusaders. And these modern crusaders, "the victorious troops of Christianity," were now both much more powerful than the indigenous population of the Holy Land, and allied to a well-organized and well-financed Jewish colonization effort that drew much of its support from the United States.

In the last half of the decade, the Zionists believed that colonization effort to be in jeopardy. Unlike the crisis of 1929, the threat did not lie only in the violent resistance of the Palestinians. Now, in the face of renewed rebellion, there was also the possibility of British concessions to Arab demands for a cessation of Jewish immigration and land acquisition. It was to discourage any concessions on the part of the British that the Zionist Organization of America mobilized American Jewish support in these years and, in addition, sought to recruit the U.S. government as an ally in this endeavor. They argued that the United States had the power to prevent such concessions based upon their interpretation of Article 7 of the Anglo-American Palestine Convention. As they read it, this article obligated the British to obtain prior American approval for any changes in the mandate.

The ZOA mobilization expressed itself on many fronts. There was the use of a mass letter-writing campaign not only from individuals, but also from Jewish and Christian organizations. These petitions were sent to newspapers, Congress, the White House, and the State Department. For instance, in the fall of 1938 the U.S. government's various branches received over sixty-five thousand letters and telegrams protesting any possible halt to Jewish immigration into Palestine. Sympathetic congressmen and senators, in turn, petitioned the secretary of state. In general, these communications deplored Arab "savagery" and also demanded that the U.S. government warn the British against any cutback in Jewish immigration to the Holy Land.[42]

The ZOA also used more personal approaches. Indeed, the organization's first effort to recruit the United States government as an ally against British concessions to the Arabs came in the summer of 1936 in the form of "personal diplomacy." In July of 1936 Will Rosenblatt of the WZO sent a telegram from London to Simon Rifkind, an associate of Senator Robert Wagner and a supporter of the ZOA. The telegram warned that the British Cabinet was considering a suspension of Jewish immigration into Palestine as a way of responding to the Arab rebellion. Rosenblatt urged American Zionists to get the American government to "make formal representations . . . against proposed suspension." The object here, according to Rosenblatt, was to give the British government the "impression that Anglo American relations might be injured" if such a suspension took place.[43]

Rifkind quickly communicated this news to Sam Rosenman, who was a personal friend and counselor to President Roosevelt (and later to Harry Truman), and who was also a supporter of Jewish settlement in Palestine. Rifkind urged a personal approach to the president because "his [FDR's] response to these matters is much more warm-hearted than that of some of his official family."[44] Rosenman complied and sent the Rosenblatt cable to FDR on July 16. He observed that "a great deal seems to be involved, if the cable is accurate, so that I am much interested." He then wondered whether Roosevelt would want "the State Department to do anything at all in the matter."[45]

On July 21 President Roosevelt referred the matter to Assistant Secretary of State (Judge) R. Walton Moore. FDR instructed Moore to "look into" the matter and, in reference to British intentions, "let me know the answer."[46] Moore, in turn, referred the matter to the Division of Near Eastern Affairs, where it was dealt with by the division chief, Wallace Murray. This routing probably would not have been to the liking of the Zionists, for Murray, and the State Department as a whole, were seen as just those elements of the "official family" that were not so "warmhearted" when it came to Jewish colonization in Palestine.

The State Department Response

Not being "warm-hearted" did not in fact mean outright opposition to Zionism on the part of the State Department. Rather, despite the ZOA's reading of the situation, it meant arguing against any official government endorsement of either the Arab or Zionist positions. In other words, neutrality and the avoidance of "entanglements." Thus, Murray, who was getting regular reports on the situation in Palestine from the consulate in Jerusalem, wrote to Secretary of State Cordell Hull on July 25 that the United States should not urge on the British any particular immigration policy at a time when "their position is extremely difficult since they must endeavor to hold a balance between two warring factions." Nonetheless, Murray understood that the American Zionists, having the ear of the president, could not be entirely ignored. So, he went on, "it might be desirable to have Mr. Bingham [Robert Worth Bingham, the U.S. ambassador in London], entirely personally and unofficially, inform Mr. Eden [Anthony Eden, the British foreign secretary] of the concern of Jewish circles in the United States."[47]

Hull was a hardworking, deliberate, and cautious secretary. However, his limited knowledge of the details of regional foreign policy outside the Western Hemisphere caused him to rely upon his division chiefs.[48] Thus he followed Murray's advice and the next day, July 26, instructed Bingham to raise the matter, "entirely personally and unofficially," with the British foreign secretary. Hull told the ambassador that he was to "stress the fact that you are not speaking for your government."[49] On the same day, Hull wrote to the president and, again following Murray's advice—and indeed sometimes using the division chief's words—argued, on the one hand, against pressing the British on the issue of immigration, but, on the other, for informing the British of American Jewish concerns.[50] The president made no objection to this approach, and on July 28, during an otherwise regularly scheduled meeting with Eden, Bingham brought the subject of Jewish immigration up in an informational way. There the matter seemed to end as far as the State Department was concerned, except that Hull instructed his subordinates "that no publicity be given to the fact that Ambassador Bingham was authorized to take this matter up with the British Government."[51] However, it is important to note that this action of the secretary of state set an important precedent. The policy of strict neutrality was subtly broken and, while it would still be often argued for, the department would nonetheless find itself repeating over and over again the "unofficial" representations of American Zionist views.

Expanding the Definition of American Interests in Palestine

Thus, it can be argued that in the summer of 1936 the State Department was not responding to American Zionist concerns over Palestine in a hostile or anti-Semitic fashion. Despite the refusal of many historians to recognize the fact, the department's leadership, and that of its Division of

Near Eastern Affairs, now understood that the efforts of American citizens in Palestine had, in effect, expanded the definition of American interests in that country.[52] For instance, in September of 1936 George Wadsworth, the American consul general in Jerusalem, acknowledged as much in a letter to the American Jewish philanthropist Nathan Straus. "Of the 400,000 who now form the Yishuv [Jewish Palestine], some 10,000, my office estimates, are American citizens. Of the $300,000,000 which I am informed the World Zionist Organization estimates as having been invested in Palestine . . . my office estimates some $33,000,000 as being today in the form of concrete American capital investment. . . . I need not assure you that these new and important American interests add much . . . to the very real interest of the work of the Jerusalem Consulate General."[53]

The reality of significant and growing American investment in the Holy Land, as well as the increasing range of American activity there, was underscored by a detailed memorandum on the subject put out by a coalition of American Jewish organizations in November of 1936. Addressed to the British government, but filed with the State Department as well, the memorandum argued that American Jews had a stake in the present and future of Palestine that could not be ignored by either government.

The memorandum's cover letter stated that "American Jews have large investments in Palestine and have sent large sums to Palestine in the way of gifts. The items summarized in the accompanying memorandum aggregate not less than $77,500,000."[54] The document went on to detail this investment in Palestinian pounds:

Land and buildings	LP 3,160,000
Citriculture	1,770,000
General investments, mortgages and credit institutions	1,600,000
Industry and handicrafts, commerce, transportation and service businesses	567,000
	LP 7,097,000
or the equivalent of approximately	$35,500,000

Thus American Jews have made the following minimum financial contributions to the development of Palestine:

In gift funds	$42,000,000
In investments	35,500,000
Total	$77,500,000[55]

There followed a detailed argument that the mandate and other treaty documents, such as the San Remo Agreements, placed Britain in Palestine for the primary purpose of turning it into a Jewish National Home. Furthermore, it was argued, the Anglo-American Convention on Palestine precluded any deviation from that path without prior consultation with and consent from the U.S. government.[56] Taken as a whole the message sent by this document was clear: Britain's job in Palestine was to secure the country for Jewish colonization, and the United States had a big enough stake in the venture to see that the British did not deviate from this end. "The participation by America in the framing of the Balfour Declaration and the Mandate . . . the treaty [Anglo-American Convention] ratified by the U.S. in 1925; the joint resolution of the Congress of the United States and the declarations of Presidents . . . [American Jewish] gifts and investments of approximately $77,500,000—all indicate a continuing and ever widening American interest in the political and economic progress of Palestine."[57]

These assertions of expanding American interests and obligations in Palestine were backed up by growing Zionist political influence. For instance, on September 7, 1936, the *New York Times* published a letter sent to the secretary of state over the signatures of seventeen senators "expressing the hope and belief that Great Britain would not interfere with Jewish immigration or otherwise hinder the rebuilding of the Jewish homeland in Palestine." The accompanying article listed thirty additional senators and representatives who had sent similar pro-Zionist messages to the State Department.[58]

Thus the letters that poured into the State Department came, in part, from dozens of the government's own influential legislators.[59] Here we see evidence of the virtual alliance between the ZOA and Congress that had been growing since the passage of the congressional joint resolution in support of the Balfour Declaration in 1922. This alliance, in turn, drew upon a deep-seated, a priori pro-Zionism that existed among a great number of governmental leaders outside the State Department.

A good example of this pre-existing attitude can be found in the case of Harold Ickes. Ickes, a lawyer and social reformer, was FDR's secretary of the interior in 1936. He had no special connection to Zionism or Palestine yet was drawn to support Jewish colonization of the Holy Land by the religio-cultural notions described at the beginning of this work. Thus, when he was asked to give a speech before a convention of the United Palestine Appeal, a Zionist fund-raising organization, his words would reveal a wide range of assumptions that supported Zionism as a movement of altruistic imperialism. Ickes told the delegates that "like any other person of broad interest I have been fascinated to watch this activity in Palestine." For him this activity was full of "social idealism." This point of view suggests that Ickes, like Louis Brandeis, may have projected into Zionist activity his own great enthusiasm for social reform. For him the Zionist undertaking became representative of "wonderful progress" bringing to the Holy Land schools, hospitals, and land reclamation. Ickes had no doubt of the right of Western Jews to colonize Palestine. Indeed, it was "the fulfillment of the destiny of a people" and "a task that is without comparison in the history of the human race." As such it was not only benefiting the Jews, but all of mankind. "We cannot but believe that the effect of a liberal, advanced civilization in the new Palestine will react to the benefit of the world."[60]

What makes Ickes's speech before the United Palestine Appeal all the more interesting is that he had submitted a draft of the talk to the State Department prior to its delivery. The draft was gone over by Wallace Murray, who asked Ickes to delete those portions of the speech which might suggest any precedent for U.S. intervention abroad on behalf of oppressed minorities. This reflected the State Department's anti-entanglement position. Ickes readily complied with Murray's request. It is to be noted that Murray (whom the Zionists did not see as a "warm-hearted" supporter) did not challenge those parts of the speech that endorsed the benefits of colonization as such.[61] There is no evidence that NEA saw anything wrong in principle with an "advanced civilization" establishing itself in Palestine. Rather the evidence suggests that the division only believed that an active public commitment to the Zionist effort to do so was not in Americans' interest.

The Arab American Countereffort

The letters found in the files of the State Department from congressmen, senators, civic leaders, and Jewish and Christian organizations, as well as the sentiments put forth in speeches such as that of Ickes, represent "facts on the ground" in the political landscape of America. As such they were the U.S. counterpart of the "facts on the ground" in Palestine itemized in the memorandum of the American Jewish organizations referred to above.

Against these facts of growing Zionist political influence, the Arab American community continued to attempt counterpressure and argument. However, in terms of letters arriving at the White House, Congress, or the State Department, those supporting the Arab position were much fewer in number than those espousing Jewish colonization. Those that did arrive reflected the sentiment not only of individuals, but also of Arab American organizations. There were, for instance, the letters, dated October 16, 1936, from Faris S. Malouf, president of the Syrian and Lebanese American Federation of the Eastern States, an organization "composed of 65 Syrian-Lebanese American clubs and representing 250,000 American citizens." Malouf wrote to both President Roosevelt and Secretary of State Hull informing them of the resolutions passed by his organization at its "fifth annual convention held in Worcester, Mass." These resolutions attempted to equate the struggle of the Palestinian Arabs in 1936 with "the early struggles of the original thirteen colonies in 1776 for independence from foreign domination."[62] Thus, while the Zionists pictured the Palestinians as the equivalent of hostile frontier Indians fighting courageous American-style colonists, the Arab Americans identified those same Palestinians with American colonists fighting against imperial oppression.

It followed then that Malouf listed among the goals of the Palestinian Arab struggle the realization of "the principle of self-determination" and "government with the consent of the governed." In a cover letter accompanying the resolutions, Malouf warned against "a great effort on the part of influential groups and members of Congress to misrepresent the cause of the revolution in Palestine and the natural and proper conduct of the Arabs." And unlike the popular press images that portrayed the Arab rebellion as a product of religious fanaticism and ignorance, the Arab Americans insisted that the uprising had been brought on by British policies, which "impose the immigration of a foreign people upon Palestine contrary to the wishes and interests of the people."[63]

In 1937, organized Arab Americans would be back again knocking at the door of the State Department. This effort involved a series of communications and delegation visits to the department that ran from February through July of that year. This was paralleled by an extensive speaking tour conducted by the Arab American poet and journalist Ameen Rihani. Rihani made it onto the New York City municipal radio station, WNYC, on June 5, 1937. He told his audience that the "the only possible and practical solution would involve a decision that the Jewish National Home was now complete, and henceforth to be developed from within and not from without. Jewish immigration and land buying would be stopped at once and a national representative government would take the place of the mandate."[64] Within days the New York City Board of Aldermen condemned the broadcast for spreading "anti-Semitism and racial hatred over a national hook-up."[65]

When it came to the State Department and the White House, Arab Americans demanded equal time with their more powerful Zionist rivals. In response to the reception of several Zionist delegations by Secretary of State Hull, Peter George, the legal adviser to the Arab National League, a successor organization to the Palestine National League (and one "composed of Arab-Americans of all countries"), secured an appointment at the State Department for representatives of his group.[66] The meeting took place on February 1, 1937. We can surmise that Hull received delegations from both sides as part of a policy to maintain a public appearance of balance and neutrality.[67]

At the February 1 meeting, the Arab American representatives (Ameen Rihani, Peter George, and the Reverend Benjamin Haffiz) presented Hull, as well as Wallace Murray and Paul Alling (Murray's assistant chief at NEA), with a five-page memorandum which challenged Zionist religious and historical claims to Palestine. They asserted that the Zionsts were succeeding as colonizers only "with money from this country, and British bayonets." They noted the evidence of the King-Crane Commission as proof that "the Balfour Declaration was forced upon the Arabs." The result was a colonization process that ran counter to America's democratic values. Indeed, the Arab Americans asserted that the Palestinian struggle expressed a universal truth, their "stand is that which every nation recognizes as fundamental and just—they want to be masters in their own house." Finally, seeking to counter popular opinion that the Arab revolt was an expression of racial animosity, the memorandum stated that "the Arabs are not against the Jews, they are against the political Zionists who would deprive them of their land."[68]

This meeting at the State Department was noted by the *New York Times* on February 2, which reported that the secretary of state had "made no comment" to the group's request that the U.S. government "turn a sympathetic ear to the voice of the Arabs of Palestine."[69] This, however, was not quite accurate. On the suggestion of Wallace Murray, Hull had resurrected the noncommittal reply made by Secretary of State Stimson to a similar Arab American delegation received in 1929 (Rihani was also on this earlier delegation and probably recognized the statement). It called upon the Arabs and the Jews to seek "a good neighbor understanding."[70]

Although Hull's response was for all intents and purposes meaningless, the Arab Americans were not ready to give up. Indeed, they seemed intent on battling American Zionist efforts step for step. Thus in July of 1937 Peter George, again acting as the legal adviser of the Arab National League, followed up the memorandum described above with a seventeen-page analysis of American interests and relations to Palestine. This was written to try to counter ZOA efforts to recruit the U.S. government into pressuring Great Britain against implementing any policies judged hostile by the Zionists. This July submission by George also served to rebut the American Jewish memorandum of November 1936, which presented an expansive view of American interests in the Holy Land.

Submitted "on behalf of Arab American citizens" the George analysis argued that "the sole concern of our government was with the safeguarding of our political and economic interests . . . together with the protection of our citizens and their property rights . . . and non-interference in the educational work . . . undertaken by our citizens in the Near East." The Anglo-American Convention on Palestine, the Joint Congressional Resolution on the Balfour Declaration, and the words of praise for Zionist colonization by various presidents did not create any legally binding expansion of these interests. In fact, according to the Arab American interpretation, the dollar amount of investment and the number of Americans resident in Palestine was not the issue. The relevant question to be asked was whether the British were reasonably respecting and protecting American political and economic rights and interests. As long as they were, the British could modify the mandate without requiring U.S. consent. George ended his long paper with a plea for the government not to be drawn into the turmoil of Palestine on any one side. "Any animus or prejudice felt [by American Jews or Arab Americans toward the situation in Palestine] should be held privately and not suffered to intrude upon the foreign policy of the country to which they owe allegiance."[71]

This plea for neutrality by Peter George on behalf of the Arab National League was, in fact, quite similar to the position taken by Wallace Murray and the Division of Near Eastern Affairs. Thus, Murray sent a detailed summary of it to Hull, Moore, and Sumner Wells.[72] Nonetheless, Murray's acknowledgment (dated July 26, 1937) sent to George upon receipt of the paper was a nondescript form letter.[73] Neutrality was the position taken even in response to an Arab American analysis supporting just that.

The 1937 Debate over Partition

Zionist Pressure Increases

The efforts of American Zionists to pressure the U.S. government into a de facto alliance intensified in 1937. Where in 1936 the issue around which this effort focused was the perceived threat to Jewish immigration, in 1937 it was the expected recommendations of the British Royal Commission, or Peel Commission, investigating the Arab uprising of the previous year. By early 1937 the commission was rumored to be preparing a recommendation for the partition of Palestine into three parts: a Jewish state, an Arab state most likely to be merged with Transjordan, and a continued British mandate for the cities of Jerusalem and Bethlehem connected to the Mediterranean Sea by a corridor to the port of Jaffa.

American Zionists broke into two camps when it came to partition. One side, led by Louis Lipsky and probably representing a majority of American Jews, took the WZO position. That is, they were wary of partition but were willing to negotiate such a proposal with the British. The other camp, led by Stephen Wise, stood adamantly opposed to partition.[74] Wise declared that partition would "strike at the very heart of Jewish hopes." To divide Palestine meant that the British were treating the Jews "as if we were just another warring tribe in Palestine even as the Arabs."[75] It was Wise and his supporters who strenuously lobbied the U.S. government.

In late February of 1937 Secretary of State Hull received a petition from 257 Orthodox rabbis protesting any attempt "to minimize or weaken the historic rights of Jewish people to their Holy Land." The petition asserted that "vital religious issues affecting millions of Jews of American citizenship are at stake. . . . It is within the power of our government to prevent the greatest injustice of modern times, by not sanctioning the curtailment of Jewish rights to Palestine."[76]

Soon thereafter, Stephen Wise met with Assistant Secretary of State Moore. At that time Moore suggested that he might ask the British ambassador in Washington to let the U.S. government know "in advance what will be the character of the report of the [Peel] Commission."[77] This offhanded remark was interpreted by Wise as a verbal contract between the State Department and the ZOA to obtain intelligence that would help the Zionists in their fight against partition or any "cantonization" of Palestine. Thus Wise, who was anxious to confirm that partition was the commission's plan early enough to prevent its ever being implemented, would now see it as acceptable to repeatedly ask, and sometimes demand, that the State Department pressure information out of the British government. Moore soon backed away from his own suggestion. But Wise simply proceeded to bypass the assistant secretary. By June 1937, concerned by "disturbing reports" out of London that the Peel Commission was considering partition, Wise was writing over and over again to Secretary of State Hull with ever-increasing impatience. "Forgive me if I repeat what I have said before, that it is of supreme importance that first our government and afterwards we, who carry the responsibility of Zionist affairs, be enabled to learn the substance of the report before it is crystallized into a decision by the British Government." Wise wanted "at least a paraphrase" of the report and demanded it "on the basis of those rights which are ours in the entire case, that is to say, our government." He reminded Hull that the ZOA's apprehension was also "the Chief's [FDR] deep concern."[78] Finally, by early July, Wise had dropped all pretense and his communications with Hull took a commanding tone. In a telegram to the secretary of state on July 2, Wise told Hull, "United States should now request summary of document [the Peel Report] for basis of any representations it may therefore desire to make. The Zionist convention just concluded unanimously adopted a strong resolution against participation cantonization or any modification of the Mandate. Urge American ambassador London be requested act immediately."[79]

Simultaneously, Wise's ZOA faction had prevailed upon the U.S. Senate to pass Senate Resolution 174, which was transmitted to Secretary of State Hull on August 12, 1937. In part it read, "Resolved, That the State Department be requested to transmit to the Senate such information as it may possess, and which it may properly give, regarding the present situation in Palestine. It is desired to know what steps are being taken by our Government to protect our interests under the treaty with Great Britain, and vigorously to represent to the mandatory, the British Sovereign, our anxiety over the situation, with a forthright indication of our unwillingness to accept any modification of the mandate without the knowledge and consent of the Government of the United States."[80]

State Department Response

The response of the State Department to this pressure will be surprising to those who assume the department's outright opposition to Zionism. Instead, the documents reveal a much more complex picture of contrasting official and unofficial policies and attempts to balance diverse interests and pressures.

Officially, the department's position was that it must decline to do what Wise and his faction of the ZOA wished—that is obtain information of British plans for Palestine and then act to stop partition by claiming the power to block changes in the mandate. One historian supporting the Zionist position has attributed this refusal to "extravagant hostility" that led men like Hull and Murray to "distort a historical record of American interest in Palestine in glaring fashion."[81] But as we have seen, the State

Department had acknowledged growing, Zionist-related, American interests in Palestine. They just balanced them against other interests and concerns, such as oil investments in Arabia and the long-standing, powerful tradition of non-entanglements.

As Hull explained to Senator Millard Tydings (one of the senators advocating the Zionist cause), what Wise and his allies asked of the State Department violated "well established international practice" which "did not permit a government to make itself a vehicle for transmission to other governments of communications from private individuals or organizations. . . . Both the Zionists and the non-Zionists . . . each have an opportunity to present their views to the British Government and to the League of Nations through the established and recognized channel of the Jewish Agency [the quasi-governmental Zionist organization representing Jewish affairs in Palestine]."[82] In other words, if the ZOA wanted to know what was in the Peel Commission report, the organization should make its own inquires through its own official channels. Of course, Wise and other Zionist leaders knew of this possibility. However, what they wanted was not just another avenue to the British Foreign Office, but an alliance with the U.S. government with all the implied influence and power this would bring their cause.

Hull took the same official position with Wise and the ZOA as he had with Tydings. Interestingly, however, he did so with great care not to offend the Zionist leadership. The original drafts of communications to Wise (probably worked up by Wallace Murray) were repeatedly toned down by Hull. Thus, following one of Wise's many demands for the government to act as an intelligence-gathering agency for the ZOA, the first-draft reply told Wise that his requests were "not proper." This was subsequently changed to read "I [Hull] have been following the matter closely but find that it is not easy to obtain even confidential advance information regarding the contents of the [Peel] report."[83]

The department's official position was only part of the story. There now existed, in fact, a two-track response to the Zionist demand that the government help oppose British partition of Palestine. On one of these tracks we have Hull's public position as described above, and also Wallace Murray working hard to lay a legal groundwork for refusing to oppose British plans in Palestine.[84] This centered on what interpretation the department would give to the Anglo-American Convention on Palestine. The Zionists reasoned that partition required a termination of the mandate and, according to the convention, that that could not be done without the prior acquiescence of the U.S. government.[85] Murray's position, on the other hand, was a much narrower one. As he explained to Judge Moore on June 10, 1937, "in my opinion . . . the sole interest of this Government at the time the mandates were being set up, as well as at the time the Iraq Mandate was being terminated [which was being used by Murray as precedent for how to react to the possible termination of the Palestine mandate], was to assure to nationals of the United States equality of economic opportunity."[86] Ultimately, the U.S. and the British governments would agree that, by treaty, the British were obligated to consult with the United States on any changes in the mandate that would impact American economic or philanthropic interests.[87] However, as long as Great Britain acted in a way that was not prejudicial to those interests in Palestine, they need not acquire prior American consent to change the mandate.

There was, however, a second important track upon which the State Department responded to Wise and the ZOA. This was to represent, most often in an informal manner, the views of American Zionists to the British government. And while this was done quietly, it was also done repeatedly. Hull summed up this activity in a letter to Senator Robert Wagner dated July 14, 1937:

For your confidential information I may say that for the past several months we have taken a constant interest in the Palestine problem. . . . on several occasions we have brought the matter informally to the attention of the appropriate British authorities. Thus last winter I asked our Ambassador in London to explain orally to the British Foreign Secretary the concern of a large section of our people in the Palestine problem. Again, on April 27 our Ambassador at London, at my direction, sought an interview with the Foreign Secretary and orally and informally advised him that Jewish groups in the United States were perturbed over rumors that the Royal Commission of Inquiry would recommend a cessation of Jewish immigration into Palestine or a system of Jewish and Arab cantons. . . . Furthermore, late in May and early in June an official of the Department conversant with Palestine . . . at my direction took up orally and informally with officials of the British Foreign Office the interests of groups of our citizens in the Palestine question. All of these conversations were, as I have explained, kept on an informal plane. . . . However, within the past few days I instructed our Ambassador at London to hand the British Foreign Secretary a written memorandum setting forth at some length the sympathy with which all our recent Presidents . . . have had in the idea of a Jewish National Home. . . . The

memorandum likewise referred to the important American colonization and investments in Palestine and concluded with the statement that it seemed fitting and proper again to bring to the attention
of the British Government at a time when it was considering the
Palestine question, the interest and concern of many of our people in
that problem.

Hull ended his letter to Wagner with the assertion that "in the light of the
foregoing, it cannot be said that we have failed to keep before the compe-
tent British authorities the widespread interest in this country in a solution
of the Palestine question.[88]

It can be argued that in its two-track approach the State Department
was wrestling with conflicting interests as well as hedging its bets. It did
not want to be forced into a confrontation with the British over the partition of Palestine,[89] nor was it able to completely ignore Zionist pressure.
Thus, on the one hand, Murray busied himself with preparing an escape
route, as described above, to avoid confrontation. On the other hand, on
at least four occasions the State Department would represent American
Jewish concerns to the British. The last of these would be rendered in a
formal written format reflecting the arguments of the November 1936
memorandum of American Jewish groups detailing U.S. interests in Palestine. These representations on the part of the secretary of state may be
interpreted as at least implying to the British that ZOA concerns were
shared by the American government. It is just as significant that Hull's
representations did not include the views of Peter George and the Arab
Americans despite the fact that their argument for not taking sides in the
Zionist-Palestinian struggle was very close to that held by the Division of
Near Eastern Affairs. Instead, "the groups of our citizens" referred to by
the American ambassador in London were exclusively Jewish Americans
and their Christian supporters. Thus, in this fashion, the strength of the
Zionist lobby forced the State Department to step away from its preferred
position of neutrality on Palestine.[90]

Murray seems to have tried hard to deny the implications of this situation. At one point in September of 1937, after the Peel Commission call for
a partition of Palestine had been made public and was being hotly debated, he noted in a memo to Hull and Moore that American Jewry itself
was far from united on how to respond to this question. As long as this
was the case, he argued, "we are in a strong position to request that they
come to some agreement among themselves before they approach us with
a view to our taking any particular line of action."[91] It was an interesting

comment, for it really does not mark a "strong position" at all. First of all, the department had taken a "particular line of action" by repeatedly representing ZOA views to the British. Furthermore, Murray's words suggest an eventual need to compromise further with the ZOA once it created a united front of Jewish Americans. Many American non-Zionist organizations had already been co-opted into an alliance with the ZOA through the auspices of the Jewish Agency. And the Zionist colonization of Palestine would gain ever more support from American Jewry generally owing to increasingly vicious anti-Semitism in Europe and the rise of immigration barriers for Jews throughout much of the Western world. In other words, conditions were growing that would only increase Zionist pressure on the U.S. government.

As for the Arab Americans, who might have expected to be among those "groups of our citizens" whose opinions the American ambassador in London represented to the British government, they were given scant attention by the secretary of state. At first glance, this appears surprising, seeing as how Wallace Murray and the Division of Near Eastern Affairs found common ground with the Arab American plea for U.S. non-intervention in Palestine. But in the end, Murray also seems to have ignored them. Why? Perhaps because the representations to the British were largely a response to ZOA political power in Congress and with the White House. The Arab Americans did not possess such power. Thus Hull never mentions the Arab Americans in his correspondence with the "Chief," knowing, as he must have, that Roosevelt's "deep concern" was not for the fate or interests of Arabs. And of course, Peter George or Ameen Rihani did not have access to the president as did Sam Rosenman and Stephen Wise.

Before we leave the State Department and its struggle to cope with ZOA pressure, one might ask if there were other groups besides the Arab Americans which sought to counter the Zionist argument? What of the American missionaries and educators who had such a historic role in the Near East? What of the oil executives who, by the mid 1930s, had as much a growing financial stake in Arabia as the Zionists had in Palestine? And were there any efforts on the part of Arab leaders in Palestine to communicate their case to the U.S. government? For the latter years of the 1930s there are only a few documents that indicate any intercession with the State Department on the issue of Palestine by these groups.

One such document is a "file note" made by Murray regarding a visit by J. A. Moffett of the Standard Oil Company of California. Moffett "expressed the fear that American support of Jewish claims in Palestine would have serious repercussions on American interests in Saudi Arabia."[92] It is reasonable that concerns over the fate of U.S. interests in Saudi Arabia were among the reasons why NEA argued against any open support of the Zionists.

Another document references a visit to the secretary of state by a delegation of four educators and clerics with connections to the Middle East. They were Professor Elihu Grant ("a well known archaeologist") of Haverford College, Professor Leland Parr ("formerly a professor at the American University of Beirut"), the Reverend R. Paul Shearrer ("formerly connected with the Presbyterian Mission in Syria"), and Mr. Harry Snyder ("who taught for years at the American University of Beirut"). They brought with them "a short letter signed by some 30 or 40 persons" including college presidents. Their position was one "sympathetic to the Arab cause," though they argued, like the Arab National League, that the United States should "refrain entirely from taking any part in the Arab-Jew controversy." In a memo describing the group to Hull, Wallace Murray portrayed the delegation as a counterbalance to Christian groups that supported the Zionists.[93]

Finally, in August of 1937 there were several communications sent to the U.S. government through the American consulate in Jerusalem from Muhammed Amin al-Husayni, acting both in his capacity as president of the Arab Higher Committee of Palestine and as the mufti of Jerusalem. The first, an official letter from Husayni as president of the Arab Higher Committee, came on August 15. The communication is interesting because it reflects a view of the United States, shared by Arab Americans as well, as a country traditionally interested in and friendly to the Arab people. This view was due to a recognition of the activities of "American centers of culture which are to be found in many of the Arab countries." It also expressed the belief that America was "remote from imperialist ambitions" and therefore able to understand that Zionism represented "a hostile and imperialistic aggression directed against an inhabited country." In an August 31 interview with George Wadsworth, the American consul general, Husayni, speaking as the mufti, expressed the fear that Jewish influence in the United States would bring the government to take the side of the Zionists and end not only the "respect and unlimited confidence" the Arabs felt toward the United States, but also endanger the "extensive business connections with the Near East and the Moslem world that are also worthy of being safeguarded and developed."[94]

While such interventions as described above probably reaffirmed the department's resolve not to advocate the Zionist cause publicly, none of these groups, nor the Arab Americans, were able to counter the reality of growing ZOA influence. Thus the State Department, while certainly attempting to balance competing pressures, did not "refrain entirely from taking any part" in the Palestine debate. Indeed, in the end, Hull was led to subtly identify the department with Zionism "unofficially and orally." Why, then, do contemporary pro-Zionist historians view the State Department at this time as "extravagantly hostile" to American Zionists? Perhaps the department's sin was its very discretion. The experience of the Holocaust seems to have encouraged an all-or-nothing criterion for support in their minds. One supports the cause completely or you stand as a real or potential enemy. Projecting this criterion back in time, subtle or occasional support of the ZOA on behalf of the State Department is overlooked. The lack of wholehearted support comes to equal hostility.

Newspaper Coverage of Partition

Newspaper coverage of Palestine in 1937 focused on the activities of the Peel Commission and the building expectation that it would recommend partition. In this coverage the *New York Times*, at least, sought to report both the Arab and Zionist responses.[95] The coverage of the other papers under consideration came mostly in the form of editorials.

In all cases, coverage of events in Palestine, as well as American Zionist activities, created what was by this time a perhaps inevitable distortive context for any occasional rendering of the Arab point of view. Thus, the reader might learn of the Palestinian Arab demand for "the establishment of an independent government constitutionally elected."[96] They might also learn that this was demanded in order to correct policies which had hitherto led to "great discrimination by the Palestine Government in favor of Jews."[97] However, as in 1936, the same reader was also faced with a description of the conflict as basically racial and religious. Take for instance the *Washington Post* editorial cartoon of July 9, 1937, which pictures a figurative Britain sawing a boat labeled Palestine in half (symbolizing partition) because it is beset with "racial problems."[98] There was also a multitude of pieces reporting Arab resistance in terms of fanaticism and extremism.[99]

Paralleling this picture of the Palestinian Arab and his motives was a growing crescendo of articles detailing support for the Zionist position by American community leaders of all descriptions. For instance, in early February 1937 the *New York Times* reported on a message sent by President Roosevelt to the Jewish-sponsored National Convention on Palestine held in Washington, D.C. As with the sentiments expressed by Harold

Ickes, FDR's remarks reflect an a priori pro-Zionism as well as the bipolar worldview that allowed Zionism to be seen as a vehicle for "freedom." The president asserted that "the American people, ever zealous in the cause of human freedom, have watched with sympathetic interest the effort of the Jews to renew in Palestine the ties of their ancient homeland. . . . [The past] two decades have witnessed a remarkable exemplification of the vitality and vision of the Jewish pioneers. . . . It should be a source of pride to Jewish citizens of the United States that they, too, have had a share in this great work of revival and restoration."[100] At the same convention secretary of agriculture Henry Wallace told the gathering that "the prophetic vision of social justice animated both the American dream of the country's future and the Jewish dream of reconstruction. . . . both dreams are astonishingly alike."[101]

Four months later the ZOA held its annual convention in New York City, and the *New York Times* prominently reported the address of Senator Robert Wagner to its eight hundred assembled delegates. Wagner asserted that "In the far flung death struggle between democracy and autocracy . . . the Jewish people and their homeland are a symbol, and democracy must protect Palestine as an outpost of civilization."[102] How this struggle for democracy was to be reconciled with the Zionist resistance to majority rule in Palestine at this time was not taken up by Senator Wagner, his audience, or, for that matter, the *New York Times*. Within the paradigm that supported the bipolar worldview, the Arabs were simply not to be counted among what Representative Hamilton Fish described, in the *Times* a month later, as "the civilized nations of the world . . . most of whom had approved" the creation of a Jewish National Home in Palestine.[103] To a reader habituated to this worldview, resistance to Zionism must have suggested being on the wrong side of "the death struggle between democracy and autocracy."

On July 8, 1937, the *New York Times* presented a long editorial on the situation in Palestine and the Peel Commission inquiry. The editorial began by acknowledging the fact that Great Britain had made "conflicting promises" during World War I to Arabs and Zionists. It even implied that one might doubt the original "wisdom of the Zionist conception." However, now that hundreds of thousands of Jews were resident in Palestine, there was "less significance" in questioning Zionism because now Jewish colonization in Palestine had to be "dealt with" as "a condition, not a theory." The *Times* editors did not think that partition was the proper way to deal with the country's "condition" in 1937. It would, they asserted, only lead to "bitter irredentism." The editors bemoaned the fact that "the voice of moderate opinion" had been "drowned out" by the "maximalist claims" of both "Zionist and Arab extremists." What then was the answer? Taking its lead at least in part from the ideas of moderate Zionist leader Judah Magnes,[104] the *Times* called for a ten-year truce between Zionists and Arabs. During this period there would be "equitable distribution of employment . . . adequate safeguards for the Arab peasant and tenant farmer in the matter of land sales . . . and most important, the fixing of a maximum of Jewish immigration over the whole period covered by the truce. . . . the number of Jews in Palestine should not exceed 40% of the total population."[105]

These suggestions constituted a recognition on the part of the *New York Times* that the Arabs of Palestine had legitimate concerns, and that these had bred more resistance to Zionism than could be safely ignored. On the other hand, the paper's ideas did not speak to the past injustices of colonialism in Palestine, or to the fact that a 40 percent ceiling to Jewish immigration would have allowed a considerable number of additional immigrants into the country. In any case, by 1937 the editors of the *Times* were whistling in the wind. There was no notable reaction to the editorial, or to Judah Magnes's similar suggestions printed in the *Times* ten days later. Indeed, those Zionists whose aim it was to muster as much opposition to partition as possible might well have seen the editorial as a helpful, if flawed, contribution to that end.

In fact, occasional recognition of the fate of the Palestinian concerns had little follow-through. Just two days later, in three short *New York Times* editorials, Arab needs and rights were forgotten and the usual themes surfaced again. These editorials described borders for the proposed Jewish state to be born out of partition, and described those areas to be left out of Jewish control. Significantly, Jerusalem was to remain part of a reduced British mandate territory, and a good part of Judea to go to the proposed Arab state. What is interesting about the *New York Times* analysis of the borders and land distribution plan is that its point of reference was biblical Israel. Thus, the paper quotes Psalm 137, "If I forget thee O Jerusalem let my right hand forget her cunning." There is then the observation that "the British plan has the new Jewish state sweeping down into old Phillistia almost half way to Gaza, whither Samson's unfortunate sex adventures brought him." And finally, there is the explanation that "the Palestinian report only follows precedent after 3000 years. . . . the beginnings of the Jewish state were in the north. There the prophet Samuel anointed the first in the person of Saul. . . . It remained for Saul's successor, David, to conquer Jerusalem. . . . At this point even an amateur may recall ten of the twelve tribes of Israel lived outside of Judea."[106] As has been shown earlier, this contextualizing of modern Palestine in terms of biblical storytelling was a common practice within a Judeo-Christian culture in which the Bible served as the major popular reference for that land. Thus we find an Associate Press release appearing in the *Los Angeles Times* of July 8, 1937, announcing "approval tonight of a Royal Commission report carving ancient Palestine into three new states."[107] Of course, what was actually being partitioned was a very different place—contemporary Palestine.

Nor did the relevance of Arab history and experience in Palestine appear in subsequent pieces that drew on more contemporary comparisons. For example, on July 10, 1937, Anne O'Hare McCormick, the first female journalist to win a Pulitzer Prize, writing in the *New York Times* told her readers that tension in Palestine was part of the larger phenomenon of rising Arab nationalism. "Native populations" are led by "exposure to foreign enterprise" to become self-conscious and nationalistic. That is to "wave flags in imitation . . . of more advanced nations," which she also describes as "their betters in Europe."[108]

Against this rising tide of supposedly not-quite-legitimate, copycat nationalism stood the more pressing and legitimate needs of the West. McCormick describes the Europeans as "the hungry, progressive, enterprising people" living in "over crowded countries while vast areas remain underdeveloped in the hands of native populations." The Zionists represented those "hungry" elements against whose needs the "imitation" nationalism of the "native population" could not prevail. Thus, "the proposal to define and circumscribe the Jewish settlement of Palestine and, by setting limits, to reconcile the Arabs to live peacefully in the shadow of an energetic and highly developed people, is a makeshift solution, obviously temporary."[109]

This was a point of view with which the editors of the *Chicago Tribune* agreed. On July 13, a *Tribune* editorial told Chicago readers that "the Arab higher committee at Jerusalem declares the [partition] plan is inadmissible because . . . [it] gives the Jews most of the fertile sections . . . while leaving the Arabs only rocky and arid territory. The Jewish reply to that might be that the Jews have shown their capacity for agricultural development as the Arabs, still a pastoral people, have not. They [the Jews] . . . have invested $380,000,000 in the development of industries and agricultural enterprises. . . . partition will deprive Jewish industries of access they would otherwise have to a market needed for their prosperity."[110] A similar attitude was expressed in the *Washington Post* of July 8, 1937. Here "staff correspondent" Clyde DuBose explained that "The Arab will have no compromise with the Jew. He will not listen to the proposal that he join the establishment of a free nation. . . . He realizes he is dealing with an intellectually and financially superior race and he sees in the future the complete submersion of his people."[111]

Finally we can return to Joseph M. Levy, the *New York Times* resident correspondent in Jerusalem. On July 25, 1937, he filed a story which was remarkable for its thorough misreading of the Arab mood in Palestine, but perfectly consistent with the Western assumption that colonialism in Palestine was a "civilizing" activity. Levy reported that he had "devoted five days to making a survey throughout the country on the true reaction of the Arabs toward the proposed partition." His conclusion was that the increasingly violent resistance to the idea, which for the first time involved Arab attacks on the British colonial administration, was the work of "a small group of terrorists—agents of certain Arab quarters backed by an interested foreign power." Here he probably meant Italy.

If violence was unrepresentative of the mood of the country, then what did he think was the true popular feeling? According to Levy, the threat of partition had finally taught many of the Palestinian Arabs that "extreme methods are not the only means of fighting for one's country." Rather, they now saw that cooperation with the Zionists was the key. The threat of partition had "brought home to the Arabs the fact that Arab-Jewish understanding would be of mutual advantage and importance to both peoples." How did this happen? The answer Levy supplies speaks to his bipolar worldview and his assumption that Zionism equals altruistic imperialism. "All classes of Arabs now understand that partition would probably deprive them forever of any hope for a return of the prosperity that they once enjoyed as a result of an influx of Jewish capital. . . . It was realization of this fact that was the real cause of the Arab protest against partition—a protest that came from all classes."[112]

In fact, the Palestinians as a community were on the verge of renewing the rebellion that had broken out in 1936 and then lapsed. The lapse was in part due to the hope that the Peel Commission would meet their demands of restricting Jewish immigration and land purchases. In addition, as early as January 13, 1937, Auni Bey Abdulhadi, a Jerusalem lawyer, had testified before the commission that "the Arabs will not compromise. . . . they will never agree to cantonization."[113] Thus, when the commission suggested partition, once more there was a resort to violence.

Joseph M. Levy had lived many years in Palestine. He was of the circle of Judah Magnes and therefore not a Zionist holding "maximalist demands." Nonetheless, he was so imbued with the assumptions of the bipolar worldview that he was incapable of understanding the situation from the point of view of the Palestinian community.

The British Temporarily Retreat

As 1937 wore on, the British government's position on partition changed. Though the British would keep it as a formal option, they decided to put off its implementation. This was done for two reasons. The first was the almost universal displeasure expressed by both Arabs and Jews. Although the WZO was willing to negotiate with the British over the issue, it was clear that the resulting mini-state would satisfy almost no one in the Zionist camp. And despite Levy's misleading reporting, the Arabs also were almost unanimously opposed to giving up what they saw as their country.

The second reason the British decided to put off partition was that when the government then in power took the proposal to Parliament, it met with significant resistance. While some of this was certainly a product of Zionist lobbying, there was also another factor at work. Partition would have required formal review by and permission from the League of Nations. As the *New York Times* reported on July 22, 1937, "One could sense the unwillingness in the House [of Commons] during the long debate to take any decision which would give to the League of Nations the last word on a British imperial problem. Privately some members said they saw no reason for the League to tell them what to do over Palestine than for it to do so in the cases of India or Ireland. The fact that in the last analysis Palestine belongs to the League of Nations seems to have made no impression upon the members of Parliament, who simply assume that it is part of the British Empire."[114]

The notion that "Palestine belongs to the League of Nations" was a popular American interpretation and also one the Zionists and their allies now put forth. Stephen Wise kept asserting that "Britain is trustee as a mandatory . . . not the owner of Palestine."[115] The pro-Zionist New York senator Royal S. Copeland was quoted in the *Washington Post* as arguing that "the British are treating Palestine as if it were English territory. Palestine does not belong to England."[116] Most in the British government, however, had never acquiesced in this view. It will be recalled that back in 1922 Arthur Balfour, the British statesman so esteemed by the Zionists, had told the League of Nations in no uncertain terms that Palestine was British by right of conquest, and they had only "imposed upon themselves" the mandate for "the general welfare of mankind." Neither the ZOA nor the WZO saw fit to challenge Balfour's assertion at the time. Balfour's position was still the prevailing one in Great Britain in 1937. Thus, the colonial secretary, William Ormsby-Gore, reminded Parliament that the Palestine mandate was "conferred . . . by the principal allied powers alone."[117] It did not matter that the ZOA, much less the *New York Times,* now had a different view. Palestine was, ipso facto, part of the British Empire until such time as the British decided to give it up.

Conclusion

As we approach the Second World War in this history, we see that the divergence of Western aspirations for Palestine and the aspirations of Palestinian Arabs for independence had grown increasingly acute. Western aspirations for, and intrusion into, Palestine were rationalized by the bipolar worldview and the notion of altruistic imperialism. They were manifested in the actions of the Zionists, which were in turn backed up by millions of investment dollars from the United States and elsewhere, and the increasingly desperate need of refuge for European Jews. Palestinian resistance was seen as unreasonable and as racially and religiously motivated.

Not surprisingly, the protests of the Palestinian Arabs, Arab Americans, and others did not result in any reassessment of the assumptions of the bipolar worldview as applied to Palestine by the American press, American politicians, or American Zionists. If anything, the rationale of Zionist colonization as an act of altruistic imperialism was called forth with ever greater energy in the words of all three parties.

The Arab Americans, tirelessly debating the issue of Palestine, made little headway against this relentless trend. Newspaper coverage in these years was largely unaffected by their efforts. Ameen Rihani could go about the country and tell all who would listen that what was going on in Palestine was a struggle against colonial exploitation. Peter George could point out that the Palestinian Arab stand was not so different from America's own revolutionary struggle against the British and that the Palestinians wanted, at least in part, what colonial Americans had wanted—national independence, freedom to develop along their own cultural lines, and perhaps even constitutional government. It made no difference. The public and the politicians simply ignored such claims, and the press did not investigate them, because they contradicted the culturally dominant imperialist assumptions. Indeed, such concepts as nation building, democracy, and freedom had already been identified with the Zionist colonialism. At this time the term *colonialism* was not associated with exploitation in the press or the popular mind, but rather with altruism and the spread of civilization. The Zionist spokesmen used the term with pride.[118] Those who resisted civilization's "pioneers" were not equated with the Founding Fathers of 1776, but rather with religious fanatics blocking the way of modernity.

All this stood as testimony to the fact that the ZOA was increasingly well organized and effective. It had created a working alliance with American non-Zionists through the auspices of the Jewish Agency. It had captured the active sympathy of Congress and the White House. And it had successfully demonstrated the very real financial and emotional stake that American Jewry had in the Holy Land. The important result of these achievements was that, in the eyes of an increasing number of Americans—both the common newspaper reader and the politically powerful—Zionist activities in Palestine were becoming defined as an extension of U.S. interests in the Middle East.

Finally, by 1936–37 the State Department had also been influenced by the ZOA lobby. While the Division of Near Eastern Affairs continued to argue for neutrality and, on occasion, the secretary of state received Arab Americans and their supporters, it was Secretary of State Hull's consistent, if discreet, willingness to represent ZOA views to the British government that bears noting. There is every reason to believe that a slow but sure erosion of the State Department's position of neutrality would have continued in the face of relentless pressure, if it had not been for the outbreak of World War II. It was the war that created new conditions that reinvigorated the department's conviction that open American support for the Zionist position in Palestine would only lead to disaster for both the United States and Great Britain.

7

The War Years

In July 1937, Britain's Peel Commission, which had investigated the causes of the Arab revolt, proposed the partition of Palestine. However, the life of this early British partition proposal proved a short one. Fascist power was on the rise both in Europe and the eastern Mediterranean area. Since 1935 and the Italian invasion of Ethiopia, Britain had been on the defensive. By the end of the decade, the British were in serious need of ways to shore up their defensive position in the Middle East. Within this context, Palestine came to be considered a pivotal asset in any future war. Keeping the area pacified was therefore an essential goal.

The question was how to best maintain peace and security in Palestine. Here British needs for Arab cooperation not only in Palestine but in the surrounding areas of Egypt, Iraq, and Transjordan came into play. German and Italian propaganda had already begun to stir up anti-British feeling in the region, and the issue of Zionist encroachment into Palestine played a central role in their message. Thus, it seemed to the British, the only way of pacifying Palestine in a manner that would also help secure the cooperation of the population of surrounding lands was to do so to the satisfaction of the Arabs. As British military strategists noted in January 1939, "We assume that . . . the necessary measures would be taken . . . in order to bring about a complete appeasement of Arab opinions in Palestine and in neighbouring countries. . . . If we fail to retain Arab goodwill at the outset of a war, no other measures which we can recommend will serve to influence the Arab States in favour of this country."[1]

Under the circumstances, partition was found to be an idea whose time had not quite come. The Arabs were absolutely opposed to it, and as we have seen, a good number of Zionists did not like it either. For the British, who were now on the verge of a new war rather than at the victorious end of an old one, it was Arab attitudes that counted most. By November of 1938 the British announced that partition was, at present, "impracticable." Then, in February of 1939, they held a conference in London of Arabs and Jews, with the proviso that if these competing parties could not reconcile their differences, the British government would "take their own decision." Predictably, the conference was unsuccessful.

The British White Paper of 1939

As a result the British issued their famous (or infamous, depending on your point of view) White Paper on May 17, 1939. In this document the British government asserted that "the framers of the Mandate in which the Balfour Declaration was embodied could not have intended that Palestine should be converted into a Jewish state against the will of the Arab population of that country."[2] As we have seen, this assessment of the motives of the "framers of the Mandate," at least in the case of Lord Balfour, is probably inaccurate. Nonetheless, the White Paper went on to set new policy that, hopefully, would appear sufficiently pro-Arab to prevent the populations of the region from supporting the fascist cause. Specifically, the White Paper promised "an independent Palestine state" within a decade. Jewish immigration would continue at a rate of 15,000 a year for five years and thereafter only with the agreement of the Arab population. This all but assured the cessation of Jewish immigration after the initial five years. The British pledged themselves to develop self-governing institutions in the ten-year period leading to independence, and since the end of the period would see the Jews constitute no more than one-third of the population, this meant a future Arab Palestine.[3]

The Arabs found the White Paper to be but half a loaf. What they wanted was immediate self-rule. Waiting a decade for the British to grant them self-determination while tens of thousands of additional Europeans entered the country was viewed with deep suspicion. By 1937 there were few Arabs who really trusted British promises.

On the other side, the Zionists saw themselves a betrayed. As one Zionist historian has put it, "Sixteen million Arabs had to be appeased, lest they turn on the British and endanger the Middle East nexus between the home isles and the Pacific part of the Empire. Just as Chamberlain had sacrificed Czechoslovakia at Munich for the sake of 'peace in our time [sic],' so he now prepared to offer up the Yishuv in the hope of maintaining good relations with the Arab world."[4] Of course, using the same logic, the Arabs could have declared that, for the sake of Jewish wartime support in 1917, Lloyd George had "offered up" the Arabs of Palestine.

Whether the Zionists felt betrayed or not, the Jews were in fact trapped. No matter what policies were adopted in Palestine, they were bound to support the British against the Nazis. Nonetheless, the Zionists pledged to resist the White Paper as much as was feasible, and, as we shall see, none were as adamantly resistant as were the American Zionists.

American Reactions to the White Paper

American Zionists geared up to oppose the 1939 White Paper much as they had opposed the prospect of partition. Numerous committees and working groups were formed, the major one being the National Emergency Committee for Palestine. Thousands of letters and telegrams from Jews and non-Jews alike were sent to the State Department, the White House, and Congress seeking U.S. intervention with Britain on this matter. Once more the U.S. government was urged to become an ally of the Zionist movement and, in this case, place that movement's interests above those of the country's strategic ally, Great Britain.

The basis of the American Zionist argument, often repeated in the communications that cascaded into Washington, was a familiar one. The May 17 White Paper represented a qualitative alteration of the mandate, and therefore, as Stephen Wise wrote to Secretary of State Cordell Hull on June 1, 1939, "the United States may properly assert that its consent is necessary."[5]

A good part of the U.S. Congress agreed. Statements on behalf of the Zionist "right" of free immigration into Palestine were signed by over 200 congressmen and 28 senators.[6] This was buttressed by a petition signed by "250 Jewish leaders from 26 states," some of whom were members of government at the state and local level, addressed to the secretary of state. The petition asked Hull to "intervene to protect American rights" by bringing about a "halt to British action in Palestine." It explained that the British White Paper would lead to an "Arab dominated state in Palestine," which would mean that "American interests and investments would suffer injury."[7] Again, the United States was assumed to have the right to intervene by virtue of its 1924 Anglo-American Convention on Palestine.

It is to be noted that, by 1939, those members of Congress allied to the American Zionists were suspicious of the State Department and frustrated by the fact that the department did not appear to be "on the same track" as they were. Typical of this attitude was a letter from Senator William H. King, chairman of the Committee on the District of Columbia, to Secretary of State Hull dated May 4, 1939. King took Hull to task because, despite the overwhelming pro-Zionist sentiment in the Congress, "the British Government had not been officially informed of the position taken by the members of the House and Senate." King then told Hull that he should let the British know "through diplomatic channels" that Congress disapproved of what the Senate described as a "liquidation of the Mandate for Palestine based on the Balfour Declaration," and that Congress believed the result would be a "new state dominated by a narrow majority." (In fact the Arabs would constitute at least 70 percent of the populace). Policy such as this, the letter continued, which would "place the Jews in an inferior position with reference to the Arab population[,] is unthinkable."[8]

From the State Department's point of view, the opinions expressed in the House and the Senate letters were not "official acts or resolutions of the Congress but merely statements signed by members of Congress in their individual capacity." In addition, the Division of Near Eastern Affairs believed that those statements misinterpreted both the 1922 congressional resolution and the 1924 Anglo-American Convention on Palestine. Zionist and congressional demands for U.S. intervention against the British White Paper forced the State Department into a relatively rare public posture. In an October 1939 press release the department pointed out that the 1922 resolution specifically asserted that "it commits us to no foreign entanglement." Further, the 1924 convention focused on American rights in commerce, property rights, philanthropic and religious establishments, "and equality of treatment with all other foreign nationals." The State Department concluded that "none of these articles empower the Government of the United States to prevent the modification of any of the mandates." For all these reasons, the department asserted that it would not be proper to make congressional protests the subject of an official communication to the British government.[9]

Thus, at this point the State Department and Congress were publicly at odds, and the resulting bickering meant that, on the eve of World War II, there was really no single U.S. policy on Palestine. The power to end the division of opinion and set a dominant and consistent policy lay, at least in theory, with the White House. Therefore, it is important to ask where Franklin Roosevelt stood, as Britain prepared to do an about-face in Palestine by implementing the 1939 White Paper.

Various judgments have been made about FDR and his relationship to the Zionists. Historians such as Selig Adler have condemned FDR as someone who cared little about the Jewish plight or Zionist plans for Palestine.[10] (Historians such as Urofsky, Grose, and Manuel generally agree with Adler.) However, while FDR did not support the Zionists as openly as they would have liked (no president before Truman did), this posture must be understood in the context of the countervailing, often wartime, conditions that Zionist historians fail to note.[11] However, there can be little doubt that President Roosevelt privately favored open immigration into Palestine. In this his position was much like that of Woodrow Wilson.

When it came to the 1939 White Paper, Roosevelt came under enormous pressure to intervene with the British on behalf of the Zionist cause. Besides the deluge of letters from the public, and the repeatedly expressed sentiments of Congress, the Zionists recruited the aging Louis Brandeis to beseech the president to "induce the British to postpone the threatened change in policy."[12] On May 10, 1939, Roosevelt told Secretary of State Hull that "I still believe that any announcement about Palestine at this time by the British Government is a mistake, and I think we should tell them that."[13] A week later, after the British had in fact announced the White Paper, FDR wrote a memorandum to Hull in which he stated that, in his opinion, the Balfour Declaration "did intend to convert Palestine into a Jewish home which might very possibly become preponderantly Jewish within a comparatively short time. . . . I do not see how the British Government reads into the original Mandate or into the White Paper of 1922 any policy that would limit Jewish immigration. . . . it is something that we cannot give approval to by the United States."[14]

Yet FDR did nothing about the British White Paper of 1939 beyond complaining to Secretary of State Hull. This posture essentially left the State Department, and specifically NEA, to carry on as it saw fit. The question is, if Congress and the public all condemned Britain for changing its prior pro-Zionist policy to one that appeared to be, at least for the time being, pro-Arab, and the president agreed that this change was "a mistake," why did he not take steps to truly pressure the British not to proceed with the White Paper?

Newspaper Consideration of the White Paper of 1939

The answer to this question can be found in the editorial comment made by the *New York Times* in reaction to the British about-face in Palestine. The *Times* editorial of May 24, 1939, noted that the British action "spells the limitation and therefore the end" of the Zionist dream of a "home to the homeless." The British took such a dramatic step because "the very existence of the Empire" now depends on "friendly relations with the Arabs." The fascist powers were strong, and war was pending. Under the circumstances, the *New York Times* suggested that the British change in policy could even be seen as in the interest of the Jews. "What would happen" to the Jewish homeland, the paper's editors asked, "if the neighboring Arab peoples passed under the influence of the Fascist Powers?"[15]

The *New York Times* asked this rhetorical question against a backdrop of general reporting on the White Paper that almost completely ignored the dilemma growing fascist power presented the British. That coverage tended to concentrate on American Zionist efforts to pressure the U.S. government to intervene with the British on their behalf, and how that campaign had the almost unanimous backing of local politicians.[16] Ironically, the very geopolitical realities that the editors portrayed as seminal were largely absent from the general coverage of their own paper. For instance, an article appearing on May 26 reported that "15 of the 25 Foreign Affairs Committeemen" called on the State Department to "protest Great Britain's proposed policy in Palestine." Representative Hamilton Fish of New York (whom we have seen as far back as 1922 orchestrating pro-Zionist resolutions) was now quoted as explaining that the British action was "in clear repudiation" of the 1924 Anglo-American Convention on Palestine and also jeopardized "$100 million in American investments in Palestine."[17] Fish, and other representatives on the Foreign Relations Committee, who at least in theory knew something about the precarious state of the world in 1939, seemed to have expressed no particular concern over the point raised by the recent *Times* editorial—that is, that the Jewish homeland, and all of its American investment, would have little future if the Arab world allied with the Germans and Italians. The *New York Times* reports, which rarely refrained from inserting viewpoints into their articles, never pointed out these concerns when covering the congressional reaction.

The situation was no more enlightening when it came to the other newspapers we have been considering. The *Washington Post* editorial on the British White Paper appeared on May 19. It described the British decision on Palestine as "the liquidation by the British government of those obligations which it assumed when it issued the Balfour Declaration in 1917." The editorial went on to praise the Zionists for making the Holy Land "blossom like a rose," an effort which according to the *Post* editors "enormously benefitted" the Arabs. Despite the beneficial consequences of this altruistic imperialism, the paper explained to its readers that the British now planned to sanction, a decade hence, an Arab Palestine. Worse yet, this was to be done at a time when European Jews were in desperate need of refuge. "At any other time," the *Post* editors concluded, "the repudiation of solemn obligations undertaken in the past would have been tragic. It is particularly so now. . . . in the process [Britain] strangles one of the most idealistic experiments of our times."[18] As to the facts of a rising fascist threat and impending war that motivated the British to "repudiate solemn obligations" we hear not a word.

The *Post*'s general coverage of American reaction to the White Paper was sparser than that of the *New York Times,* but of the same character. It too centered around American Zionist efforts to "appeal to Roosevelt" to "act in Palestine."[19] Here too there is little reference to geopolitical realities.

The *Los Angeles Times* and *Chicago Tribune* also offered editorials on the White Paper of 1939. In its editorial of May 19, the *L.A. Times* did suggest that "Britain appears motivated more by the needs of her war preparation program than by a sense of justice to the hapless Jews." The paper went on to suggest that for the British to do "anything less would probably plumb them [the Arabs] forthwith on the side of the Axis powers." Then, ignoring the possible implications of such a development, the *L.A. Times* editors concluded that British policy will leave the Jews of Palestine "at the mercy of their enemies." The Zionists will, however, "put up vigorous opposition" and this "may bring about a fairer settlement. It is to be hoped so."[20]

The *Chicago Tribune* editorial appeared on May 23 and proceeded to blame "radio technology" for the British White Paper. The paper's editors explained that it was German and Italian radio propaganda that had made it impossible for the British to keep knowledge of their previously pro-Zionist position in Palestine from the Muslims in the rest of their empire. As a consequence, Muslim anger was able to pressure a change in policy.[21]

Both the *L.A. Times* and the *Chicago Tribune* editorials hint, in qualified fashion, that Britain faced a dilemma in the Middle East. However, the sparse general reporting of these two papers on the White Paper issue restricted itself to the same topics as found in the *New York Times* and *Washington Post*. Coverage was concentrated on Zionist anger over the denial of alleged Jewish rights, and the effort to get the United States to intervene on their behalf. By failing to support their editorial explanations of the British position (where such occurred) the newspapers in effect negated the geopolitical context of events. They also failed to consider the right of Palestinian Arab self-determination as a possible legitimate end for British mandate policy. In this way the coverage of all four papers was bound by the parameters of the bipolar worldview.

The Position of the State Department

The State Department and its Division of Near Eastern Affairs have been harshly condemned by many American historians for their wartime opposition to the Zionist position on Palestine. As early as 1949, Frank E. Manuel charged the "permanent officials of the Department" with anti-Semitic feelings toward the Zionists. In his opinion, these feelings were "expressed with a vehemence of language hardly defensible. . . . State Department officials were writing with extravagant hostility and distorting an historical record of American interest in Palestine in glaring fashion."[22] In the 1970s Phillip Baram carried forward the same argument when he accused NEA of a "subjective animus" toward Zionism with the result that, during World War II, the State Department as a whole became "the lesser of the world's anti-Jewish evils."[23] In the 1980s Naomi Cohen weighed in with the assertion that NEA's attitude toward Zionism "bore unmistakable traces of anti-Semitism."[24] Other historians such as Selig Adler, Melvin Urofsky, Peter Grose, and Michael Cohen have followed the same line.[25]

What was NEA's position on the British White Paper of 1939, as well as Zionist activity between the years 1939 and 1945? Given that the evidence suggests that the division's position up to this time had been one of neutrality toward Zionism, is it accurate to assert that its position starting in 1939 was motivated by "subjective animus" and "anti-Semitism"?

We can begin with a memo written by the head of NEA, Wallace Murray, to Secretary of State Hull on February 9, 1939. The background to this communication includes, first, the State Department's awareness of growing fascist power and impending war; second, the fear that the Arabs might turn against the British and join forces with the fascists; and third, a concern for deteriorating U.S.-Arab relations as pro-Zionist sentiments were expressed more openly, especially in Congress. Thus Murray wrote to Hull,

> It is apparent that the British cannot arrive at a decision which would make lasting enemies of the Arab states bordering Palestine. . . . if the Arabs are pressed too hard by the British it is quite within the bounds of possibility that they would decide to cast their lot with Germany and Italy. A mere glance at the map will indicate the dangerous position of the British in the event of a large-scale conflict in which the Arabs joined up with the totalitarian countries.
>
> In the light of the foregoing, and bearing in mind the European situation since Munich, it seems altogether undesirable for us to take

any action which would further weaken the British position. . . . With German and Italian pressure in Europe and Japanese pressure against the British in the Far East, a weakening of British strength in Palestine might well be the final blow which would bring about a collapse. Furthermore, a British collapse in the Near East would undoubtedly mean the massacre of all the Jews in Palestine.

Likewise, from the point of view of American interests in the Near East there would seem to be sound reason for our refraining from pressing further the Zionist demands. We have scores of reports from our diplomatic and consular officers of the unfavorable reaction of the Arabs to what they consider the partial views of this Government in favor of Zionism.[26]

To this end, Murray and NEA had been asserting a narrow definition of American interests and obligations in Palestine. As he explained in a memo, again to Hull, dated June 17, 1940 (but referencing previous State Department public statements of October 14, 1938, and May 26, 1939), "this Government has consistently refused to assume formally any obligations with respect to the realization of the Jewish National Home, this Government having limited its formal intervention at all times to the safeguarding of American rights and interests. It has never been considered that the realization of the Jewish National Home was connected with the safeguarding of American rights and interests. . . . [Rather] it must be emphasized that the underlying and sole concern of this Government in all the original negotiations over mandated territories was that of assuring equality of treatment for its nationals."[27]

As of 1941, the situation in the Middle East appeared to be getting worse. Assistant Secretary of State Adolf Berle noted in April of that year that "there is a pro-German government in Syria which probably will not do very much to resist German infiltration . . . [and] the position of Ibn Saud is still in doubt. . . . the consideration that prevents Arabs . . . from backing the Allies is their fear of increased political dominion by Zionist groups." His memo goes on to say, "the head of the Zionist movement, Dr. Weizmann, is in the United States now. He ought to be able to see the main desideratum, namely, that if the Mediterranean is closed, the extermination of the Zionists in Palestine is only a question of time. If he does see this, it might be possible to get him to take a more reasonable attitude than he has taken heretofore."[28]

The State Department proceeded to make contact with the World Zionist Organization so as to arrange a meeting. However, initial discussions took place not with Weizmann, but rather with Emanuel Neumann of the ZOA. The first meeting took place on April 15, 1941. At that time Assistant Secretary Berle suggested to Neumann that "in light of the present unfavorable moves" which saw the "Germans . . . attacking Egypt . . . the British might be so hard beset that they did not have the force available to defend Palestine." Under these circumstances "it would seem that some sort of understanding with the Arabs might . . . become a crucial necessity." Neumann could not manage more than a noncommittal response to this logic.[29]

The Zionists were, in fact, never really moved by State Department concerns. Rather, they used the opening offered them by Berle to begin an ongoing wartime dialogue with the department and NEA. The Zionist position was that the British simply needed to commit whatever force was necessary to ensure the Zionist position in Palestine, and they needed to reverse the 1939 White Paper. This done, "the power of the Jewish economic machine [could be] harnessed to the war effort."[30]

As the dialogue continued (sometimes carried on by Chaim Weizmann, Moshe Shertok, Nahum Goldman, and Louis Lipsky), the Zionist position supporting an alliance between the Jews and the Allies was elaborated to include the following arguments: (1) that the Jews were against Hitler, which was more than can be said of the Arabs, and that therefore the Allies should defer to Zionist wants rather than Arab wants; and (2) that Jewish Palestine constituted part of the "progressive world," which was not the case of the Arab Middle East, including Arab Palestine, and that therefore, to the extent that the Allies were fighting for a more civilized world, the Zionists, and not the Arabs, were their natural allies.

At one point, however, the Zionists admitted that there was a "question of justice" that arose in Palestine and presented the West with a "dilemma." As Moshe Shertok put it to NEA representatives in a meeting on March 3, 1943, there exists two alternatives in Palestine, either to be unjust to the Arabs, or to be unjust to the Jews. However, "there is less injustice to the Arabs involved in awarding Palestine to the Jews than there would be injustice to the Jews in not allowing them to have Palestine. . . . The Arabs are an undeveloped people. There is plenty of opportunity for them in a developed Palestine which would create employment. Their fears are unjustified."[31]

It is unclear whether Shertok actually believed this or was just using it as a point of argument. He knew, of course, that the Jewish economy in Palestine was evolving into an ethno-religiously segregated one. On the other hand, as most of their arguments indicate, he and the other Zionist negotiators were as locked into the bipolar worldview and its corollary of altruistic imperialism as most other Westerners. Perhaps even more so, for their absolute devotion to their cause as, among other things, a vanguard of Western civilization in the Middle East seemed to have overridden even recognition of the threat of rising fascist power laid out by Berle and NEA staffers. Perhaps the Zionists assumed that they could rally Western popular opinion sufficiently to prevent British abandonment of Palestine even if, for instance, German forces took Egypt.

Just as the State Department's argument about the need for the Zionists to compromise in the face of fascist threats brought no change in Zionist thinking, so the Zionists' arguments failed to convince the State Department. By the 1940s NEA personnel knew that Shertok's assertion that Palestinian Arab "fears are unjustified" was misleading. They had evidence that Zionism was not really altruistic when it came to the Arabs. Wallace Murray noted in 1940 that the weight of evidence collected by NEA and American diplomats in Palestine led to the conclusion that "the Jews with some conspicuous exceptions among non-Zionists, would appear to have been lacking any sense of responsibility for the fate of that part of the population whom they are seeking to displace."[32] It was not that State Department personnel like Murray had somehow escaped the bipolar worldview and its corollary of altruism. It is that they had realized that Zionism wasn't living up to the ideological premises of that belief system.

Nor did the Zionist arguments about being more anti-German than the Arabs change the need to prevent Arab ambivalence from becoming open support of the Axis powers. In November 1943 we still find Murray reminding everyone who will listen that "the Near East is still an important theater of war and that it is as important as ever that it should remain quiet."[33] It was this conviction about the importance of the Middle East both to the war effort and to long-term U.S. interests that drove the State Department to continue its search for some "understanding" between the Arabs and the Zionists.

The Place of Ibn Saud in American-Zionist Wartime Relations

Beyond dialogue with the Zionists, one further State Department strategy was to try to facilitate negotiations between Chaim Weizmann and the king of Saudi Arabia, Ibn Saud. This effort began in December of 1942. On the 4th of that month Weizmann called on Assistant Secretary of State Sumner Wells. Of all the State Department staff, Wells was the most sym-

pathetic with the Zionist cause. Weizmann told Wells that Winston Churchill desired to "make Ibn Saud the boss of bosses in the Arab world" on
condition that the Saudi king would be willing to work out with Weizmann "a sane solution of the Palestine problem." Weizmann further asserted to Wells that Churchill claimed "the President [FDR] was in accord
on this subject."[34]

Wells informed Murray at NEA of this conversation and asked for his
opinion. Murray's initial reaction was one of skepticism. He pointed out
that British influence with the Saudi king was small. Certainly it was not
sufficient to "make him anything he did not want to be." And Murray
doubted if Ibn Saud had any ambition to be the "boss of bosses" of the
Arabs, because he had little interest in "town Arabs" beyond those of the
Hejaz. As to working out a "sane solution" in Palestine, Murray was
again doubtful. He doubted whether what the Zionists would regard as a
"solution" would come anywhere near what Ibn Saud would regard as
"sane."[35]

Nonetheless, Murray seemed to be intrigued by the possibility of initi-
ating some sort of Jewish-Saudi dialogue. After all, a deal had almost been
worked out between Weizmann and Emir Feisal back in 1919. Thus, he
suggested to Wells that productive conversations might take place on the
basis of the bi-national statehood ideas of Judah Magnes, president of
Hebrew University. Magnes had long ago rejected the goals of "political
Zionism," which sought Jewish domination of Palestine. Rather, he
wished the Jews to live as equals with the Arabs in a state that would allow
the former to cultivate their religion and culture. Murray found great
merit in these ideas. Back in July of 1942 he asserted that they possessed
both "breadth and wisdom." Murray believed that Magnes understood
that "In any area of the Arab world where the Jews might be admitted in
large numbers, the Arabs will always be in the majority and consequently
there must be established between the two semitic races full confidence
and a mutual give-and-take, rather than any thought that Jewish ascen-
dancy can be achieved or maintained either by foreign bayonets or the
power of Ibn Saud himself." Murray concluded his memo on Churchill's
"boss of bosses" proposal by asserting that if any approach was to be
made to the Saudis, it should be "a joint American-British one." He detailed American interests in Arabia and observed that while "Ibn Saud
would not be disposed to enlarge his . . . dependence on Great Britain," he
would "welcome a far greater American participation in his country."[36]

Discussions between the Zionists and the State Department continued
on into 1943. While Murray might have liked to use the opportunity to

move Weizmann and his collegues away from "political Zionism," this proved naive. For them, Magnes was little more than a traitor and his ideas had no currency. Despite this, the plan to initiate an approach to the Saudi king went forward.

At a meeting held between Zionist leaders and NEA personnel on January 19, 1943, Weizmann urged that "the matter of holding discussions with Ibn Saud should be explored immediately, and the way must be paved by American and British Governments." Yet at the same meeting the Zionist leader stated categorically that "Palestine . . . could never be an Arab land again."[37] How did Weizmann plan to win Ibn Saud's cooperation to such an anti-Arab position? Weizmann felt that Ibn Saud could be enticed by the idea of an "Arab federation of which Ibn Saud would be the head and in which a Jewish Palestine would cooperate." In addition he suggested "granting of a credit of 20 million pounds to Ibn Saud for development purposes in the Arab federation, the loan to be raised from Jewish communities in the United Nations."[38]

At this point NEA balked at the scheme. Murray recognized that Ibn Saud might well see the Weizmann-Churchill version of an Arab Federation with a Saudi ruler at its head as "a throne . . . obtained by giving Palestine to the Zionists," and the development loan as a "slush fund" to be used by Ibn Saud to "overcome opposition among the Arabs to the plan." Murray asserted that Ibn Saud was a "deep believer in and exponent of Arabism; he is a Moslem puritan; and he is on record as being wholly opposed to Zionist ambitions. The first question which arises therefore, is whether Dr. Weizmann has mistaken his man. If so the King would not only reject the bargain but might well be displeased with anyone and everyone who had anything to do with it." Under the circumstances, Murray opposed the United States taking on the role of intermediary in such a scheme. He concluded this way: "I believe that the less we have to do with the present specific proposals of Dr. Weizmann the better."[39]

Murray's insight into Ibn Saud's attitude was supported by a formal communication sent by the king to FDR in May of 1943. In this letter, Ibn Saud denounced Zionist ambitions in Palestine as contrary to the Atlantic Charter.[40] The Atlantic Charter entailed "common principles" agreed upon by the United States and Great Britain in August of 1941. Among these was a restatement of the Wilsonian principle of self-determination in the form of an affirmation of the right of all peoples to select their governments and approve or disapprove of territorial changes affecting them.[41] The king also expressed his worry over "the persistent news that these

Zionists do not refrain from bringing forth their wrong and unjust claim" and thereby "mislead by propaganda."[42] Ibn Saud was very much aware of American Zionist activities and influence with the American public and its politicians.

Further indications that Murray's assessment of Ibn Saud was accurate came in May of 1943. On May 6 the chargé d'affaires at the American embassy in Saudi Arabia, J. Harold Shullaw, wrote the secretary of state to tell him that the Saudi king's dedication to Islam and the cause of Arab independence meant "there is little likelihood that Ibn Saud under any circumstances would receive a Jewish delegation," nor "could it be expected that the King's position would be altered by any communications addressed to him by the Zionists."[43]

However, in what was to set a precedent, President Roosevelt ignored the opinions of those in the government who knew most about the regional attitudes of Middle East leaders. Roosevelt met with Weizmann in early June 1943, and, as Secretary of State Hull described it, "as a result of this discussion, the President believes that the time has come when an approach should be made to Ibn Saud with a view of seeing whether any basis for settlement [in Palestine] can be found."[44]

Why should Roosevelt ignore the warnings of the State Department and instead go with the arguments of Weizmann? One reason, of course, was that American Zionists constituted a powerful domestic lobby that supported Weizmann's scheme. Another possibility is that the president never read, or was briefed on, the opinions of Murray and his colleagues. However, even if FDR was aware of NEA's arguments, he may very well have ignored them because they conflicted with his own stereotyped view of Arabs.

What was Roosevelt's opinion of the Arabs? His view is revealed in the minutes of the president's June meeting with Weizmann. At that meeting Weizmann had described the Saudi king as "a desert prince . . . very much removed from world affairs." The fact that Ibn Saud's May letter to FDR indicated considerable knowledge of American-British agreements as well as Zionist activities in the United States seemed not to have served to contradict this assessment in Roosevelt's mind. Weizmann went on to assert that because of this provincialism it was necessary that "the democracies" tell the Arabs directly that they "mean to affirm the Jewish rights to Palestine." The meeting minutes continue this way: "at this stage the President made several remarks: a) that the Arabs have done very badly in this war; b) that although the Arabs have vast countries at their disposal, they have done very little towards their development; c) that possibly the Jews might help with the development; just as the United Nations would. He then said that he believes that the Arabs are purchasable." In other words, FDR had a stereotypical Western view of the Arabs as a backward people who needed Western (Zionist) help to "develop." And that they were of such character that they could readily be bribed. Roosevelt went on to suggest the idea of a conference with Ibn Saud, and it was agreed that the U.S. government would send someone to talk to the king "to prepare the ground." The difficulty FDR felt was "finding Arab leaders" to deal with. Despite all, Ibn Saud was clearly both the Zionists' and the president's candidate for a "purchasable" Arab with whom to negotiate.[45]

Thus, on the very same day as FDR's meeting with Weizmann, we find Secretary of State Hull informing the American embassy in London that the president proposed to send Lieutenant Colonel Harold B. Hoskins of the U.S. Army "to Saudi Arabia to initiate discussions" on Palestine. "Hoskins is thoroughly familiar with the current situation in the Near East . . . and for a long time has been a close student of the Arab-Jewish problem. He speaks Arabic fluently."[46] Hoskins would leave the next month, July, with directions issued by Hull that told him "In your conversations with the King you should confine yourself exclusively . . . to obtaining the King's reply to the following specific question: Will King Ibn Saud enter into discussions with Dr. Chaim Weizmann or other representatives selected by the Jewish Agency for the purpose of seeking a solution of basic problems affecting Palestine acceptable to both Arabs and Jews?"[47]

Hoskins spent the latter part of the summer of 1943 in Saudi Arabia. And as Murray had predicted, he failed completely in securing Ibn Saud's agreement to meet with the Zionists. Even before Hoskins had arrived, the king had been informed of Churchill's idea of making him "boss of bosses" within an Arab federation, and the Zionist proposal to offer him a large amount of "development" money. Again, as Murray had foreseen, the king interpreted it all as an attempt to bribe him. In his report back to Roosevelt, Hoskins noted that Ibn Saud believed that FDR had offered to act as "guarantor of payment" if the king agreed to the deal. The president expressed "surprise and irritation" at hearing this, "since there was of course no basis in fact" for this belief.[48] However, considering Roosevelt's opinion that the Arabs were "purchasable," such a role for him does not appear beyond possibility.

The whole episode seems to have given FDR pause about what was and was not possible in Palestine. He told Hoskins in September of 1943 that now "his own thinking leaned toward a wider use of the idea of trusteeship for Palestine—of making Palestine a real Holy Land for all three religions. . . . He said he realized it might be difficult to get the agreement of the Jews to such a plan but if Moslems and Christians of the world were agreed he hoped the Jews could also be persuaded."[49]

Roosevelt stayed away from the Palestine controversy until he met personally with Ibn Saud on February 14, 1945. The meeting took place on the cruiser *Quincy*, anchored in the Suez Canal, during FDR's return journey from the Yalta Conference. The president was even then convinced of his personal ability to cut some sort of deal with the Saudi king over Palestine. As the story goes, FDR had "an exceedingly pleasant meeting with Ibn Saud," and he and the king "agreed about everything until I [FDR] mentioned Palestine." After listening to the president describe the benefits of development that would supposedly come with cooperation between the Arabs and the Zionists, the Saudi king brought the U.S. president back to reality by informing him that "the Arabs would choose to die rather than yield their land to the Jews."[50]

What is not often related about this meeting is the king's suggestions for resolving the "Jewish problem." As related by William A. Eddy, then serving as U.S. minister plenipotentiary to Saudi Arabia, and also interpreter for FDR and the king at their meeting, FDR told the king of Jewish suffering at the hands of the Germans. He then asked Ibn Saud what suggestions he had as to how to help the Jewish survivors. Ibn Saud replied, "give them and their descendents the choicest lands and homes of the Germans who had oppressed them." FDR replied that the Jews did not wish to stay in Germany after the war, and in any case, they had "a sentimental desire to settle in Palestine." Ibn Saud responded, "What injury have Arabs done to the Jews of Europe? It is the Christian Germans who stole their homes and lives. Let the Germans pay." The king now neatly reversed the Zionist argument that the Arabs had so much land that they could afford to give up little Palestine. He noted to Roosevelt that Palestine had already "been assigned more than its quota of European refugees." If the president did not like the idea of giving the Jews part of Germany, he should keep in mind the fact that the "allied camp" had "fifty countries" in it. Surely they could manage to take the remaining Jewish survivors.[51]

These suggestions might have seemed naive to President Roosevelt, but in truth they can be judged as no more so than Zionist aims sounded to Arab ears. As it was, FDR came away from the meeting rather shaken. According to Harry Hopkins, Roosevelt was "greatly shocked" at the Saudi king's refusal to see the logic of his arguments. According to Hopkins the one thing FDR did learn was "the Arabs meant business" when it came to Palestine.[52] In the end, it was not the "King of the desert" but rather the U.S. president who made concessions. Both during their conversations on board the *Quincy*, and later in a letter dated April 5, 1945, Roosevelt affirmed to Ibn Saud that "no decision [would] be taken with respect to the basic situation in that country [Palestine] without full consultation with both Arabs and Jews." And further, that Roosevelt would "take no action in my capacity as Chief of the Executive Branch of government which might prove hostile to the Arab people."[53]

When he returned home, Roosevelt made an official report on the Yalta Conference to Congress and in it he included comments on his meeting with Ibn Saud. "I learned more about that whole problem, the Moslem problem, the Jewish problem, by talking with Ibn Saud for five minutes than I could have learned in an exchange of two or three dozen letters."[54] As a consequence, it is probably true that Roosevelt was less inclined to see Zionist ambitions as fully achievable.

Roosevelt's meeting with the Saudi king caused great consternation among the Zionists and their supporters. The loudest protests were heard in Congress, where the comments revealed something of the intellectual level of the debate at the time. For instance, Edwin C. Johnson, Democrat from Colorado, made the following comment, "with all due respect to the President and King Ibn Saud, I must say that the choice of a desert king as expert on the Jewish question is nothing short of amazing. . . . I imagine that even Fala [the president's dog] would be more of an expert."[55] Then there was the comment made in a letter to the *New York Times*, which probably reflects popular American opinion at the time. The writer asked, "what record as to the historic right of the Jewish people to Palestine is more authentic, the Bible or Ibn Saud?"[56] For these commentators the Arabs seem to have no relevance to the "Jewish question" in Palestine.

The American Zionist leadership was so upset with the president that soon after his return from Yalta Roosevelt deemed it politically necessary to grant an interview to Stephen Wise and Abba Silver. At the meeting FDR authorized the Zionist leaders to make public a statement in which he reaffirmed the U.S. government's "greatest sympathy" for the realization of a Jewish National Home in Palestine.[57] This statement, in turn, brought protests from the governments of Saudi Arabia, as well as Egypt and Iraq, to which the State Department had difficulty replying. Roosevelt, caught between the dual realities of Zionist domestic strength and Arab adamance on the issue, was simply sending out mixed messages, and satisfying no one.

NEA and Non-Zionist Jews

While Roosevelt sought to promise something to both the Arabs and the Zionists, the State Department held to more consistent positions. Throughout the war they had made the argument that any formal or public commitment to Zionism on the part of the U.S. government would undermine the British position in Palestine. Also, they believed that it would do irreparable damage to American interests throughout the Middle East.

Were these positions inspired by anti-Semitic prejudice? While arguing against open support for Zionism, NEA in fact supported Judah Magnes and his idea of a bi-national state. Wallace Murray repeatedly voiced his admiration and support for Judah Magnes's effort to arrange a peaceful settlement between Arabs and Jews. In 1938 he encouraged the American consulate in Jerusalem to facilitate negotiations between Magnes and Nuri Pasha, the Iraqi leader. At that time, Magnes sought to arrive at some formula, acceptable to the Arabs, that would allow for continued Jewish immigration into Palestine.[58] Murray also backed Magnes's long-standing advocacy of Arab-Jewish civil and political equality in Palestine.[59] In 1942 Murray recommended Magnes's ideas to Secretary of State Hull as ones "representative of the conservative majority of American Jewry."[60]

However, none of this verbal support was to have much impact. Besides saying encouraging things about Magnes in internal State Department memos, Murray and NEA did little to actually promote his moderate views beyond the executive branch of government. In particular, they made no effort to promote Magnes's views in the U.S. Congress. This limited range of activity reflects the State Department's limited concept of its own role. Except up and down the chain of command within the department and, through the secretary of state, to the White House, it did not see its role as a proactive one.

Murray and NEA also established an ongoing dialogue with Morris Lazaron and Elmer Berger of the American Council for Judaism, as well as Morris Waldman of the American Jewish Committee. Both of these were active organizations of anti-Zionist Jews. NEA established these contacts in part because Murray and others believed that, while the American Zionists were politically influential, they were ultimately unrepresentative of American Jewry. In an October 1943 memo to then assistant secretary of state Edward Stettinius, Murray estimated that there were 5 million Jews in the United States, yet only 50,000 were "paid-up" members of the ZOA. He observed that "a sharp distinction must be made between those who favor a national life for the Jewish people and those who do not. The Zionists are well organized, militant, and highly vocal. The non-Zionists are relatively poorly organized."[61]

Murray's feeling about the unrepresentativeness of Zionism was not just based on wishful thinking. It was supported by the Zionists themselves. The July 1939 issue of the official ZOA organ, *New Palestine*, editorialized that "only a small number [of American Jews] are affiliated with the Zionist movement. . . . Only a handful appreciate the significance of Zionism . . . [and] are able to see how closely knit together all of Jewish effort is with the building of the Homeland." In April 1941 Emanuel Neumann admitted to Murray that "the number who were formally connected with the movement was not as large as one might wish."[62]

It was this situation that led Murray and NEA to hope that the anti-Zionists might eventually prove viable competitors for the support of American Jewry. In December of 1942, Murray focused on the American Council for Judaism, which, he noted, took the position that Judaism was a religion rather than a nationality. He cited the organization's assertion that "We are definitely opposed to a Jewish state, a Jewish flag, or a Jewish army. We are interested in development of Palestine as a refuge for persecuted Jews but are opposed to the idea of a political state under Jewish domination in Palestine or anywhere else."[63]

The council's leaders engaged in a dialogue with NEA just as the Zionists did. They wrote to and solicited interviews with the secretary of state as well. They published editorials and op-ed pieces in, among other publications, the *New York Times*[64] and *Life* magazine.[65] All of this won Murray's approval. Noting, in late 1942, Morris Lazaron's public declaration that "no pledges as to the future political status [of Palestine] can be made; that must be determined by Palestine's Jews, and Christians, and Moslems," Murray remarked, "my own view is that it would be an act of far-seeing statesmanship to follow Rabbi Lazaron's suggestion. The effect would, I believe, be powerful and instantaneous rallying Arab and Moslem opinion to the cause of the United Nations. We have . . . over a considerable period of time been warned . . . of the alarming deterioration in Great Britain's political position in the Near and Middle East because of the Zionist question."[66]

NEA's support of moderate, anti-Zionist Jews who favored Palestine as a Jewish refuge, but not a Jewish state, argues that the division would have liked to see a compromise solution which would have situated the Jews as members of a bi-national Palestine wherein Jews and Arabs had equal rights. What NEA could not support was a maximalist Zionist solution giving Palestine to the Jews and thus sparking civil war. This, they be-lieved, would push the Arabs into the hands of the fascists and do real harm to the Allied war effort. It also risked identifying the United States exclusively with the Zionist cause and thereby seriously undermining American interests in the entire Middle East region. While NEA's stands supporting both bi-nationalism and anti-Zionist Jews upset the Zionists, both at the time and later, neither can be judged positions reflecting a racial dislike of Jews.

Further American Zionist Wartime Efforts

The inability of contemporary historians to identify NEA's true position on Palestine may have much to do with how the Holocaust came to color wartime events. Of course, long before the Holocaust, the Zionist move-ment had dedicated itself to obtaining Palestine for the Jews, and Zionists would have continued on this path if the Holocaust had never occurred. As it was, however, the magnitude of the disaster wrought by Nazi anti-Semitism so strengthened Zionist resolve, and so popularized the goal of a Jewish Palestine, that anything that got in the way led to all-out opposi-tion on the part of the movement and its supporters. This was true even if the obstacles were aspects of British war strategy against the fascists, or the prospect of a postwar democratic government for Palestine.

The Biltmore Program and the American Palestine Committee

This aggressive posture was readily apparent at the 1942 Biltmore Confer-ence. The background of this conference lay in the plethora of planning that the war gave rise to. The Allies had hundreds of committees and commissions not only planning wartime activities, but also planning what the postwar world was to look like. Britain's 1939 White Paper was itself a manifestation of this activity. Early in the war the Zionists realized that they too had to join this process lest their cause be undercut by other planners who did not share their interests.[67]

Thus, on May 9, 1942, Zionist leaders from Europe and America met at the Biltmore Hotel in New York. This gathering was attended by 586 American delegates led by Stephen Wise, Abba Silver, and Louis Lipsky. Sixty-seven Zionist leaders came from abroad, including Chaim Weiz-mann and David Ben Gurion. The purpose of the conference was to set forth a definitive outline of the Zionist program for postwar Palestine. As Ben Gurion told the meeting delegates, there were three principles that should guide that program: (1) reestablishment of Palestine as a Jewish

Commonwealth, (2) immediate granting of authority to the Jewish Agency to control Jewish immigration and the "upbuilding" of the country, (3) "complete equality for all inhabitants of Palestine, civil, political, and religious."[68] Not surprisingly the final declaration of the conference paid attention to only the first two demands. It also, once again, tied the entire Zionist movement to the process of Western colonial expansion, the bipolar worldview, and the rationalizing notion of altruistic imperialism.

> In our generation . . . the Jewish people have been awakened and transformed their ancient homeland. . . . their pioneering achievements have written a notable page in the history of colonialization. . . . The Conference calls for the fulfillment of the original purposes of the Balfour Declaration and . . . affirms its unalterable objection of the White Paper of 1939 . . . [which] is in direct conflict with the interests of the Allied war effort. The Conference demands that the gates of Palestine be opened; that the Jewish Agency be vested with control of immigration . . . [and] the necessary authority for upbuilding the country . . . and that Palestine be established as a Jewish Commonwealth integrated into the structure of a new democratic world.

The conference's final declaration made no direct reference to Ben Gurion's third principle, "complete equality of inhabitants." Instead, it offered the claim that "Arab neighbors have shared in the new values thus created" by the Zionist presence in Palestine, and that "the WZO expresses the readiness and the desire of the Jewish people for full cooperation with their Arab neighbors."[69]

The Biltmore Conference declaration made official what the Zionists already held to be the "maximalist" goals of their movement. To achieve them, they had launched an organizing campaign that would span the war years and be galvanized by the horrors of the Holocaust. Several new committees had emerged; chief amongst them was the Emergency Committee for Zionist Affairs, created in 1939 to coordinate the wartime activities of various Zionist organizations. After Pearl Harbor, and the American entry into the war, the Emergency Committee became an increasingly militant advocate of American Zionism. By the time of the Biltmore Conference it fully backed the program put forth by Ben Gurion.

One other new committee that was of particular importance in recruiting large numbers of important American political, economic, and social leaders to the Zionist cause was the American Palestine Committee (APC). Originally created in 1932 as an organization of Christian supporters of

Zionism, the APC was reorganized and reinvigorated in March of 1941. Within a month its membership included 70 U.S. senators, 120 congressmen, a number of Cabinet members, including Attorney General Robert H. Jackson and Secretary of the Interior Ickes, 21 state governors, clergymen, civic leaders, and other "men of affairs," such as William Green, head of the American Federation of Labor.[70] The committee was chaired by the energetic Robert F. Wagner of New York, who told the *New York Times* on March 28, 1941, that "the purpose" of APC "will be to support the movement for developing Palestine as an outpost of freedom and social justice, and to prepare for large scale colonization of Jewish refugees."[71]

Both Wagner's plain speaking, and the rapid growth of the APC, were a source of worry for the British government and a number of Middle Eastern states. An official from the British embassy in Washington called at the State Department on April 21, 1941, to express concern that German propaganda directed at the Arab world would use the APC's work to assert that "the United States would force Great Britain at the end of the war, if Great Britain is victorious, to open up all of Palestine to Jewish settlement." (This, of course, was exactly what the Zionists would soon urge the U.S. government to do.) If "prominent persons high in the [U.S.] Government" started publicly advocating that position, "very great unrest will be created in the Arab world."[72] The next day the Turkish ambassador delivered essentially the same message.[73]

APC's activities, combined with increasing congressional support, would greatly complicate the lives of NEA staffers and U.S. diplomats in the Middle East. They were never able to convince Arab leaders that the APC's goals were not official U.S. policy when scores of congressmen, senators, and other government officials all were publicly proclaiming that "the Jewish National Home in Palestine has been a world-sanctioned experiment in democracy. It must be protected and cherished. . . . Its continued upbuilding must be a vital part of a just world order when the present conflict is over."[74]

The work of the APC, the Emergency Committee for Zionist Affairs, and other Zionist lobby groups successfully marshaled public and private support for the Zionist movement and brought it to a fever pitch.[75] Particularly as the extent of Nazi persecution became known, the support of Jewish claims to Palestine became something like a moral imperative. This created a context, particularly within the U.S. Congress, where the possible detrimental consequences of official government support for Zionism, both to the war effort and to U.S. long-term interests in the Middle

East, were most often overlooked. Likewise, NEA efforts to call attention to such dangers were soon considered tantamount to anti-Semitism.

This attitude can be seen in the behavior of Representative Emanuel Celler in 1943. Frustrated by NEA's consistent refusal to support open Jewish immigration into Palestine as the only answer to Nazi persecution, Celler wrote to FDR accusing the State Department of attempting to "nullify and destroy the numerous declarations, mandates, and treaties in which we, directly and indirectly, are participants, and which would permit rescue of Jews in Axis devastated lands." He accused NEA of being "Arab appeasers" and taking part in a "cabal . . . to discredit the work of Jews in Palestine." Then he threatened a congressional investigation unless "the State Department ceases its absurd opposition to Palestine as a haven for the Jews."[76] Celler's threat of an investigation proved a bluff, but the often angry division of opinion between Congress and the State Department remained ongoing for the rest of the war.

The Congressional Resolutions of 1944

In 1944 that difference focused on a series of proposed congressional resolutions on Palestine. On January 27, 1944, Representatives James A. Wright of Pennsylvania and Ranulf Compton of Connecticut introduced a resolution in the House that urged the U.S. government to take "appropriate measures" to induce the British to allow unlimited Jewish immigration and colonization so that Palestine might be ultimately reconstituted "as a free and democratic Jewish Commonwealth."[77] On February 1 an identical resolution was introduced into the Senate by Robert Wagner of New York and Robert Taft of Ohio. Upon submitting the Senate resolution, Senator Wagner placed it within a liberally reinterpreted historical context: "this resolution reaffirms the historic policy of the Government of the United States formulated by Congress in June 1922 when it unanimously passed a joint resolution sponsored by the late Senator Lodge. . . . The Lodge resolution confirmed the Balfour Declaration, establishing in Palestine a homeland for the Jewish people. Although it was issued in the name of the British Government it was as a matter of fact a joint policy of the Governments of Great Britain and the United States."[78]

As we have seen, besides President Wilson's offhanded approval, the U.S. government had nothing to do with the issuance of the Balfour Declaration. Nonetheless, at the public hearings on the House resolution, held in February, Senator Wagner's version of history was both supported and contested. Appearing in support of the resolution were Stephen Wise,

Abba Silver, and other Zionist leaders. Appearing in support of open im-
migration, but in opposition to a "Jewish Commonwealth," were John
Slawson of the American Jewish Committee and Morris Lazaron of the
American Council for Judaism. And appearing in opposition to the reso-
lution altogether was Professor Philip Hitti of Princeton University and
Faris S. Malouf, president of the Syrian-Lebanese American Federation of
the Eastern States. Malouf was also a past president of the Arab National
League.

Professor Hitti's testimony, given on February 15, aimed at discrediting
the Zionist position. He asserted that "the Arabs have the natural right of
occupancy to their country" and noted that "the third article of the Atlantic Charter respects the right of people to choose their own government."
And then, in answer to earlier Zionist testimony claiming that "the Arabian Empire was sparsely populated and therefore could spare one percent
of its land which Palestine represented," he asked the congressmen if the
argument should not be applied elsewhere. "Why doesn't the U.S. open its
immigration to Jews, for instance, on the plains of Arizona and Texas?"
These areas would require the displacement of far fewer people than in
Palestine.[79]

Arab American opposition made no more difference in 1944 than it
had in 1922. Indeed, when the hearings began, the Zionists and their
congressional supporters were confident of a near-unanimous victory.
Even the sometimes skeptical editors of the New York Times, now confronted with the human catastrophe of the Holocaust, weighed in in support of the resolution. In an editorial published on February 12, 1944, the
paper's editors declared that "The increasingly desperate state of those of
Jewish faith in Europe has made it more than ever evident that . . . doors
of any place of refuge . . . should be open wider." Ignoring the U.S.
Congress's own refusal to allow for the immigration of significant numbers of Jewish (or any other) refugees at this time, the Times took Great
Britain to task for its "arbitrary ban" on immigration into Palestine. The
editors demanded that it "should be lifted and immigration be permitted
on the most generous terms possible." The New York Times editors then
asserted that "the case for American intervention in this question is stronger than it was five years ago. The presence of our troops and supply
depots in the Near East and our vital concern in peace and order in this
strategic area give us a greater right to urge that the White Paper should
now be abrogated."[80]

This argument ran counter to the reasoning used by NEA, in which
concern for troops and depots led to a desire not to interfere with British

policy in Palestine. And in fact, the logic of this latter position would eventually lead to the temporary demise of the congressional resolutions. Even prior to the House hearings, opposition to the resolutions had come first from the War Department and then from the State Department. In a letter dated February 7, Secretary of War Henry Stimson wrote to Senator Tom Connally, chairman of the Senate Foreign Relations Committee, to let him know that "the subject of this resolution is a matter of deep military concern to the War Department. I feel that the passage of this resolution at the present time, or even any public hearings thereon, would be apt to provoke dangerous repercussions in areas where we have many vital military interests."[81] Secretary of State Hull followed this up on February 9 with a letter of his own to Connally suggesting that "no further action on this resolution would be advisable at this time."[82]

Arab governments had made it quite clear to American authorities that they considered pro-Zionist resolutions provocative. Protests were lodged with the U.S. legations in Egypt, Iraq, Transjordan, Saudi Arabia, Lebanon, Syria, and Yemen. The Iraqi government also communicated by cable directly with Senators Taft, Wagner, and Connally. The Iraqis informed the senators that "immigration of Jews into Palestine with the idea of turning it into a Jewish state would lead to disturbances there and would aid the efforts of enemy propagandists."[83] This was essentially what General George Marshall, then army chief of staff, told the Senate Foreign Relations Committee in executive session on March 4.[84]

While Marshall's objections were sufficient to cause the withdrawal of the resolutions, the sponsors, particularly Senator Taft, were indignant and angry over being thwarted. Not being able to direct that anger at the War Department, Taft lashed out at the Iraqis for having had the audacity to offer their concerns to the U.S. Congress. He told the *New York Times* that "the Congress of the United States, which for more than a century has been able to reach its own conclusions without advice from officials of foreign nations, is fully able to reach a wise conclusion in this matter which will be in accord with the wishes of the American people."[85]

The sponsors' anger also eventually led them to question Marshall's advice. Later in March, according to the *New York Times,* Taft "took issue with the military critics of the proposal [the resolutions] who suggested that the action might weaken the position of Allied troops in North Africa and the Middle East." After confessing that "I am no expert on military affairs and I do not know enough about military conditions in North Africa to affirm or deny the alleged position of the Secretary of War and General Marshall," Taft proceeded to do just that, deny the "alleged position." He said, "I strongly suspect that the real objection is political and not military."[86]

Within a week President Roosevelt himself proceeded to muddy the waters when he appeared to contradict his own military experts. On March 10 he met with Stephen Wise and Abba Silver and authorized them to release a statement that said, "the American Government has never given its approval to the White Paper of 1939 . . . and that when future decisions are reached full justice will be done to those who seek a Jewish national home, for which our Government and the American people have always had the deepest sympathy."[87] This release renewed Arab concerns and sent the State Department scurrying for an explanation of the contradictory positions within the government.[88] In Wallace Murray's opinion, as well as that of the Office of Strategic Services (the wartime predecessor of the CIA), the behavior of the U.S. Congress when it came to pro-Zionist resolutions "led to a material weakening in the American psychological position in the Near East."[89]

The pro-Zionist congressional leaders either did not believe, or did not care about, that opinion. Therefore, they used Roosevelt's March 10 statement to resurrect their resolutions. By the end of March they were arguing that FDR's statement "overruled . . . the Chief of Staff [Marshall]" and therefore Congress could proceed to reconsider the Palestine resolutions.[90] This position was furthered when, over the summer of 1944, both the Republican and Democratic party platform committees inserted planks favoring the "opening of Palestine to unrestricted immigration and colonization."[91] As a consequence, Palestine resolutions were back in the House and Senate by November.

By that time, however, Arab diplomatic protests over the issue had become charges of betrayal. They referred specifically to FDR's promise that no decision would be taken altering the status of Palestine without prior consultation with both Arabs and Jews.[92] Once again, Roosevelt, the State Department, and the War Department were forced to intervene to have the resolutions shelved. This time the argument was that they were "unwise from the standpoint of the general international situation."[93]

Failure to achieve passage of the resolutions caused dissension within the Zionist establishment. A split developed between Stephen Wise and Abba Silver. Wise felt that the preservation of Roosevelt's good will (and his own personal relationship with FDR) would best serve the Zionists in the long run and was therefore more important than the resolutions. Silver was much more the firebrand and insisted that the resolutions be pushed forward even if it meant alienating the president. It was he who had worked to get the House and Senate to resurrect the resolutions toward the end of 1944. And when those resolutions too were withdrawn under pressure, it was Silver whom the other Zionists blamed for the strain and embarrassment the whole episode caused the Roosevelt administration. As early as May 19, 1944, after the first set of resolutions had been set aside, Nahum Goldman, chairman of the World Jewish Congress, told Wallace Murray that "the guiding spirit behind the introduction of those resolutions . . . was Rabbi Silver. [But] so long as the war gave an excuse for the Arabs to 'make trouble,' the military authorities would oppose any action which might incite the Arabs." Goldman went on to explain that he and Stephen Wise "quite understood this point of view," but both had been away from Washington, and their absence had left "Rabbi Silver free to press for the resolutions."[94]

The saga of the 1944 resolutions points to the fact that Congress, even in the midst of global war, lived in an altogether different world than did the State Department. While the members of Congress seldom looked beyond the constituencies of their own districts or states, the State Department dealt with international realities and their contending forces. Thus Hull, Stettinius, Murray, and those who staffed NEA saw the potential damage the resolutions were likely to have first on the strategic Allied military position in the Middle East, and, later, on the long-term overall interests of the United States. Murray itemized some of the negative possibilities in February 1944. The resolutions, if passed, would probably "precipitate armed conflict in Palestine and other parts of the Arab world, endangering American troops." And they would "seriously prejudice, if not make impossible, important pending negotiations with Ibn Saud for the construction of a pipeline across Saudi Arabia, a development of utmost importance to the security of the United States."[95]

It is hard to escape the conclusion that neither the Zionist leadership nor their supporters in Congress paid any attention to the State Department's perspective. On the contrary: to Congress, the Allied military position in North Africa and the Middle East, much less U.S. regional interests in that area, seemed to be absent until George Marshall forced the congressional leadership to begrudgingly take them into consideration. Here, it would seem, we have an example of the fact that the forces that shape behavior in the U.S. Congress, even in the midst of war, are basically parochial. Zionism may have been a danger to U.S. interests abroad, but it had become a vital asset to parochial interests of congressmen and senators at home. Therefore it, and not U.S. national interests as defined by the foreign policy arm of the government, defined their behavior.

The Question of Immigration

A shared concern for the fate of European Jews suffering the horrors of the Holocaust helped further solidify the alliance between the U.S. Congress and Zionism. The anxiety of the American Jewish community over the issue, and the passion of the ZOA and its affiliates to do something related to the Holy Land in the face of it all, helped make Palestine the domestic issue it surely was by the 1940s. As Edwin C. Johnson, the Democratic senator from Colorado, put it to the *New York Times* on March 28, 1944, "the problem must be met. If we cannot send the refugees to Palestine they must be sent somewhere else to get them out of Hitler's hands. If we don't do something we must share his guilt." Johnson then advocated immediate passage of the congressional resolutions on Palestine.[96]

This raises the issue of, If not Palestine, then why not "somewhere else?" We have seen that both Arab leaders and Arab Americans such as Philip Hitti had made specific suggestions as to where that "somewhere else" might be found. Hitti had pointedly told Congress in his testimony of February 15, 1944, that the refugees should be admitted to the United States.

Many volumes have been written on this question.[97] The consensus is that America as a nation failed to do all that might have been done to facilitate the escape of millions of innocent victims, Jews and non-Jews, of the Nazi regime. Certainly America's immigration policy was part of the problem. As David Brody tells us in his incisive piece "American Jewry, the Refugees, and Immigration Restriction, 1932–1942," American immigration laws had become tighter and tighter as the economic depression of the 1930s deepened.[98] But the war changed economic conditions, if not frames of mind. With mass conscription and the gearing up of industry to wage world war, unemployment was no longer an issue. As Seymour Maxwell Finger points out in his study *American Jewry during the Holocaust,* "during the last three years of the war nearly 400,000 German prisoners of war were interned in camps across the United States. Most were used in civilian industries, particularly agriculture, to alleviate labor shortages. This makes it difficult to argue that . . . the Jews who might have left Europe in that period . . . could not have been similarly interned to save them from death."[99] Nonetheless, an unnecessary fear of job competition from immigrant labor lingered, helping to keep "the doors of the U.S." closed to Jews, while correspondingly contributing to organized labor's strong support for the Zionist movement.[100]

Most historians also see the State Department as part of the problem. It will be recalled that Phillip Baram characterized the department in these years as "the lesser of the world's anti-Jewish evils." David Wyman, in his book *The Abandonment of the Jews,* tells us that there were "two aspects of the State Department's response to the Holocaust" that led to inaction. "One was the visa policy that shut the U.S. to all but a tiny trickle of refugee immigration. The other was the Department's quiet, but unwavering, support for Britain's policy of very tight limits on refugee entrance to Palestine. Thus, two of the most likely havens of refuge were virtually closed. And other countries were provided with justification for their own barred doors."[101]

Wyman's criticism is in fact misleading. He, like virtually all who have commented on this subject, fold together the actions of the State Department's Visa Bureau, headed by Breckinridge Long, and Wallace Murray's Division of Near Eastern Affairs. In truth there was a qualitative difference between the responsibilities, motivations, and actions of these two departments. Breckinridge Long was, to use Wyman's characterization, "an extreme nativist, especially with regard to Eastern Europeans."[102] It is probably true that Long disliked Jews. He also disliked everyone else who did not fit into his narrow vision of what America should be like. He was, in essence, a bigoted man who in turn empowered the bigotry of many of his subordinates. However, the result was not a distortion or perversion of the American popular will. For, as David Schoenbaum tells us in his book *The U.S. and the State of Israel,* "the same year as the so called kristallnacht pogrom of November 9, 1938, 83% of American respondents answered No when asked their willingness to raise immigration quotas to admit refugees. A year later . . . a bill to admit 20,000 children above the quota failed in both the House and Senate."[103] Long was a bigoted man in a bigoted age.

Nor was the reaction of most American Jews, American Zionists among them, very different from that of their fellow citizens when it came to real changes in immigration policy. Through the 1930s major American Jewish organizations opposed any influx of Jewish immigrants because of the prevailing depression conditions.[104] By 1939, however, those same Jewish organizations realized that increased immigration would not have a serious economic impact. At the same time they were increasingly aware of the dire situation of the Jews in Europe. Nonetheless, they failed to back several efforts to liberalize immigration laws put forth by Jewish congressmen.[105] The consensus is that these organizations would have liked to see more refugees admitted, but were hampered by a fear that any influx of European Jews would lead to a dangerous increase in anti-Semitism in the

United States. This opinion was shared by Zionist leaders. Stephen Wise told a congressional hearing in 1939 that "I have heard no sane person propose any departure or deviation from the existing [immigration] law now in force."[106]

The dilemma posed for American Jews, caught between a desire to aid Jewish refugees in Europe and the overwhelming American opposition to substantive changes in immigration policy, was real and painful. However, there was a seemingly convenient and, for the Zionists, ideologically powerful solution to be had. That solution was Palestine. How much easier it must have been to rail against the 1939 British White Paper than against American immigration laws.

Thus, according to David Brody, the efforts of those few American Jews who did seek to challenge the country's restrictive immigration laws largely cease by 1940, and most Americans interested in the fate of Jewish refugees become fixated on Palestine.[107] It was the logical road to take because it was the road of least resistance in terms of America's own immigration politics and popular opinion. However, by abandoning the effort to liberalize American immigration laws, American Jews acceded to the same bigotry and nativism that motivated the behavior of men like Breckinridge Long.

The position taken by NEA staff in reference to Palestine should not be equated with the bigotry of the Visa Bureau personnel, despite the fact that that is exactly what many historians do.[108] There is no evidence that Wallace Murray and his collegues at NEA opposed mass Jewish immigration into Palestine because they were anti-Semitic. As we have seen, there were good strategic, military, diplomatic, and economic reasons for their opposition, and these formed a legitimate basis for their position, especially within the context of impending and actual world war.

Wallace Murray clearly understood, and on occasion articulated, the need for the resettlement of Europe's Jewish population. "I believe that the most likely way to alleviate [the consequences of anti-Semitism] . . . is to provide . . . for the orderly settlement in some suitable territory of the greater part of European Jewry."[109] And we have seen that he was quite willing to work toward any compromise, such as that put forth by Judah Magnes, that would maximize Jewish immigration into Palestine without risking widespread Arab rebellion and harm American interests as well. Yet he, and NEA as a whole, are lumped together with the likes of Breckinridge Long and branded as evil anti-Semites.

There is something troublesome about this treatment of NEA. Stephen Wise and the rest of the American Jewish establishment largely failed to confront U.S. public opinion over the need to liberalize immigration because they feared inflaming U.S. anti-Semitism. Yet American historians, most of whom are supporters of the Zionist position, condemn the NEA for failing to confront the British over their 1939 White Paper. These historians choose not to recognize that NEA's position arose from the division's fear that the same liberalization of Jewish immigration into Palestine would inflame the Arabs, and thus undercut the British position in relation to the fascists. Is there not at least the suggestion of hypocrisy in condemning others for failing to do what your own group had not the courage to do?

Activities of Arab Americans

While the American Jews did not want Europe's Jewish refugees flooding into the United States, but rather wished them to go to Palestine, Arab Americans could not understand why Palestine should be made to bear a burden America refused. As they had in the 1920s, Arab Americans tried to compete with the Zionists and present the Arab point of view. By the latter part of the 1930s a number of Arab organizations were engaged in this effort. Foremost among them was the Arab National League, which was still under the leadership of Fuad Shatara. There also existed an allied group of non–Arab Americans sympathetic to their position called American Friends of the Arabs. This group was led by Elihu Grant.

The Arab National League was in regular contact with the State Department. Documented meetings took place in October of 1938, January of 1939, and April of 1941, and there were probably others.[110] At these meetings, and in numerous letters addressed to President Roosevelt and Secretary of State Hull,[111] their message was the same as in the past. They argued that increasingly close ties between government officials (particularly in Congress) and the Zionists jeopardized the good will Arabs had built up for America over time. Over time this erosion of good will was bound to negatively affect trade relations. They also asserted that it was fundamentally unjust to "relieve the oppression of the Jews by resorting to methods which resulted in the oppression of the Arabs." What was called for was a worldwide effort to save refugees by "humane people of all countries." And finally, they asserted that it was imperative that the U.S. government "maintain an attitude of impartiality" toward the struggle in Palestine. Taking the Zionist side was not only unfair but played into the hands of fascist propagandists seeking to undermine the Allied position in the Middle East.[112] These arguments corresponded closely to those being made by Arab leaders in the Middle East[113] and were taken seriously at NEA.[114]

In April of 1941 the State Department sent Harold Hoskins to New York City "to discuss with the leaders of certain Syrian [American] organizations there, their attitude toward this country and the war." Hoskins reported that these Arab Americans were "extremely loyal to the United States." He went on to emphasize that "none of these [Arab American] organizations is asking the U.S. government to do anything for the Arabs, but all appear equally anxious that the U.S. government not take any position officially in support of the Zionist movement."[115] This information was incorporated into a memo from Wallace Murray to Secretary of State Hull and Assistant Secretary of State Wells in which he argued for the same position of neutrality toward Palestine.[116]

Thus, by the late 1930s a convergence of views existed between NEA and organized Arab American groups such as the Arab National League. However, because the State Department did not actively seek to educate Congress and other branches of the government to this position, this convergence was of little aid to Arab American efforts. Nonetheless, Arab American leaders tried tirelessly to build on this foundation. Not only did they communicate their views to the government, they also picketed Zionist public meetings,[117] and even attempted an appeal to Chaim Weizmann. On behalf of the Arab National League, Faris Malouf wrote to Weizmann on April 21, 1941,

> In the present world war, though a Hitler victory will in all probability eliminate political Zionism from Palestine, the Arabs nevertheless have refrained from activities which will play into the hands of the totalitarian states . . . thereby weakening the cause and forces of democracy. . . . You well know there is resentment throughout the Arab world against political Zionism and that this furnishes fertile soil for Axis agents and propagandists. . . . [Therefore] your insistence on abrogating the Palestine White Paper . . . [is] unfair, opportunistic and dangerous in the face of the present emergency. . . . We trust you will appreciate the responsibilities and implications of your activities and call a halt to them in the interest of Jews, Arabs, and all the forces fighting against totalitarian aggression.[118]

There is no evidence that Weizmann answered this letter or gave any consideration at all to its appeal.

Other contacts were made between Arab Americans and anti-Zionist Jewish leaders such as Morris Lazaron of the American Council for Judaism.[119] However, little seems to have come from these communications. By the 1940s even those American Jews who stood against the notion of a Jewish state favored the reversal of the White Paper and unlimited immigration rights into Palestine for Jews.

Toward the end of the war, clearly facing overwhelming odds in terms of competing with the Zionist message, Arab Americans remained organized and active. In November of 1944 the Arab National League sponsored a two-day conference in New York involving "150 representatives of societies with a total membership of 200,000 Arab Americans."[120] At the end of the meeting the attendees sent a telegram to the secretary of state. In this message they noted that "any approval of a Jewish state . . . in Palestine against the will of its native Arab inhabitants . . . is irreconcilable with the principles of democracy." They then called for "a truly democratic government in Palestine based on proportional representation."[121]

The themes of democracy and the Palestinian right of self-determination were the most consistent and long lasting of the Arab American positions. They remained valid even as the Allies eliminated the fascist threat in the Middle East. However, except for NEA, Arab American pleas fell on deaf ears. This was because, as we have seen, the Palestinian population was either invisible to or considered backward by the politicians and media of the day.[122] Palestinian Arab aspirations were not recognized as representative of a modern national movement, so it made little difference what Arab Americans claimed. Indeed, the right of self-determination and democratic expression in Palestine had already been appropriated, in the eyes of the American public, by the Jews despite the fact that only a small minority of them resided there.

Conclusion

The deference shown to the British White Paper of 1939 by the executive branch of the American government flew in the face of the growing influence and power of the Zionist movement in the United States. What held that power at bay was wartime contingencies in North Africa and the Middle East. NEA recognized those contingencies and sought to keep the government focused on them, albeit in a quiet way that penetrated little beyond the State Department. It must be emphasized therefore that during the war years it was immediate military reality that frustrated the capture of America's Palestine policy by the Zionists, and not any broad influence of NEA. Take away the war emergency, and replace it with a refugee emergency accented by Western guilt over the Holocaust, and you have a setting for the defeat of NEA's position on Palestine. Under such new circumstances the long-pursued desire of American Zionists to have their ends define America's national interests in Palestine would be realized.

8

1945–1948

Zionism Triumphant

There can be little doubt that at the end of his life Franklin Roosevelt did not favor the partition of Palestine. Instead, he favored the notion of a United Nations trusteeship for the Holy Land. This was an idea that he had put forth after the failure of Harold Hoskins's diplomatic mission to Ibn Saud in 1943. As late as March of 1945, just weeks before the president's death, he told Hoskins that he believed that the Zionists in Palestine were such a demographic minority that they could not successfully defend themselves if it came to civil war. When Hoskins told Roosevelt that the State Department had worked up a preliminary plan for Palestine based on the president's suggestions that "the country be made an international territory sacred to all three religions," FDR replied that "he thought such a plan might well be given to the United Nations organization after it had been set up."[1]

It is uncertain whether FDR would have been able to sustain this plan. We have already seen that, upon his return from Yalta, the intense political pressure of the American Zionists had led him to publicly reiterate his support for the Zionist effort in Palestine. He was first and foremost a politician, and, on the subject of Palestine, American politics was firmly in the hands of the Zionists. This situation may very well have led Roosevelt to support Zionist desires in the end, but the point is really moot. In April of 1945 President Roosevelt died and his vice president, Harry Truman, assumed power.

The White House versus the State Department

President Truman's formal introduction to the situation in Palestine seems to have come in the form of a memo dated April 18, 1945, from Secretary of State Edward Stettinius.

It is very likely that efforts will be made by some Zionist leaders to obtain from you . . . commitments in favor of . . . unlimited Jewish immigration into Palestine and the establishment there of a Jewish state.

As you are aware, the Government and people of the United States have every sympathy for the persecuted Jews . . . and are doing all in their power to relieve their suffering. The question of Palestine is, however, a highly complex one and involves questions that go beyond the plight of the Jews in Europe. . . . therefore, I believe you would probably want to call for full and detailed information on the subject before taking any particular position. . . .

There is continual tenseness in the situation in the Near East largely as a result of the Palestine question and as we have interests in that area which are vital to the United States, we feel that this whole subject is one that should be handled with the greatest care.[2]

On the face of it, this communication was simply informing a new president of a sensitive situation. However, Truman appears to have read much more into it. One can readily see this from statements he made to Rabbi Stephen Wise during a fifteen-minute interview on April 20. Though brief, his candid remarks to the Zionist leader effectively predicted Truman's evolving attitudes toward both Palestine and the State Department. He was "skeptical . . . about some of the attitudes assumed by the 'striped pants boys' in the State Department," he told Wise. In essence, they had their priorities wrong. "It seems to me that they didn't care enough about what happened to thousands of displaced persons [Europe's surviving Jews] who were involved" in the Palestine question. He also told Wise that he was quite familiar with both the Balfour Declaration and Roosevelt's statements on the issue.[3]

One interpretation of Truman's statements entails the assumption that he, a man of the people, had a dislike of the moneyed class from which most of the State Department personnel, "the striped pants boys," were supposedly drawn. In addition, he seemed not to like being told what to do by "experts."[4] This attitude led the veteran Washington correspondent for the Associated Press, Jack Bell, to describe the new president as "always [having] a chip on his shoulder."[5] Thus, it appears that Truman took Stettinius's memo as an insult. "The striped pants boys warned me, in effect, to watch my step. They thought I really didn't understand what was going on over there."[6]

This was almost certainly not the secretary of state's intent, but that made little difference. Truman was never to have a good working relationship with the State Department. In terms of Palestine, the difference between him and the "striped pants boys" was soon defined by his well-known propensity to identify with the underdog, in this case the Jewish displaced persons now under the care of Allied forces in Europe.

The issue of Europe's postwar Jewish refugees had a twofold appeal for Truman. First, he was probably genuinely interested in their plight and earnestly wanted to help them. We can give him the benefit of the doubt here despite the fact that Truman seems to have decided to give priority to this concern for persecuted Jews only at the end of the war.[7] His desire to help also led him, at a later stage of his presidency, to make perfunctory efforts to increase the number of refugees who could immigrate into the United States, though these efforts never significantly altered the country's restrictive immigration laws.[8]

Truman showed no similar concern for the situation in which the indigenous people of Palestine found themselves. Indeed, consistent with a bipolar worldview orientation, Truman called into question the legitimacy of Arab demands for self-determination in the Holy Land by placing the term *rights,* when referring to the Arabs in Palestine, in quotation marks.[9] Given such an attitude, he never squarely faced the fact that helping the Jewish refugees in Europe to immigrate to Palestine (rather than the United States) was acting against the express will of the majority population of the Holy Land.

Ironically, this unconcern flowed from the fact that Truman, like so many presidents before him, considered himself a self-made expert on Palestine. He had studied the Bible and read much of the available English-language (Christian) literature on the subject.[10] In his mind Palestine was really an extension of the Judeo-Christian world and the proper home of the Jewish people. The State Department's balancing of other interests against those of European Jews seeking relief through refuge in Palestine was out of sync with that assumption. It suggested to Truman that "they [the State Department experts] were an anti-Semitic bunch over there, they put the Jews in the same category as Chinamen and Negroes."[11]

Secondly, the refugee question could serve Truman well politically. Truman was a politician with a strong ambition to win election to the White House based on his own merits. Coming to the presidency in the shadow of the great Franklin Roosevelt meant Truman had an uphill battle toward this goal, and his public opinion poll ratings (which sometimes went as low as a 35 percent favorable figure) reflected this. Quickly, then, the potential of the Jewish displaced-persons issue to secure American Jewish/Zionist political support came together with Truman's underdog sympathies, unconcern for Arabs, and dislike of "striped pants" experts. Mixed together, they produced a mind-set that would dominate his approach to the issue.

Reinforcing this scenario was Truman's choice of White House advisers. Primary among them was Clark Clifford, a lawyer and fellow Missourian. Clifford, who served as "special presidential counsel," had a single-minded goal of getting Harry Truman elected as president in 1948. To achieve this goal he believed that it would be necessary to secure the votes of America's five million Jews, who were allegedly politically pivotal in states such as New York. To this end he became a staunch Zionist supporter, and would spend a lot of time both arguing against the State Department's position on Palestine and demeaning Arabs.[12] There is evidence that he was involved in using political blackmail to bring about a favorable UN vote for the partition of Palestine,[13] and that he assisted in writing both Israel's 1948 request for U.S. recognition and the U.S. government's official and favorable reply.[14]

Two other advisers were important in developing Truman's pro-Zionist domestic and foreign policy. One was Max Lowenthal, who served as an assistant to Clifford. Lowenthal had always been a strong supporter of Truman, and had played a role in having him selected as FDR's running mate for the 1944 election. Lowenthal was Jewish and was considered to be the White House staff expert on Palestine. Finally, there was David Niles, who served as the president's "adviser on minority affairs." Niles was a Polish Jewish immigrant who had grown up in Boston. He was Truman's and Clifford's liaison with various Zionist organizations and was most likely leaking to them State Department communications that came to the White House.[15]

The general line taken by both Truman and his advisers was that their policy on Palestine was a product of humanitarian concerns and the strategic interests of the United States.[16] However, this was not the way a good number of other government officials saw it. As we shall see, the various secretaries of state that served under Truman constantly argued that American support for a Jewish state in Palestine ran counter to national interests. And James Forrestal, Truman's secretary of defense from 1947 to 1949, considered the administration's policy to have nothing to do with either national interest or even humanitarian relief. In his opinion it was motivated by "squalid political purposes."[17]

While Truman's White House advisers were shaping a pro-Zionist policy on Palestine, the State Department's Office of Near East and African Affairs (NEA was now a branch of this office) was refining its own stand. On August 24, 1945, the office director, Loy Henderson, sent a memo to Secretary of State James Byrnes outlining four different scenarios for Palestine: rule by Arabs, rule by Jews, partition, or UN trusteeship. Henderson and his staff argued that while they understood that "Palestine has become a problem in American internal politics" and that "they would not presume to give advice in this regard," the least harmful solution for U.S. national interests in the Middle East was to support trusteeship. This solution would also be least damaging to what NEA saw as American principles. Henderson told Byrnes bluntly that

> We feel . . . that we would be derelict in our responsibilities if we should fail to inform you that in our considered opinion the active support by the Government of the United States of a policy favoring the setting up of a Jewish State in Palestine would be contrary to the policy which the United States has always followed of respecting the wishes of a large majority of the local inhabitants with respect to their form of government. . . . At the present time the United States has a moral prestige in the Near and Middle East unequaled by that of any other great power. We would lose that prestige and would likely for many years to be considered a betrayer of the high principles which we ourselves have enunciated during the period of the war.[18]

Thus, by the spring of 1945, with Harry Truman in the White House barely a month, the lines were drawn for a policy battle over Palestine. In this battle the State Department's arguments focused on U.S. foreign policy issues: U.S. support for Zionism undercut growing national interests in the Middle East while undermining the country's prestige and violating long-held principles such as the right of self-determination. While the State Department's view may have been accurate in terms of international relations, it failed to take into consideration American popular perceptions. The Arabs were a "desert people" far away, while the Jews were victims of German violence and worldwide neglect who had a strong lobby in the United States. Congress saw Zionism and Palestine as domestic issues and had a long tradition of ignoring or rationalizing away all of the State Department's arguments. The executive branch of government had traditionally tried to walk a middle road. The president was called upon to respond to competing interests, such as war-related demands, that precluded unmitigated support for Zionist ambitions. Both Wilson in

World War I and FDR in World War II experienced these restraints. But now World War II was over and the Western world confronted the consequences of the Holocaust. Truman was a president looking for votes in an environment that, at least from the point of view of him and his advisers, presented no convincing, competing interests to Zionism. In other words, in 1945 the presidency would go the way of Congress on the issue of Palestine. The State Department was effectively isolated.

The State Department Ignored

Despite receiving a large number of State Department communications, Truman often ignored NEA's views on Palestine. For instance, on August 31, 1945, the president wrote to Prime Minister Clement Attlee of Great Britain suggesting that the British admit into Palestine "as many as possible" of the Jewish displaced persons (DPs) then in refugee camps in Europe. This letter, which explicitly offered Palestine as a solution to Europe's Jewish DP issue, was written without prior consultation with the State Department. Nor was the department advised when the letter was dispatched.[19]

Truman's letter was a reaction to two things. First was the findings of Earl Harrison, who had been sent to Europe to report on the status of displaced persons. The mission had been David Niles's idea, and Harrison's camp tours had been in the company of Zionists.[20] Harrison had indicated that perhaps as many as 100,000 Jewish DPs, who were living in deteriorating refugee camp conditions and knew they had little chance of reaching the United States, would go to Palestine if they could. The other factor was that the American Zionists had taken up their cause by calling for the immediate admission to Palestine of 100,000 Jews.

The British were greatly upset by Truman's letter, which soon became public. According to the White Paper of 1939, they had promised the Arabs that there would be no additional Jewish immigration after 1944 without the acquiescence of the native population. They had not been able to deliver on this promise (if they ever truly intended to) because of the consequences of the Holocaust and the sensitive question of what to do with the survivors. But as Ibn Saud had pointed out, the Arabs had nothing to do with the Holocaust and did not feel that compensation for European sins should come at the cost of Arab land. Arab reaction to Truman's request was, of course, sharply negative.[21] Thus, Truman's letter only heightened the Arab-Zionist dilemma the British sought to manage. It seemed to London that the American president was pressing for an action the consequences of which he was unwilling to take responsibility for (Truman had ruled out the use of American troops to keep the peace in Palestine). As the British well knew, the immediate admission of 100,000 Jews to Palestine in the summer of 1945 would spark certain civil war.

Behind the scenes, the personnel of NEA were also upset. The division staff now rightly suspected that they were being marginalized. As Gordon Merriam put it to Loy Henderson in a memo dated September 26, 1945, "It seems apparent to me that the President (and perhaps Mr. Byrnes [the secretary of state] as well) have decided to have a go at Palestine negotiations without bringing NEA into the picture. . . . I can see nothing further we can appropriately do for the moment."[22]

Henderson, however, refused to stay quiet on the issue. On October 1, 1945, he sent yet another memo, this time to the acting secretary of state, Dean Acheson, reminding him of the pledges made by FDR to consult with Arabs and Jews before making any decisions on Palestine. In the memo he stated bluntly that Truman's demand of the British that they permit the influx of a large number of European Jews into Palestine constituted a breach of that pledge. He pointed out that "The mere resentment of the Near Eastern peoples towards the United States on the ground that we have decided to disregard the Arab viewpoint with regard to Palestine would be unpleasant. It would be much more serious, however, if we should give them ground to believe that we do not live up to our firm promises already given."[23]

Acheson pushed Henderson's concerns forward to the president. In his communication to Truman he summarized NEA's concerns and again suggested that the department prepare "a full summary of the situation, including our recommendations."[24] Once more, Truman ignored the department's offer. There was at this time a witticism going about the capital that went "to err is Truman."[25] One can only assume Henderson was in full agreement with this sentiment.

The Joint Anglo-American Inquiry

It was at this stage (October 19, 1945) that the British proposed a joint Anglo-American inquiry into the Palestine problem and the situation of Jewish DPs in Europe. Even though this may have been an effort, as one investigator has put it, "to delay any major decisions as long as possible," or was perhaps a move to lure the United States into joint responsibility for Palestine, the British plan still served to confirm Truman's semi-official linkage of the two issues.[26] Both the Zionists and the Arabs were unhappy with the idea, though of course for different reasons. The Zionists saw it as a delaying tactic, while the Arabs did not want any reconsideration of the problems of Palestine that might lead to further erosion of the 1939 White Paper.

Nonetheless, the joint investigatory committee was formed in January of 1946 and proceeded to both try to ascertain the desires of the DPs and look into conditions in Palestine. It was to conclude its investigations in 120 days. Like all other past efforts to bring together the aspirations of Zionists and Palestinians, this attempt too would lead to unworkable recommendations.

At roughly the same time, the Truman administration, unable to fully escape Roosevelt's past pledges of prior consultation with Arabs and Jews, began to lay the groundwork for rendering them meaningless. This was important because if, as Truman and his advisers hoped, the Joint Anglo-American Inquiry paved the way for the admittance of 100,000 DPs into Palestine, the government should have a response to whatever charges of breach of promise might arise. Prior consultation with Zionists, of course, had been an ongoing affair since 1917 and was never really an issue. It was the promise of consultation with the Arabs that was troublesome. Thus, in December of 1945 Truman had James Byrnes, who was back at his post as secretary of state, instruct U.S. embassies in the Middle East that "In discussing this Government's Palestine policy with Arab or other leaders you should make it plain that full 'consultation' with both Arabs and Jews . . . does not mean prior 'agreement' with Arabs and Jews."[27]

This message to the Arab governments was sent within a context that clearly indicated that prior agreement had already been reached between the United States and the Zionists. This seemed obvious not only from President Truman's statements at press conferences, where he repeatedly declared that "we want to let as many Jews into Palestine as possible,"[28] but also by virtue of Congress's joint resolution, passed on December 19, 1945, calling for the "free entry of Jews . . . so that they may freely proceed with the upbuilding of Palestine."[29] It is no wonder then, that the Arabs anticipated the worst from the Joint Anglo-American Inquiry. As the Saudi foreign minister, Faisal ibn Abdul Aziz, told an American official, "Your government has permitted itself to be placed in the position of urging the British government to break their pledges [those made in the 1939 White Paper] to us."[30]

The inquiry commission brought in its report on April 30, 1946. As an exercise in squaring circles, it perforce was made up of contradictory parts. The report called for a unitary Palestinian state under a UN trustee-

ship with equal protection rights for all citizens. Though not the full independence the Arabs demanded, they might have been persuaded to go
along with what amounted to a democratic state except that this constituted only half of the inquiry commission's solution. The other half proposed the immediate entry of the controversial 100,000 Jewish DPs, and
an end to restrictions on land purchases by Jews. This guaranteed Arab
rejection of the plan.

However, it should be understood that by spring of 1946, the inquiry
commission report was first and foremost a political football in U.S. domestic politics, as well as a corresponding irritant in American-British
relations. The last thing it can be considered was a workable solution to
the dilemma in Palestine. As if to demonstrate this point, President Truman immediately chose only that part of the report that corresponded to
what he wanted, and publicly pushed it forward. Without prior consultation with the British, or the State Department, he came out in support of
the plan's call for admittance of 100,000 DPs and the removal of land-sale
restrictions. This, of course, once more angered both the Arabs and the
British, whose reluctance to comply with these selective demands set off a
series of vitriolic attacks from the U.S. Congress.[31] It also once more left
NEA feeling ignored. NEA had, a bit naively, urged immediate adoption
of the complete report as one that had something for everyone, and en-
compassed an end point that precluded a Zionist state.[32] It was at this
point, with Truman's selective treatment of the report, that many NEA
staffers started to suspect that the president had, in essence, decided to
sacrifice U.S. national interests in the Middle East for the sake of his sympathy for the DPs and his domestic political needs.[33]

Although the British were suspicious and annoyed with Truman's response to the inquiry commission report, it proved to be the only game in
town. Again, perhaps to delay, perhaps to draw the Americans into further
responsibility for Palestine, the British continued to work with Washington. The result was yet another investigatory body, this one the Morrison-
Grady Commission, whose purpose was to figure out how some variant
on the Anglo-American Inquiry report might be implemented. Neverthe-
less, Herbert Morrison and Henry F. Grady seemed to have a deeper understanding of the complexities of the Palestine problem. Thus on July 24,
1946, they recommended a delay in any mass influx of European DPs.
Other countries should be asked to absorb greater numbers of refugees,
including the United States.[34] The commission also called for Palestine to
be restructured as a series of "semi-autonomous zones" under a continuing British "trusteeship."

The British were pleased with these conclusions, but the Zionists and their allies were greatly displeased. The American Zionists, at least at this point, found the idea of accepting only part of Palestine repugnant. It would leave them with a "Jewish ghetto" in Palestine, they declared.[35]

With mid-term elections coming up in the United States the president was especially susceptible to the resulting American Zionist pressure to reject the Morrison-Grady report. This meant that, for the moment, any scheme to divide Palestine was politically harmful to Truman. Thus, by the end of July, Dean Acheson was in London informing the British that "in view of the extreme intensity of feeling in centers of Jewish population in this country [the United States] neither political party would support this program."[36]

However, things were about to reverse themselves as to the idea of partition. The resulting deadlock between Britain and the United States, along with the escalating war between the Jewish underground and British forces in Palestine, now led the World Zionist Organization to take a less stubborn stand on partition than their American Zionist counterparts. At a meeting of the WZO leadership in Paris in the first week of August 1946 (from which the Americans were absent), they agreed to a tactical retreat from the Biltmore Declaration by proposing to accept the partition of Palestine. Having taken this decision, Nahum Goldman of the Jewish Agency traveled to Washington and formally proposed partition to the American government. He said that he could guarantee American Jewish support for the plan if it resulted in an end to British rule and in a Jewish state that controlled its own immigration.[37]

In a rare moment of agreement, Dean Acheson, who was once more acting secretary of state, and Harry Truman both liked the idea. As we shall see, however, NEA had serious doubts about it. Truman accepted the partition scheme on August 9. As far as the documents show, no one bothered asking about how the Arabs, who had rejected partition in the past, might take the news.

The momentary agreement between president and State Department did not last long. Truman and his advisers quickly sought to turn their approval of Goldman's proposal to political advantage. Given Truman's precarious domestic political position, this is not surprising. Also there was a strong suspicion that the president's Republican opponent, Thomas E. Dewey, was on the verge of making a pro-Zionist announcement. Thus, over State Department objections (Acheson, while entertaining the notion of partition, did not want any precipitous U.S. public announcement), Truman decided to announce his support for the creation of a "viable

Jewish state" occupying an "adequate area of Palestine," and to do so on the eve of the upcoming Jewish holiday of Yom Kippur.[38]

Truman gave the British prime minister less than twenty-four hours' notice of his intentions, which brought an immediate and urgent reply that the president delay until "the British government could acquaint you with the actual situation [in Palestine] and the probable results of your action."[39] The president dismissed the plea and proceeded to make public what was, for all intents and purposes, a call for the partition of Palestine. His actions sent American-British and American-Arab relations to a new low. Prime Minister Attlee felt betrayed and, as one historian has put it, believed that "Truman was playing domestic politics with an issue of enormous peril to British interests."[40] King Ibn Saud of Arabia sent a sharp letter of protest, pointing out that "Your Excellency and the American people cannot support right, justice, and equity and fight for them in the rest of the world while denying them to the Arabs in their country, Palestine."[41]

None of this moved Truman, who responded to both the British and the Arabs with the claim that he was acting out of humanitarian concern for the Jewish victims of Nazi persecution. Ibn Saud responded to Truman that he seemed intent "in the name of humanity" to "force on the Arab majority of Palestine a people alien to them, to make these new people the majority, thereby rendering the existing majority a minority."[42] Truman did not respond to this point.

Truman's action also further alienated NEA. Gordon Merriam put NEA's position this way: "U.S. support for partition of Palestine as a solution to that problem can be justified only on the basis of Arab and Jewish consent. Otherwise we should violate the principle of self-determination which has been written into the Atlantic Charter, the Declaration of the United Nations, and the United Nations Charter—a principle that is deeply embedded in our foreign policy. Even a United Nations determination in favor of partition would be, in the absence of such consent, a stultification and violation of UN's own charter."[43] Loy Henderson agreed with Merriam. He told Acheson that "Of course, we have practically been forced by political pressure and sentiment in the U.S. in the direction of a viable Jewish state. I must confess that when I view our policy in the light of the principles avowed by us I become uneasy."[44]

There is no reason to doubt that Henderson and Merriam believed what they said about self-determination being a sacred U.S. principle. It was, of course, a naive assertion when placed against the history of American foreign policy. And as Woodrow Wilson's behavior had made clear, Palestine in particular had always been an exception to this rule as far as American politicians were concerned. Nonetheless, according to Evan Wilson, who worked at NEA at the time, the blatant assertion that Zionism ran counter to sacred U.S. principles was politically explosive enough to cause Acheson to inform Merriam that his memo would "not be placed in the Department's files and that all copies [would] be destroyed—except for the original which he said the author might keep for himself."[45]

The British Pass Palestine On to the UN

By 1947 the British were losing the struggle for Palestine on two fronts. All efforts to persuade the United States to cooperate with Great Britain in Palestine, either by relenting on its steadfast pro-Zionist stand, or by sharing in the responsibility of that stand by contributing materially to the maintenance of law and order in Palestine, had failed. Truman had ruled out deployment of U.S. troops in the Holy Land as well as any idea of an American co-mandatory status with the British. Nonetheless, the mounting pro-Zionist pressure on England to implement partition and immigration, coming from a White House and Congress that refused to accept any American responsibility for the consequences, was unrelenting. And it is clear that this position was supported by the American public.[46] By 1946 there had even arisen threats to retaliate against Britain's reluctance to open Palestine to the Jews by withholding U.S. postwar loans and aid.[47] In Palestine itself, Zionist attacks on British forces had rapidly escalated. These attacks, which the *New York Times* had no trouble labeling terrorist actions, included the July bombing of the King David Hotel in Jerusalem.[48]

By early 1948 the British government saw the situation as intolerable. No longer in a financial position either to further alienate the United States, or mount a major military campaign to pacify Palestine (as they had done in 1936), the British decided on retreat. To do this in a face-saving fashion they announced on February 14, 1947, that they were intent on turning over responsibility for Palestine to the United Nations. Later, they set May 15, 1948, as a date on which they would unilaterally withdraw from the territory. In announcing these plans in Parliament, Foreign Minister Ernest Bevin laid ultimate responsibility for Britain's untenable situation at the feet of Harry Truman. Recalling the president's refusal to cooperate with Great Britain on the issue of his Yom Kippur announcement of support for partition, Bevin told Parliament that "In international affairs I cannot settle things if my problem is made the subject of local [U.S.] elections."[49]

Britain's decision led to a special session on Palestine of the UN General Assembly in April of 1947. At that time the UN created the UN Special Committee on Palestine, or UNSCOP, yet another in a long line of investigatory committees. It was ordered to report back to the General Assembly by September with a plan for Palestine's ultimate disposition. During its investigation, the Arabs boycotted UNSCOP. They asserted that the UN had no authority to decide the fate of Palestine's Arabs. This may have been a legitimate argument at the level of principle, but the assertion of principle had never saved the Arabs of Palestine from foreign manipulation before, and it would not now. The Zionists pressed hard for partition.

UNSCOP issued its report on August 31, 1947. The committee had split, and therefore the General Assembly received both a majority and minority report. The majority report recommended the partition of Palestine into independent Jewish and Arab states. The minority report recommended a unitary government for a Palestine made up of Arab and Jewish cantons. The General Assembly would have to decide between the majority and minority recommendations, and do so by a two-thirds vote.

At this point NEA again made its strong opposition to partition clear. Loy Henderson repeatedly emphasized a series of points. The first was that "it seems to me and all members of my office acquainted with the Middle East that the policy which we are following [support for partition] . . . is contrary to the interests of the United States. . . . we are forfeiting the friendship of the Arab world . . . [and] incurring long-term Arab hostility towards us." It seemed inevitable to NEA that such a turn of events would negatively impact U.S. commercial and strategic interests in the region. The second point was that the support for Zionist ambitions in Palestine undermined the "integrity of the United States" by casting doubt on the "many pronouncements that our foreign policies are based on the principles of the Charter of the United Nations." As we have seen, NEA was seriously concerned with principle, and the trustworthiness of American diplomatic personnel in the eyes of the Middle Eastern peoples. And finally, Henderson and NEA believed that partition could only be implemented through the use of force, which would require a long-term UN mission that would draw in both U.S. and Soviet forces. "It seems to me that . . . we ought to think twice before we support any plan which would result in American troops going to Palestine. The fact that Soviet troops under our plan would be introduced into the heart of the Middle East is even more serious."[50]

Truman's response to Henderson's prodding did not consider the substance of his arguments. Arab disenchantment with America's alleged lack of principle left him unmoved. He has been reported to have once told a gathering of American Middle East diplomats that "I am sorry gentlemen, but I have to answer to hundreds of thousands who are anxious for the success of Zionism; I do not have hundreds of thousands of Arabs among my constituents."[51] As we have seen, this opinion was factually incorrect. There were hundreds of thousands of Arab American voters in the United States. But they were as invisible to Truman as were the Arabs of Palestine. Nor did he seem to take seriously Henderson's other arguments. Rather, Truman's reaction was one of annoyance and distrust. He suspected Henderson of disloyalty and ordered him to stop working against the president's wishes.[52] Later, Henderson's opposition to Zionist ambitions in Palestine, and the president's support of them, would lead to bitter public attacks upon him, and a concerted effort on the part of Truman and his advisers to remove him from the State Department.

The UN Vote on Partition

Predictably, the Arabs rejected both the majority and minority proposals of UNSCOP. "Many people may be . . . homeless and they may covet the homes of others and love to have them for their own," Jamal al Husseini, vice chairman of the Arab Higher Committee of Palestine, told the General Assembly on October 18, "but neither homelessness nor love can give a right to possess the homes of others. . . . The right of self-determination in Palestine is our right and we shall stick to it."[53]

The Zionists, on the other hand, accepted the majority report. Chaim Weizmann told the General Assembly that "this solution . . . has profound relevance to the Jewish problem which weighs so heavily upon the conscience of mankind." Then he added that "the smallness of the state will be no bar to its intellectual achievement. Athens was only one small state and the whole world is still its debtor."[54] This statement can not be taken seriously. Weizmann's acceptance of the "smallness of the state" was nothing but a tactical maneuver on the part of the Zionists. The majority of them, both in and out of Palestine, had always seen the possession of the entire area on both sides of the Jordan River as their goal. Partition was but a temporary compromise in the face of the diplomatic and military realities of the moment. This can be clearly seen in the bickering that went on in the Zionist camp in Palestine over the issue of partition. The Irgun leader Menachem Begin, who at this time was generally considered throughout both the Middle East and the Western world as a terrorist, bitterly opposed "the bisection of our homeland." He claimed that all of Palestine, including Transjordan, had to become part of a Jewish state. David Ben Gurion, leader of the mainstream Zionist community in Palestine, did not disagree. He was just more tactically skillful. He urged acceptance of partition while pointing out, though not for public consumption, that the Zionist movement's acquiescence on this point was not final, "not with regard to regime, not with regard to borders, and not with regard to international agreements."[55]

President Truman was also tactically skillful on the issue, at least from the standpoint of domestic U.S. politics. Under his direct orders, the American delegation at the UN announced its support for partition on October 11, 1947. American Zionist acclaim was immediate. Even the hard-line firebrand Rabbi Abba Silver—who once had the audacity to thump on the president's desk and yell at him—described Truman's announcement as "American statesmanship at its best and noblest."[56] Soon thereafter, Truman was encouraged to believe in the political correctness of his stand by a long memorandum by Clark Clifford detailing how the president's "flagging popularity" could be improved by supporting a Jewish state in Palestine. It was a move "calculated to win the backing of Jews and liberals."[57]

As if to offer constant reinforcement of this conclusion, the American Zionists mounted an intense publicity campaign in support of partition that would run right up to the UN vote on November 29, 1947. As the historian Kathleen Christison explains, "membership in the various U.S. Zionist organizations had grown to just under one million. . . . These members . . . were not passive but were letter writing, lobbying, money-contributing activists who blanketed the country." The result was that "during the second half of 1947, the White House received 135,000 telegrams, postcards, letters, and petitions on the Palestine issue."[58]

When it came to the UN vote on partition, pro-Zionist pressure did not restrict itself to benign, if intense, lobbying. On November 24, Truman had instructed his own staff, and the State Department, that he "did not wish the United States Delegation [at the UN] to use threats or improper pressure of any kind on other Delegations to vote for the majority report favoring partition of Palestine."[59] However, within days he may have been undermining his own directive. David Niles contacted the U.S. delegation shortly before the UN vote and "speaking at the request of the President" instructed them that "he [Truman] wants the resolution to succeed, and that we had just better make sure it does."[60] Was this really the president speaking? If we are to believe Truman's memoirs, the answer is no. He tells us that he would never approve of such tactics because "I have never approved of the practice of the strong imposing their will on the weak." He suggested that "improper pressure" as applied at the UN was the work of "extreme Zionists" who "were even suggesting that we pressure sovereign nations into favorable votes in the General Assembly" (what he was referring to was economic blackmail applied to such states as Liberia and the Philippines).[61] It is likely, however, that members of his own staff were among those "extremists." According to former undersecretary of state Sumner Wells, who back in December of 1945 had come out "in favor of a Jewish commonwealth in Palestine," pressure was exerted. He said that during the lead-up to the UN vote on partition, "by direct order of the White House every form of pressure, direct and indirect, was brought to bear by American officials upon those countries outside the Moslem world that were known to be either uncertain or opposed to partition."[62] If the "direct order" did not come from Truman, then David Niles and Clark Clifford are the next-best candidates.[63]

Whoever gave the order, the result was that up to seven countries whose votes were uncertain, or leaning against partition, ended up voting for it.[64] That was enough of a shift to carry the day for the majority report, which received official General Assembly approval on November 29, 1947. The consequences for Palestine were almost immediately negative.

Back in September of 1947 Loy Henderson had predicted that "any plan for partitioning Palestine would be unworkable."[65] Now he and NEA were proven correct in their fears. Partition turned out to be less a solution to the problems of Palestine and more an incitement to war. The Zionists had actually anticipated this consequence and commenced to implement several sequential plans the aim of which were to mobilize Zionist forces first to defend, and then expand beyond, the UN-designated borders of the Jewish state.[66]

Truman, while disturbed by the resulting violence, seemed incapable of understanding his own role in bringing it about. He blamed the deteriorating situation on everyone but himself and the Zionists. Speaking of the early days of 1948, he observed that "every day brought reports of new violence in the Holy Land." In his opinion this was because the UN could not successfully answer the Zionist call for an "international police force" to impose partition; because the British would "enforce it [partition] only if both Jews and Arabs agreed"; because the Arabs had announced that they would "defend their 'rights'"; and because Arab leaders had "flatly" rejected his call for them to "preserve the peace and practice moderation." Therefore, what could the Zionists do? According to Truman, "the Jews, realizing that there was little chance to get international enforcement, announced that they would establish a Jewish militia force."[67]

Truman's Momentary Retreat

In the face of civil war, and along with it growing anti-Americanism throughout the Arab world, it was the State Department, and not Truman and his White House advisers, that sought to adjust U.S. policy so as to ameliorate a deteriorating situation. For NEA and its supporters at the State Department, that meant abandoning partition and supporting a UN trusteeship at least until stability could be restored in Palestine. This argument was laid out in detail by George F. Kennan, director of Policy Planning at the State Department, in a long, top-secret memorandum dated January 19, 1948. In this document Kennan repeated what NEA had said many times before, that a one-sided pro-Zionist position, now symbolized by the government's support of partition, threatened U.S. economic and military interests throughout the Middle East. "As a result of U.S. sponsorship of the UN action leading to the recommendation to partition Palestine, U.S. prestige in the Moslem world has suffered a severe blow and U.S. strategic interests in the Mediterranean and Near East have been seriously prejudiced. Our vital interests in those areas will continue to be adversely affected to the extent that we continue to support partition."[68]

This position was supported by a CIA report of February 28, 1948. That agency's report stated bluntly that partition "cannot be implemented." Various Arab nations were preparing to invade Palestine to prevent the creation of a Jewish state, while Zionist organizations such as the Irgun were calling for an invasion of Jordanian and Egyptian territory in order to "claim all of Palestine." Under the circumstances, the CIA recommended that the whole issue of Palestine be taken back to the Security Council of the UN and a "new solution" sought on the basis of the UNSCOP's minority report.[69] Kennan's questioning of partition was given further support by the Defense Department and the Joint Chiefs of Staff. The military expressed fear that if partition were enforced from outside by a UN force, this would lead to the introduction of Soviet troops into the Middle East. They also stood against the use of American troops to enforce partition.[70]

President Truman and his advisers now found themselves trapped by events. On the one hand, they felt politically dependent on American Zionists, whose support, they believed, was vital for winning the upcoming presidential election. On the other hand, Truman belatedly discovered that "a serious threat to the world's peace was developing in Palestine."[71] The State Department was alarmed about what this was doing to American interests, and it now had the backing of the CIA and the Defense Department. The situation, and the opinions of all of these departments, could not just be ignored.

Under the circumstances, Truman tried to find maneuvering room between the two conflicting points of pressure he found himself under. He agreed with the State Department that, if partition could not be implemented except by force, he would allow the United States to shift its policy to the support of a temporary trusteeship which would be used to stabilize the situation. Truman made it clear that in his mind "this was not a rejection of partition but rather an effort to postpone its effective date until proper conditions for the establishment of self-government . . . might be established."[72] By agreeing to this he showed more sensitivity to the complexities of the situation in Palestine than did the leaders of Congress. When they were approached by Secretary of Defense Forrestal about the possibility of supporting a temporary trusteeship, they flatly rejected the idea and all the arguments in support of it.[73]

Truman, who was quite aware of the political risks that prevented the congressional leaders from even thinking about abandoning partition, knew he was on thin ice. Thus he wanted any announcement of such a shift in policy to be made in such a way that it would not appear to be such an abandonment. He told Secretary of State Marshall on February 22, 1948, "I approve in principle this basic position. I want to make it clear, however, that nothing should be presented to the Security Council that could be interpreted as a recession on our part from the position we took in the General Assembly [in favor of partition]."[74] This was, of course, a demand that the United States appear to be saying yes to partition even as it said yes to trusteeship. It was all confused and convoluted but reflected well the impossible contradictions Truman faced. After all, Truman was a politician and his political career was on the line. To give himself some distance from the mounting pressures the situation generated, he gave orders to his staff that he would see no more Zionist lobbyists. Their behavior, even towards Truman, had of late become "quarrelsome and emotional."[75]

Truman's brief refusal to see any more Zionist spokesmen did not, however, extend to the Zionist spokesmen on his staff. Thus in these early days of 1948 Clark Clifford continued to argue for steadfast support of partition. In a memorandum put forth on March 8, 1948, he claimed to be offering advice based only on "what is best for America. . . . What I say is, therefore, completely uninfluenced by election considerations." Clifford justified the administration's support for partition as "in conformity with the settled policy of the United States," by which he meant it somehow flowed from the Balfour Declaration and the various pro-Zionist congressional resolutions. Then, ignoring the fact that the prospect of partition had aggravated interethnic rivalries to the point of civil war, he declared that "partition offers the best hope of a permanent solution of the Palestine problem that may avoid war." Asserting that partition was the policy (rather than just a recommendation) of the United Nations, he explained that world peace depended on upholding that body's decision. The United Nations, Clifford said, was a "God given vehicle . . . to resist Soviet aggression," and any backing away from partition would mean the "jettisoning of the United Nations." This in turn would lead to a feeling of "complete lack of confidence in our foreign policy from one end of this country to the other and among all classes of our population." Thus, Clifford concluded, "It is utterly unthinkable for the United States now to back the Arabs and openly oppose a decision of the United Nations Assembly, arrived at at your own [Truman's] insistence. The only alternative is, therefore, to back up the United Nations so that there will be peace in Palestine."

What of those American interests in the Middle East that the State Department believed were being severely undermined? Clifford denied that they existed. The United States' real interests lay only in South America and Europe, therefore it had no vital interests in the Middle East that required accommodation of the Arab peoples. The Arabs would sell oil to the United States no matter what its policy because "they must have oil royalties or go broke." And in any case, to take Arab concerns seriously put the United States "in the ridiculous role of trembling before threats of a few nomadic desert tribes. This has done us irreparable damage. Why should Russia . . . or any other nation treat us with anything but contempt in the light of our shilly-shallying appeasement of the Arabs?"[76]

Clifford's memo, including its racist overtones, is clearly reflective of the man's bipolar outlook. It also represents a Machiavellian tour de force, if only because he was probably incapable of setting aside the upcoming election when making recommendations. The whole exercise was no doubt an effort to get Truman to stay the course on partition so as not to jeopardize Jewish electoral support. In the end, however, it was not just

Clifford's persuasiveness that would confirm Truman's support of partition. It would also be the president's suspicions of the "striped pants boys" and the alleged failure of the State Department to abide by his instructions that any move toward trusteeship must not appear to be what it really was.

On March 8 Truman met with Secretary of State Marshall and Undersecretary Robert Lovett. This was the same day as Clifford's memo, but it is unclear if Truman had read it prior to this meeting. At the meeting he orally reaffirmed his approval of a move toward temporary trusteeship if an upcoming meeting of the Security Council scheduled for March 19 could not agree on a plan to implement partition.[77] Beyond that fact, the meeting was plagued by miscommunication. It would seem that Truman assumed that he would be notified before the American ambassador at the UN, Warren Austin, made an announcement. Even though the president had seen an outline of a proposed statement that Austin might present, he probably did not consider the wording finalized. In any case, Marshall and Lovett were not aware that Truman wanted prior notification, nor did they feel that the wording of the statement was in doubt.[78] Thus Marshall informed Austin that Truman had approved the announcement of U.S. support for trusteeship "if and when necessary."[79]

American Zionist leaders were well aware of the fact that Truman was wavering on partition. However, Truman was now refusing to see them. Nonetheless, they found a way to finally reach him. They did so by working through Truman's old friend and business partner Eddie Jacobson. Leaders of B'nai B'rith had flattered Jacobson, and thereby recruited him to go to the president so as to convince Truman to see Chaim Weizmann.[80] The meeting took place on March 13, and apparently, despite Truman's annoyance with Zionist pestering, Jacobson had little trouble getting the president to violate his own ban. Explaining how Weizmann was "perhaps the greatest Jew who ever lived," a man Truman himself had described as "a great statesman," and finally how Weizmann was "an old man and a very sick man" who had "traveled thousands of miles to see you," he easily persuaded the president to see the Zionist leader. "When Eddie left I gave instructions to have Dr. Weizmann come to the White House as soon as it could be arranged" for a meeting that was to be "entirely off the record."[81]

Like Clifford, Weizmann saw the need to shore up the president's support for partition. He did so by affirming for Truman the historical rightness of the bipolar worldview and altruistic imperialism. The two men met on March 18, and Weizmann proceeded to tell the president of all the great and glorious things that the Zionists would do when they got a state of their own, how important it was that the state include the Negev, which, he claimed, the Zionists were even now turning from a desert to fertile land, and how "the Jewish state . . . will quickly become an object of development and would make a real contribution to trade and commerce. . . . one can foresee a day when a canal will be built from some part of the eastern Mediterranean coast to Akaba. . . . This would become a parallel highway to the Suez Canal." And on Weizmann went, mesmerizing the president with a "fantastic" view of the future. "I was extremely happy," Weizmann observed, "to find that the President read the map [I was drawing] very quickly and very clearly."[82] And indeed, Truman had read the map in the enthusiastic manner of a Westerner who ardently believed that bringing progress to the Middle East was the inevitable result of Zionism. "Dr. Weizmann was a man of remarkable achievements and personality," Truman reported. "His life had been dedicated to two ideals, that of science and that of the Zionist movement."[83] Zionism and science—how could a Jewish state not equal modernity? By the time Weizmann left the White House, Truman had reaffirmed American support for partition.

However, the president did not tell the State Department of this renewed commitment. Indeed, he had not even told the State Department of Weizmann's visit. Thus, unaware of this latest development, and having a green light from Secretary of State Marshall, Warren Austin made his announcement the next day at the United Nations. He stated, "The Security Council now has before it clear evidence that the Jews and Arabs of Palestine and the Mandatory power cannot agree to implement the General Assembly plan of partition through peaceful means. . . . My government believes that a temporary trusteeship for Palestine should be established . . . to maintain the peace and to afford the Jews and Arabs of Palestine, who must live together, further opportunity to reach an agreement regarding the future government of that country."[84]

Austin's statement, and the State Department position which it reflected, was in fact an unrealistic one. The Jews and Arabs of Palestine had been, theoretically, seeking an agreement on the government of the country for the prior thirty years. The result had been the creation of entrenched positions based on what each side perceived as uncompromisable principle. There was no evidence that a UN trusteeship could do what the British mandate could not do—that is square the circle of these irreconcilable demands. On the other hand, the State Department (or at least NEA) probably did not truly believe a trusteeship would bring reconciliation. It would, however, move the United States back into a neutral position that would be less hazardous to U.S. interests in the area.

Austin's statement was also unrealistic because it defied the wishes of an American Zionist lobby that had, by now, proven itself politically dominant when it came to the issue of Palestine. The American Zionists and their allies in Congress and, as we shall see, in the media, had long ago ceased to be meaningfully concerned with those interests that preoccupied the State Department. Indeed, for those in Congress, the State Department's interpretation of U.S. national interests in the Middle East were now clearly in contradiction to their reading of their own local political interests. Those were tied to public opinion, and public opinion was on the side of the Zionists.[85] The Zionists at this point wanted only one thing—partition of Palestine. Therefore, when Austin made his announcement, the Zionists and their allies did not bother with a textual analysis of the statement. They completely ignored the fact that Austin had called for a "temporary trusteeship." All they saw was betrayal on the part of the administration.

Considering how dangerous this reaction was to Truman's political ambitions, he was understandably upset. However, he was not upset at the Zionists, his domestic advisers, or himself. He was upset at the State Department. After all, it was the State Department that had given Austin the go-ahead. "This morning (March 20) I find that the State Dept. has reversed my Palestine policy. The first I know about it is what I see in the papers! Isn't that hell? I'm now in the position of a liar and a double crosser. I've never felt so in my life. There are people on the 3rd and 4th levels of the State Dept. who have always wanted to cut my throat. They have succeeded in doing it."[86]

Thus, if the Zionists felt betrayed by the president, Truman felt betrayed by the State Department. However, was Truman's anger at NEA (the third- and fourth-level people) reasonable? He ignored his own poor management of events leading up to Austin's announcement. He had not made it explicitly clear to Secretary of State Marshall or Undersecretary Lovett that he wanted prior warning of Austin's statement. Nor had he made it clear that he was dissatisfied with a draft of the statement which he had seen in late February.[87] Austin's announcement was contextualized as best it could be to meet the president's political need to appear to be saying yes to trusteeship while not saying no to partition. That is why emphasis was placed on the temporary nature of trusteeship proposal.

Marshall, seeking to exercise damage control, reemphasized the temporary nature of any trusteeship on March 21. He would later reintroduce the idea that the chaotic state of the region could provide an opening for Soviet influence. On March 25 Truman himself met the press and made some of the same points.[88] What Truman failed to realize was that these qualifications would make no difference to the Zionists, Congress, or the press. By 1948 most of the Congress and a good part of the press could conceive of no acceptable solution that did not meet the minimum requirements of the Zionist program. Thus, the Zionists, the Congress, and the press saw only vacillation and weakness in the administration's shift to trusteeship.[89] In his frustration with this hostile reaction, Truman turned on NEA.

Over the next month Truman would reluctantly stick by the trusteeship proposal. To do otherwise would make him appear all the more vacillating. Increasingly, however, he and his advisers would characterize trusteeship as a scheme of NEA's and particularly the devious work of Loy Henderson. A White House meeting that took place shortly after the UN announcement deteriorated into an angry shouting match between Clifford and Niles on the one side and Henderson on the other. According to the White House advisers, Henderson and NEA were more sensitive to "the British internal situation than to ours."[90] Because of his failure to equate U.S. national interests with the political interests of the president, Henderson became targeted by Clifford, Niles, and pro-Zionist congressmen as well. All would subsequently work for Henderson's removal from his State Department post.[91]

Confrontation over Recognition

In practical terms, however, the whole issue of trusteeship was rendered moot when, on May 14, 1948, the Zionists unilaterally declared the State of Israel's existence. Faced with a fait accompli, attention immediately shifted to the question of recognition of the new state. Here was an issue through which the president might redeem himself with the American Zionist establishment.

Once more there was a difference of opinion between the State Department and Truman's domestic advisers. The State Department wanted to delay recognition until the situation in Palestine stabilized and the United States knew exactly what kind of state the Zionists were erecting and whether it would survive. However, with polls showing Truman losing the upcoming presidential election no matter who the Republicans put up against him, Clifford argued, at a White House meeting of May 12, that the administration should grant immediate recognition as soon as the expected announcement of statehood was made. The Soviets were planning on quick recognition, he said, and the United States should make sure to recognize Israel before the Russians did.[92]

The State Department did not believe that Clark Clifford had any real interest in growing American-Soviet competition. Lovett replied to Clifford at the same meeting that immediate recognition was "premature" and that Clifford's proposal "was a very transparent attempt to win the Jewish vote." Secretary of State Marshall, who was also present on that day, was even more forceful. Taking up such a "transparent dodge to win a few votes" would mean "the great dignity of the office of the President would be seriously diminished. The counsel offered by Mr. Clifford was based on domestic political considerations, while the problem which confronted us was international."[93]

Marshall's statement got to the crux of the matter. The State Department, and particularly NEA, had always believed the events in Palestine should be viewed as separate from the political interests of congressmen, senators, or presidents. The United States had well-defined interests in the Middle East which were philanthropic and economic. The latest manifestation of the latter was growing oil interests in Saudi Arabia—oil interests which, immediately after World War II, were seen as vital to the Marshall Plan and its goal of European reconstruction. National movements of basically foreign origin, such as Zionism, simply did not qualify as a U.S. national interest. How one dealt with such movements was an "international" issue. However, Marshall, Lovett, and Henderson seemed not to have grasped just how fundamentally the American Zionist movement had changed these calculations. The Zionists had long ago transformed Palestine into a powerful domestic issue. Truman knew that, Clifford knew that, but the State Department leaders, while certainly aware of American Zionist influence in politics, refused to accept it. It was they who were out of touch with the domestic political realities of their own country.

For the president, there was no doubt about what he wanted to do on this issue. He had already instructed one of his veteran political advisers, Sam Rosenman, to let Chaim Weizmann know that, if the UN proved incapable of establishing a trusteeship in Palestine, and the Zionists proclaimed their state, that he would recognize it immediately.[94] It was only out of deference to Secretary of State Marshall that Truman refused Clifford's earlier advice to grant recognition even before the state was proclaimed.[95]

On May 14, 1948, Clifford met with Lovett and laid the president's position out for the State Department leader. The president was "under unbearable pressure to recognize the Jewish state promptly." Such an action was "of the greatest possible importance to the President from a domestic point of view." Lovett protested that such "precipitate action" would create a "tremendous reaction . . . in the Arab world." Clifford was unmoved. He indicated that a formal request for recognition was expected that afternoon and there was to be no delay in responding. He refused Lovett's request of a delay of one day to allow for prior notification of allied governments. Lovett came to the conclusion that Clifford was determined to "at least make him [Truman] the midwife" of the new State of Israel.[96]

Thus, once more ignoring the advice of the State Department, President Truman granted Israel de facto recognition at 6:11 P.M. Eastern Standard Time on May 14, 1948. This was eleven minutes after the Jewish state had been proclaimed. It represented what Lovett described as an act of "indecent haste . . . that might [cause us to] lose the effect of many years of hard work in the Middle East with the Arabs and . . . that would probably bring our missions and consular representatives into personal jeopardy."[97] This was not just alarmist posturing. Back in December of 1947 a Syrian mob had likely set a precedent by attacking the U.S. embassy in Damascus and destroying the American flag.[98]

The fact that consideration for the safety of American diplomatic personnel apparently meant less to the president and his White House advisers than "the domestic point of view" resulted, in the words of one historian of the period, in "nearly open revolt within the State Department."[99] On May 24 Marshall told Truman that he was having difficulty "in preventing a number of resignations among the members of our delegation to the United Nations and the State Department." The president told the secretary of state that "he was unaware of this and much perturbed at the possibility."[100] It is difficult to believe that Truman was sincere in this statement. He had already come to the conclusion that NEA's behavior was unacceptable. He resented their attempt to prioritize U.S. relations with the Arab world as of greater importance than his domestic relations with the Zionists. As he states in his memoirs, "The difficulty with many career officials in the government is that they regard themselves as the men who really make policy and run the government. . . . Too often career men seek to impose their own views instead of carrying out the established policy of the administration. . . . I wanted to make it plain that the President of the United States, and not the second and third echelon of the State Department, is responsible for making foreign policy, and, furthermore, that no one in any department can sabotage the President's policy."[101]

Ironically, Truman's quick recognition of the Jewish state was not as pivotally important to his reelection as Clark Clifford assumed. The American Jewish community would support Truman in the upcoming November presidential election, but with less enthusiasm than it had supported FDR. Truman would win about 75 percent of the Jewish vote as against FDR's record of 90 percent, and Truman lost New York State.[102] Nonetheless, against all odds, he would win reelection.

Regardless of how the Jewish vote did or did not factor into Truman's reelection, his triumph also marked the ultimate triumph of American Zionism. Truman's victory appeared to confirm the political importance of Zionism to any serious national politician. As a consequence the American Zionists' goal of making U.S. national interests in the Holy Land synonymous with their interests was also achieved. In 1948 the Zionists actually won two states, the State of Israel and the United States of America.

Newspaper Coverage

Newspaper coverage of Palestine picked up in the years immediately following World War II. All four papers under consideration covered the rising level of violence in Palestine (particularly Jewish-British violence), Anglo-American negotiations on Palestine, the partition debate, and the declaration of the State of Israel. Also, all four papers melded their Palestine coverage with reporting of what was interpreted as President Truman's erratic policy on Palestine.[103]

Most of the coverage was of a pro-Zionist nature, and most of the editorial positions taken were also pro-Zionist. The real difference among these newspapers was quantitative, not qualitative—that is, in the amount of detail supplied to the reader. Here, as usual, the *New York Times* was the most prolific. For instance, in the seven weeks that followed the United Nations' vote on partition, the *Times* ran no fewer than 360 articles on Palestine and related issues.[104] Many politicians, and the American Zionists as well, recognized the extent of this coverage by acknowledging that interested Americans often "got the Palestine story" from the *New York Times*. President Truman paid particular attention to the paper, calling it "the Bible of informed opinion."[105]

Postwar Attitudes

On December 17, 1945, the *New York Times* reported that the United States Senate had "overwhelmingly adopted . . . a resolution urging the U.S. to use its good offices toward the establishment of a Jewish commonwealth in Palestine and for the free entry of Jews there."[106] The next day the *Times* reported that the House of Representatives "unanimously gave its approval . . . to the Palestine resolution passed by the Senate."[107] Thus, Congress positioned itself to support the final act that would see the transformation of Palestine into a Jewish state.

The *New York Times* itself had already come out in support of this position, at least in terms of immigration. The *Times* editorialized on November 14 that "the civilized world, viewing one of the ghastliest crimes of all history, Hitler's war of extermination against the Jews, may take some comfort from [the fact that] . . . the Anglo-American Committee of Inquiry . . . has the task of not only examining conditions in Palestine but of carrying out a similar investigation in Europe." (Thus the *Times* found "comfort" in that which the Arabs had always insisted was illegitimate, the connection of the problem of European anti-Semitism with the problem of Palestine.) The *Times* then reasserted the argument of altruistic imperialism that, since the early twentieth century, had always accompanied this linkage and seemed so logical to the Western mind. "It may be argued that Palestine could profitably accept many more [Jews] than this [the present rate of immigration] and that if the land and resources of the country were fully utilized in a modern manner very many more could live there without hurting Arab interests—indeed with positive economic benefit to the present Arab population."[108]

That the Arabs insisted, as the Arab Information Service in Washington, D.C., put it on December 18, 1945, that such alleged altruism would inevitably result "in . . . the disposal of an Arab country against the express desire of its people"[109] had always been lost on the Congress, the press, and the American people. On the contrary, at the end of the World War II, as in the 1920s and 1930s, Zionism continued to be viewed, in Sumner Wells's words, as "one of the noblest ideas of modern times."[110] And some influential journalists described it as nothing short of Americanism reborn into the Holy Land. The celebrated reporter Anne O'Hare McCormick still traveled about this new frontier transforming it into a mixture of Wild West and suburban development. In an op-ed piece published in the *New York Times* on January 6, 1945, she wrote that the city of Tel Aviv "was proof of what urban Jews can make grow on barren ground." And what had they grown? "One of the world's youngest cities, better planned, more modernistic than the Florida boom towns it resembles." It was a place that "American boys" find resembles "a home town." McCormick explained,

Palestine in general and Tel-Aviv in particular, is a leave center for thousands of officers and GIs from all over the Middle East, Africa, and Italy. The main leave camp is within a few miles of Tel-Aviv. Boys on furlough flock to this town, where they see American movies . . . meet girls who speak English, and stroll on streets that look like main street. . . . The so-called Arab world isn't their world. They feel alien and uncomfortable in its strange sights, sounds and smells. Here [in Tel Aviv] they feel at home. "It sure feels good to see something like an American town," said the inevitable boy from Texas. . . . "this is the best place I've seen since I waved good-bye to Old Lady liberty."

McCormick draws the obvious conclusion from this, and thereby reinforces it for her readers. "The result of this experience is likely to make these soldiers strongly Zionist when they get home."[111]

"Likely" was, if anything, an understatement. McCormick's own perceptions of what was going on in Palestine, so widely disseminated through the "Bible of informed opinion," were themselves an expression of the bipolar worldview's overwhelming power to contextualize the history of Palestine's present moment in "orientalist" terms. Along with biblical identification, there was the assumed fact that Zionism was a manifestation of American culture, and therefore its cities "Florida boom towns." What need was there to liberalize American immigration laws in order to show the United States' concern and sympathy with Jewish DPs? There was no need for them come to America when Palestine itself was in the process of becoming American.

The message was phrased more generally by the American Council on Public Affairs in April of 1946. Reiterating the imperialism-as-altruism outlook of the *New York Times'* 1945 editorial, and also resurrecting the "full-belly" approach to colonialism, this representative liberal organization explained that the escalating violence that now threatened to engulf Palestine "can be reduced by intensive development of the economic potentialities of that country." Not considering, probably out of ignorance, the fact that the Jewish economy of Palestine was designed to be ethnically exclusive, the council asserted that Zionism "can serve the whole Middle East as a progressive, Westernizing influence. . . . They can be an outpost of Western culture without being an outpost of Western imperialism."[112] This last statement only reflects how Zionism became exempted from the negative stigma imperialism acquired in the American mind after World War II. To the Arabs, Zionism was an obvious product of European imperialism. Certainly the British understood its success as part of their own imperialist activities following World War I. But the council quite ignored the fact that the Zionists had ridden into Palestine in the baggage train of the British army. In any case, the Jews were no longer allies of the British. They were, in fact, often compared "to the American patriots of Revolutionary times." As one letter to the *Times* put it, "It is entirely in keeping with the circumstances that the gallant young Hebrews of modern Palestine, fighting for the rescue and survival of their stricken fellow-Jews [the Jewish DPs], should be compared to the American colonists."[113]

The Jewish DPs

If one wanted proof for the argument that Zionism was indeed a European imposition in the Middle East, one needed to look no further than Europe's displaced persons' camps. Over and again the press reinforced the connection. This great "stockpile of misery,"[114] the plight of which would "move the hearts of men of stone,"[115] ought properly to go only one place, and that was Palestine. However, the press did not describe this proposition as a mid-twentieth-century twist on imperialism. Rather, this population transfer from Europe to the Middle East, now put forth by President Truman and the Zionists in the form of a demand for an initial, immediate, transfer of 100,000 DPs, was an expression of "the highest considerations of statesmanship and humanity," the realization of which would be "a victory for the progressive and liberal forces which have fought so long for justice to the Jews."[116]

The rhetoric on this issue too was dominated by the bipolar worldview. A good example of this came from Governor Dewey, who would soon contest the presidency with Truman. As was the case with Truman, Dewey understood the political value of the DP issue and was soon competing for Zionist support. On October 7, 1946, the *New York Times* reported on a speech of the governor in which he claimed that "large scale and immediate Jewish immigration" was "the solution to the Palestine problem." The speech, which the paper printed in its entirety, never mentioned the Arabs of Palestine, and of course, it is only by perceptually depopulating that land of its indigenous population that the governor was able to turn what the Arab world considered "the problem" into "the solution."[117]

Under the circumstances, those who dared argue that the 100,000 DPs really constituted a crisis-producing influx of aliens were denounced. In August of 1946, the *Times* reported "angry Senate clamor," and the "severe criticism" of the British government for not immediately letting in the 100,000. Also, "the U.S. State Department's Near East Division was criticized by Republicans and Democrats alike, who accused it of helping the British to delay admission of the Jews."[118]

The attacks by Congress and American Zionists pushed the British to respond with their own angry accusations. Thus on June 13, 1946, Foreign Minister Bevin was reported to have remarked "regarding the agitation in the U.S. . . . for 100,000 Jews to be put into Palestine, I hope it will not be misunderstood in America if I say . . . that that was because they did not want too many of them [Jewish DPs] in New York."[119]

Actually, Bevin was correct in as much as the U.S. government had not seen fit to significantly liberalize its own immigration statutes. The following September, in an editorial on the subject of immigration, the *New York Times* noted that Congress behaved as if admitting DPs into the United States was "a menace." President Truman's request for "a fixed number" (3,900 a month) to be granted "permanent resident" status had been greeted by Richard Russell, chairman of the Senate Immigration Committee, as "a dangerous precedent."[120] These were the same DPs whose admittance to Palestine was supposed to be the premier cause of the civilized world. The *New York Times* stated that it disagreed with Russell and supported Truman's request, but other papers did not immediately follow suit. It was not till a year later, in November 1947, that the *Washington Post* editorially complained that that year's Congress had adjourned without addressing the immigration issue.[121] Nearly a year after that, in May of 1948, the *Chicago Tribune* came out flatly against any liberalization of immigration. Its reason was that the United States had a housing shortage, and new immigrants would only exacerbate this situation.[122] Thus, one must sadly admit that Foreign Minister Bevin was accurate in his assessment—except when it came to his naming New York City. On September 16, 1946, the *Times* had reported on an offer by that city's Mayor William O'Dwyer to create "a haven" for 250,000 refugees within "100 miles of New York city."[123] New York and its environs was probably the only major urban area in the United States that was likely to have welcomed the refugees.

Partition

The plight of the refugees, set against the rising tide of Zionist violence, dominated news reporting on Palestine well into 1947. The American Zionists often grew annoyed at the *New York Times* because its detailed coverage included the terrorist acts of their Palestine comrades. For instance, the *Times* had no trouble labeling those who, in July of 1946, blew up much of the King David Hotel as "Jewish extremists" and the action itself as "terrorism."[124] Yet it was not those labels which put off the Zionists. Perhaps they felt that the American people would make allowances for any violence which could be portrayed as a result of British refusal to relieve the misery of the DPs by allowing open immigration. What really worried them about the attention paid to their violent actions in the Holy Land was that it gave credibility to the State Department's argument that a continued UN trusteeship was needed in Palestine.[125]

Since August 1946, trusteeship, or for that matter continuing the mandate, had been unacceptable to the Zionists. They were now focused on partition as a first step to creating the State of Israel. As the United Nations became involved in deciding the fate of Palestine, press attention shifted away from the continued terrorist nature of Zionist and Arab violence in Palestine, and focused on the debate leading to the General Assembly's vote on partition in late November 1947. However, the reporting on this issue was plagued with contradictions hardly noticed then or since.

Newspaper reporting of the debate leading to the partition vote readily noted the "heavy pressure" that was being put on various delegations to vote for partition. Indeed, the *New York Times* estimated that "unless the U.S. makes strenuous efforts to win over some of the delegations," partition "had little chance."[126] The *Chicago Tribune* even described this pressure as coming in the form of "economic threats."[127]

What the press saw as unusual was not that such pressure was being used, but rather that it was necessary at all. For instance, the *Washington Post* chastised such "doubtful states" as the Philippines and Liberia for even considering voting against partition. The *Post* reminded its readers that such countries "owe their independence to the U.S." and are economically "still leaning on us." Because of these points the exercising of independent judgment by these governments on the matter of partition seemed to the *Post* to be acts of ingratitude. It appeared "incredible that they have reached their decision on Palestine without taking into account the American stand." In fact, it seemed so incredible to the *Post*'s editors that they concluded it had to be the product of some conspiracy that went beyond the capitals of these countries. Who was really to blame? It could not be the Russians, for they too favored partition. "The mystery is fathomable only in terms of the attitude of State Department officials. . . . It looks to us as if . . . the Philippines and Liberia have had a high sign to take no notice of the pro-partition stand. . . . no other explanation . . . makes any sense."[128]

It can be argued that what made even less sense was the conspiratorial "logic" of the editors of the *Washington Post*. They seemed to have never asked themselves why these countries might have considered voting against partition in the first place, if such an act ran counter to the desires of their patron and placed their economies at risk. In other words, why should it take "heavy pressure" to bring them around? Did the editors of the *Post* ever consider that the men who ran Liberia and the Philippines might have been moved, at least for a brief moment, by a distaste for the precedent that would be set by partition? Perhaps they agreed with Mohammad Fadill Jamali, the Iraqi foreign minister, who had just days before characterized partition as an impending "act of conquest by the UN" that would result in placing tens of thousands of Arabs "under the subjugation of a Jewish state."[129]

This explanation never seemed to cross the minds of the *Post* editors, because they, and so many other American opinion-makers, could not get beyond the bipolar worldview that subordinated non-Western peoples to the causes of "civilization," "modernity," "progress," and the like. It seemed to the *Post* that to vote against partition was to vote against these virtues, and no sensible government would do that. The *Post* editors also seemed to be unable to understand their own country's foreign policy within a historical context that would make sense to the Filipinos. Looked at from the non-Western side of the bipolar divide, the Philippines "owed their independence" to the United States only because the United States had held the islands as an imperialist colony for almost fifty years. Should gratitude for this fact require compliance with U.S. wishes on what many in the non-Western world looked upon as a new act of imperialism?

The partition vote in the General Assembly came on November 29, 1947. The "heavy pressure" had proved effective, yet the vote just barely achieved the required two-thirds majority. Fifty-six percent of Palestine would go to the Jewish minority. What the Arabs saw as a UN-sanctioned "act of conquest" was hailed by the American Zionists and their supporters as "a high moment in the life of the UN." It was a moment that would, according to Chaim Weizmann, who was ever attuned to the argument of altruistic imperialism, open the way for the Zionists to "contribute to the regeneration of the Middle East and the welfare of mankind."[130]

The *Los Angeles Times* reported that "many saw in the vote a strong portent of permanent world peace based on peaceful adjudication of international issues."[131] But just ten days earlier, the *L.A. Times* had reported that the Arabs had warned the General Assembly that a partition vote would require the UN to "rule by force" in the Holy Land.[132] Given that the vote in the General Assembly had been so close, and achieved only with the help of "economic threats," the prediction of permanent peace and peaceful adjudication of issues printed in the *L.A. Times* seemed as fanciful as the conspiracy theories coming out of the *Washington Post*. As if to prove this point, by the end of the year the *L.A. Times* would carry a headline announcing Arab attacks on U.S. legations in the Middle East.[133]

As questionable as were the tactics used by the Zionists and the United States to bring about the favorable decision on partition, the *New York Times* in an editorial on the vote printed on November 30 sought to legitimize the whole affair as an expression of world opinion. Describing how "history was written" by the vote, the editors asserted it was only taken after "a thorough investigation and a full and fair debate." What of the "heavy pressure" that the paper itself had reported on? The editors ignored this factor, and attributed the closeness of the count to the fact that some delegations were put off by the absence of an enforcement plan for partition. Nonetheless, "doubts must now yield," the editors said, "the Assembly has made its choice, and its decision should command the acquiescence, the respect and the loyal support of all nations and all peoples."[134]

In truth, partition barely commanded the acquiescence of the American Zionists, who, for all their celebration of the vote, also expressed a feeling of somehow having been cheated by partition. Emanuel Neumann, now president of the Zionist Organization of America, told the *New York Times* that "the decision does not fully satisfy the just claims and historic aspirations of the Jewish people." Meir Grossman, president of the United Zionist Revisionists of America, was even more explicit when he told the *Times* that the vote had, in effect, "reduced the Jewish national territory from 44,000 to 5500 square miles." He declared that the fight would continue for "a Jewish state within the historic boundaries of Palestine."[135]

Despite the obvious fact that the Zionists did not see the partition vote as the end of the process of establishing state borders, but rather the beginning, the opinions one found expressed in the press assumed that, to make partition work, acquiescence had to come mainly from the Arab side. It is no surprise that this was the opinion of American Jews. For instance, Rabbi William F. Rosenblum, president of the Synagogue Council of America, stated that he hoped "that upon mature reflection they [the Arabs] will accept the decision of the Assembly and thus indicate that they too want to make the world safe for democracy and human rights."[136] This was also the opinion of seasoned reporters. Thomas J. Hamilton, the *New York Times* correspondent at the UN, asked, "will partition work?"

He then answered his own question this way: "The answer depends primarily upon the Arabs of Palestine and the neighboring states. If they accept the Assembly decision, it will work."[137] Rosenblum's convenient avoidance of Zionist territorial aspirations can be understood. However, for Hamilton to have been either ignorant or unmindful of the statements of Neumann and Grossman, printed in his own paper, is less understandable. Similar Zionist expansionist plans being discussed by leaders such as David Ben Gurion and Menachem Begin in Palestine, and discoverable by even half-hearted efforts at investigative reporting, were similarly not given much attention by the reporters or editors of any of the papers under consideration.

Declaration of the State of Israel

Support of partition led to the support of the declaration of the State of Israel issued on May 14, 1948. This support also flowed naturally from long adherence to the bipolar worldview that dominated American attitudes toward Palestine in 1948, as it had in 1917. On May 15, 1948, a *New York Times* editorial quoted the Israeli proclamation of statehood and then offered the following: "in these words, addressed to the nations of the world from the seaport city of Tel Aviv, itself a living testimonial of the industry and deep faith and burning zeal with which much that was barren land has been transformed into a thriving modern civilization, do the pioneers who have long sought 'a national home' in Palestine announce their intention to fill the vacuum created by the surrender of the British Mandate with the creation of an independent state. . . . No one can question the courage or the high purpose of this act of self-assertion, or doubt that partition . . . is now a living fact."[138]

The *Washington Post* offered two editorials, one on May 14 and another on May 16. The first placed the Arabs in the usual semi-barbaric posture while correspondingly offering promise for the future from the West.

> To be sure trouble is bound to keep the Holy Land in ferment. . . . Arabs harassed the British and the Jews in the thirties and sought to upset the British position in Iraq during the war. In those days the men who are now the self-styled leaders of Arab Palestine . . . were the particular troublemakers. . . . Arabs who used to be a restraining influence in Arab Palestine have been bumped off by the Mufti's gunmen. They used to cooperate in the union movement in Palestine. Now there is a chance, if American policy will encourage it, of turn-

ing Middle East opinion toward a wider union based upon the common interest . . . [now that] old fashioned imperialism has wound up.[139]

The second editorial continued the theme that only something of the West can bring redemption to an otherwise "feudal" part of the world. Beginning with a quote from Senator Arthur Vandenberg, the *Post* editorialized that U.S. recognition of Israel

"takes account of the reality that no other authority can fill what otherwise would be a cruel and dangerous vacuum in this area of Palestine." The Jewish state is an accomplished fact and the only alternative to anarchy. Its declaration of independence . . . evidences a strong determination for survival, but also promises restraint. Social and political equality are pledged to all citizens. . . . Peace and amity are offered to all neighboring states and people. And "the state of Israel is ready to contribute its full share to the peaceful progress and reconstitution of the Middle East". . . . Peace in the Near East is now unquestionably dependent upon the Arabs' sense of realities. It would be naive to ignore the clash of traditions and culture when the dynamic Jews develop a state alongside the Arabs' feudal civilization. But the new order can work to the advantage of both if there is the will to seek peaceful accommodation.[140]

In these editorials we find the bipolar worldview plainly operative. The Arabs are "troublemakers" and "gunmen," who for a long time have been "harassing the British and the Jews." They are products of a "feudal civilization." The Zionists, on the other hand, are "pioneers" transforming "barren land." They act with "high purpose." They offer an "alternative to anarchy" as well as "peace and amity." They represent "modern civilization."

Interestingly enough, the editorials in the *Chicago Tribune* and *Los Angeles Times* are much more equivocal. This might be because, in each case, the proclamation of the State of Israel was an excuse for an editorial about something else. In the case of the *Tribune* it was an opportunity to attack President Truman and the fact that his "haste in recognizing the new state" was not principled, but rather done "with an eye to the Jewish vote in the metropolitan cities of the east, particularly New York." The *Chicago Tribune,* in using the opportunity to go after Truman, had nothing against Israel. "We hope that Israel will flourish and that her relations with her neighbors will soon become peaceable." But then the editors added this prescient statement: "having recognized Israel, Mr. Truman may expect one of these days to be told that he has an obligation to defend the boundaries of the new country, wherever they may be located. . . . It seems likely that Mr. Truman's answer will be dictated, like his other answers to the Zionists, by his political ambitions."[141] The applicability of this prediction would not be restricted to the Truman administration.

In the case of the *Los Angeles Times,* the editorial on the new state was an opportunity to worry over Russian intentions in the Middle East. The editorial quoted at length from an article that had recently been published by Hannah Arendt. Arendt was a philosopher of renown and an iconoclastic Zionist. She worried that the conditions under which Zionism had evolved and the new State of Israel born had produced a militaristic Jewish community that did not care much about the rest of the world. However, she also speculated that "Russia might be our ally for a certain period." The *L.A. Times* immediately focused on this minor part of Arendt's analysis. "The key words here are those about Russia—the key words for the United States—Russia itching for Middle East." The *L.A. Times* editors got so worked up over this prospect that they concluded that "the United States seems bound to do something." Yet the best the editors could recommend was that the war in the Holy Land be stopped, and all the parties go back to some undefined settlement under the auspices of a "UN trusteeship."[142] The paper's support of the trusteeship idea was belated and momentary.

These two editorials did not mean that either paper had somehow escaped the parameters of the bipolar worldview. In both cases their general coverage was pro-Zionist and Arab rights were never seriously discussed. For the *Chicago Tribune,* the most conservative of the four papers considered, even the ironic fact that "financial contributions from American Jewry . . . have made possible the foundation for the world's newest socialist republic"[143] did not prevent the paper from expressing "the hope that Israel will flourish."[144] In the case of the *L.A. Times,* the paper's main columnist, who went under the pen name of Polazoides, described the founding of Israel as "one of the great events in world history."[145]

Sources of Opposition: The Anti-Zionist Jews

As was the case in the 1930s and early '40s, there was American Jewish opposition to partition and the creation of the State of Israel. One can find mention of it among the more general pro-Zionist reporting, particularly in the ever-detailed coverage of the *New York Times.* Some of the anti-

Zionist Jews' activities are also recorded among the documents of the State Department. Their 1940s efforts have also been documented in Thomas Kolsky's book *Jews against Zionism*.

On September 30, 1945, just as the war ended, Morris S. Lazaron, whom we have already seen in close contact with NEA, reiterated much of the American anti-Zionist position in a long letter to the *New York Times*. He noted that Jews were divided over the question of a Jewish state in Palestine. Those who saw the issue from a non-Zionist point of view felt that Judaism was a "universal religion" and not a "national religion." This had led to a long-term concern of Lazaron and his compatriots that a Jewish state would undermine the citizenship rights of Jews in other countries. They also felt that the Zionists' "maximum" demands would inevitably lead to escalating "violence and bloodshed."[146]

The issue of violence was a particular concern of the anti-Zionist American Council for Judaism, with which Lazaron was affiliated. Its president, Lessing J. Rosenwald, would, in July of 1946, publicly warn that Palestine was "approaching anarchy." He asserted that "American Jews know that to turn to machine guns as final arbitrators is tragic, criminal folly; they will have nothing to do with terrorism or violence."[147] Unfortunately, he was wrong. In October of 1947 Judah Magnes would charge that American Jews were financing terror in Palestine. By doing so, he said, they had made their religion into "pagan Judaism."[148] Even Chaim Weizmann would come out and criticize American Jews for supporting "Jewish extremists."[149]

The American Council for Judaism wrote to President Truman in August of 1946 and declared that "any policy that sanctions and strengthens the forces of segregation and division among those living in Palestine would mean the perpetuation of antagonistic nationalistic conflicts and endless violence."[150] And Rosenwald publicly petitioned Secretary of State Dean Acheson to inform the British government that the Jewish Agency "cannot represent those Jews who are profoundly concerned about their co-religionists but who are fundamentally opposed to the Zionist program." More than just the views of the Zionists need to be considered, he asserted.[151] Later, they would charge that "the overwhelming concern of American Jewry for the plight of European and Palestinian Jewry has been manipulated and maneuvered to suggest support of political Zionism. Humanitarianism, not political ideology, is the one and only issue on which Jewry is united."[152]

The Zionists scorned the American Council for Judaism and charged Lazaron with "calculated mischief against the wretched Jews of Europe."[153] It was a fratricidal wrath they felt toward those who, while part of the faith, had turned into traitors to the sacred cause. Actually, the Zionists exaggerated the dangers represented by men like Lazaron and Rosenwald. While it is true that they opposed a Jewish state, they were by 1945 thoroughly marginalized both in terms of the U.S. government and the American Jewish community at large. As to the government, their only ally was an equally isolated NEA. And as for American Jewry, they had indeed been traumatized by the horrors of the Nazis, and simultaneously hemmed in by their own country's inhumane immigration policies. Palestine appeared to be the only place left for the Jewish survivors. This apparent fact also trapped the anti-Zionists.

Thus Lazaron and other anti-Zionist Jews agreed with the Zionists on a "need to find homes for the stateless and dispossessed" and "the ability of Palestine to absorb a large proportion of such unfortunates." They also agreed with the Zionists as to the "justice of the claim that Palestine should be open to such immigration."[154] Thus, the anti-Zionist Jews too were working within the parameters of the bipolar worldview. However, they did not want Palestine turned into a Jewish refuge in such a way that would drive the Arabs to war. Indeed, what Lazaron wanted was a binational state very much like that proposed by Judah Magnes.[155] However, both the Zionists and the Arabs knew that it was impossible to separate out the massive immigration of Europeans into Palestine from the cause of Zionism. It was Zionism, and not humanitarianism, that was the organizing principle that guided the refugees to the Holy Land. Humanitarianism would have created pressure for open immigration into the United States and other countries, and not sent the DPs willy-nilly into a war-torn zone such as Palestine. Thus, the cries for moderation and reason issued by the anti-Zionists found little audience in either camp.

Other Sources of Opposition: The Arab Americans

One of the objectives Arab American organizations had set themselves was to convince the U.S. government to "maintain an attitude of impartiality" toward the conflict in Palestine. They had never been able to do this when it came to Congress, and with the accession of the Truman administration the effort was, for all intents and purposes, a failure. Nonetheless, Arab Americans continued the debate with the American Zionists. In terms of organizations, the Arab National League disappeared from the news and was replaced in 1945 by another organization, the Institute for Arab American Affairs. This organization, headquartered in New York and led by Faris Malouf and Khalil Totah, described its purpose as the "promotion of friendly relations between the U.S. and the Arab Lands."[156]

In March of 1945, having learned of a recent visit to the White House by Stephen Wise, the institute solicited an interview with President Roosevelt. The Arab Americans, who traditionally could not get past the State Department level, were rebuffed. Despite the fact that FDR was readily willing to see Zionist leaders at this time, Malouf, under whose signature the request had gone out, was told that "I am sure you will appreciate that the limitations on the President's time . . . render it quite impossible for him personally to meet with representatives of all organizations."[157]

They had no better luck with President Truman, so the institute released a public letter to the new president in August 1945. The letter returned to the theme of democracy in Palestine that had been one of the constants in the Arab American argument. "Zionists are anxious to form a majority in Palestine, after which the conversion of the whole of Palestine into a Jewish state will be automatic. It is then and only then that the Zionists will concede to let the principles of free election and majority rule operate in that country. The position of the Arabs, in accordance with the best tradition of American democracy, is that the rules of free election and legislation should be given the right of way now, before it is too late."[158]

Another letter to Truman went out from the institute in October 1945. This one protested the Zionist demand for unlimited immigration into Palestine as a solution to the plight of Jewish refugees in Europe. The Zionist demand was an opportunistic one, the institute insisted, and of a "purely imperialistic and political character." Zionist ambitions in Palestine "antedated the refugee problem by many years and only utilized the plight of the refugees as a subterfuge for its political ends."[159]

There is no evidence that these letters were ever read by Truman, and their arguments were never seriously taken up by either the president or his aides. No Arab American ever gained access to the White House to have the opportunity to counter the positions put forth by scores of Zionist visitors and lobbyists.

In 1946 warnings came to the U.S. government from Arab leaders such as King Ibn Saud of Saudi Arabia and Abdul Rahman Azzam Pasha, secretary general of the Arab League. They cautioned that continued sponsorship of Jewish immigration into Palestine would inevitably "risk incurring not only the enmity of the Arabs but the enmity of all Moslems as well."[160] This, of course, was the point that NEA had been trying unsuccessfully to get across to Truman. The Arab warnings, the accuracy of which was now being reflected in setbacks for U.S. business in the Middle East,[161] made no impact on the president.

Against the background of these warnings from the Arab states, spokesmen for the Institute for Arab American Affairs engaged in a number of public debates with Zionist leaders. The first encounter, sponsored by the Overseas Press Club of America, took place at Town Hall in New York City on the evening of April 13, 1946. It was a raucous event at which Khalil Totah represented the institute. Also involved was Rabbi Elmer Berger of the anti-Zionist American Council for Judaism. Among the Zionists present was Louis Lipsky. Not much of substance was discussed at this debate because the audience "hooted down" much of what the non-Zionist speakers tried to say. Things got so unruly that "a policeman had to walk up and down the aisle and motion to those jumping from their seats to sit down."[162]

A second, more sedate debate took place in November 1946 at the Waldorf-Astoria Hotel in New York, under the auspices of the Foreign Policy Association. With an audience that was perhaps prescreened, a real exchange of views took place between Nahum Goldman of the Jewish Agency and Khalil Totah. Goldman stated that the demand for an Arab state in Palestine was not possible because "the Jewish minority in Palestine, nearly 700,000 Jews, will never recognize Arab rule." Instead, he insisted that the solution lay in "territorial compromise," or partition. "That would satisfy the aspirations of both people." Goldman knew, of course, that in the long run the Zionist leadership had no intention of being "satisfied" with this initial partition of Palestine. However, he did not elaborate on this but instead suggested that, if the Arabs accepted a Zionist state, the result might be the growth of "one of the greatest centers of human civilization in the world."

For his part, Totah told the audience that "Zionism means war" because the Arabs would fight to prevent the establishment of any Zionist state. He said that there was, however, a way to prevent war and that was to institute immediately a democratic government in Palestine. "The Zionists are clamoring for a free democratic Palestine. So are the Arabs. Why not inaugurate democracy at once?"[163] Nahum Goldman's response, if any, went unreported.

In 1946 the activities of the Institute for Arab American Affairs were complemented by the activities of another Arab effort, known as the Arab Office, in Washington, D.C. Headed up by Cecil Hourani, the Arab Office sought to create an Arab lobbying presence in the American capital. Hourani also wrote letters that were published in the *New York Times*, and, in this fashion, sometimes rebutted statements made by Zionists. For instance, in September of 1946 Hourani wrote to the *New York Times* in order to lay out the Arab argument against the partition of Palestine. Partition would "undermine the integrity of the Arab world," Hourani asserted, and therefore was impossible for Arabs to accept. He also pointed out that it was foolhardy for President Truman to think that his support for partition would lead to a real solution to the Palestine problem. This was because "it would not be the intention of the Zionists to make it final. The fact that the Jewish Agency has accepted partition does not mean that it has given up the whole of Palestine. It is not difficult to imagine the policy of the Jewish Government in its own area. The floodgates of immigration would be opened, the Hagana would flourish unchecked, the alienation of land . . . would be encouraged. The day would come when the Jewish state would be obliged by its own inner forces to expand, and it could only expand at the expense of the Arabs."[164]

Finally, in 1947 Arab Americans were joined by some of their non-Arab fellow citizens who sympathized with their cause. These included Bayard Dodge, Harold Hoskins, and Kermit Roosevelt, among others. They too wrote letters to the newspapers and publicly debated the Zionists.[165] This too represented an ongoing effort, evidence of which we have seen in the interwar period.

That these efforts did not prevail does not mean, as some historians have suggested, that they lack historical significance.[166] The contemporary assumption that Zionism always had unanimous support in the United States is rendered suspect by the reality of the efforts of the Arab American community and its allies. Though Zionism was certainly close to the hearts of a large majority of Americans who paid attention to the Holy Land, and though it fit neatly within the parameters of the bipolar worldview that dominated most Americans' view of the non-Western world, it did not go unopposed. The Arab American community was not passive. And because there was debate on Palestine from 1917 to 1948, a proper understanding of the history of American popular perceptions of Palestine cannot be had without taking this opposition into consideration.

9

Colonizing the American Mind

The American perceptions and attitudes that supported Zionism from 1917 to 1948 were the same as those that upheld Western imperialism and colonialism. The American Zionists and their supporters in these years were quite open about this connection. They consistently used the terminology of colonization for Zionist activities in Palestine. Newspaper coverage of those same activities approvingly placed them within the context of altruistic imperialism. It was only after World War II, when "old-fashioned imperialism" fell out of fashion, that this language disappeared, and Zionists began to ignore the colonialist nature and roots of their enterprise. This contemporary use of selective memory notwithstanding, the historical evidence presented in this work makes clear the fact that the Zionist venture in Palestine is, historically, an imperialist and colonialist phenomenon.

Perceptions of imperialism and Zionism were held within the context of a bipolar worldview that assigned positive attributes such as development, modernity, and good government to the West in general and the American model in particular. Correspondingly, negative attributes such as backwardness, fanaticism, and a warlike posture were assigned to non-Western peoples such as the Muslims of the Middle East. To the extent that the West imperially dominated the Non-West, the West was seen as disseminating its positive attributes, and thus could claim that colonialism was an altruistic process. This point of view strongly shaped American views of Zionism and its role in Palestine.

Religion also influenced the way Americans perceived Palestine. The Judeo-Christian heritage of the West, as represented in biblical literalism, had long ago defined Palestine as the Holy Land. By the time of World War I, Palestine's status as a religiously significant extension of the Judeo-Christian world was well established, and thus it became a prime candidate for imperial appropriation and colonization.

American popular acceptance of this process was also facilitated by the fact that, since the nineteenth century, orientalist literature and missionary propaganda had rendered the Muslim majority of Palestine of little or no account to Westerners. In this sense the area had been "perceptually de-populated."

The vacuum created by the discounting of the native Muslim popula-tion was filled by the Zionists, who were at once representatives of a "biblical people" and the "progressive" West. Thus, as both Jews and Westerners, the Zionists were believed to have a religiously legitimate claim to Palestine, and, as important, in realizing that claim they would bring to the Holy Land the allegedly positive attributes of the West. This made the "up-building" of Palestine, to use the Zionist term, part and parcel of altruistic imperialism. In turn, this particular rationalization of the act of conquest was useful in categorizing indigenous resistance. When eventually the Muslim majority rebelled against the influx of tens of thou-sands of Europeans, their doing so seemed to prove their backward, fa-natical intransigence to civilization itself.

Into the Present

Have the American perceptions and attitudes that supported Zionism in the years leading up to the creation of the State of Israel significantly changed? After all, the age of empire, as traditionally understood, is over. It is now assumed that the basically racist beliefs that were associated with that age are also a thing of the past. However, in the case of Palestine/Israel it may not be so easy to give up these traditional attitudes. If Israel is in fact a product of Western colonialism that is still popularly supported by Americans, many of the attitudes that rationalized its establishment would need to be held as valid into the present.

We have already seen some early clues that an updated version of a bipolar perception as applied to Palestine/Israel would carry over after World War II. Thus the forward-looking American Council on Public Affairs stated in April 1946 that Zionism "can serve the whole Middle East as a progressive, Westernizing influence . . . an outpost of Western culture without being an outpost of Western imperialism."[1] This arbitrary separation of cause and effect was seconded by the *Washington Post's* 1948 notion that "old-fashioned imperialism has wound up"[2] (that is, finished) yet the "Jewish state is . . . the only alternative to anarchy" in Palestine. It represented an avenue to "peaceful progress and reconstitu-tion of the Middle East."[3]

Certainly into the 1960s Americans maintained this image of Israel as a progressive Western outpost, and the Israelis as a modern people redeeming a land rightfully theirs. Visually, this conviction came through clearly in the acclaimed 1960 film *Exodus* (based on Leon Uris's book of the same title). In 1961 words were put to the popular theme music of the picture. The words, in part, went as follows:

> This land is my land, God gave this land to me
> This brave and ancient land to me
> And when the morning sun reveals her hills
> Then I see a land where children can run free. . . .
> To make this land our home
> If I must fight, I'll fight to make this land our own
> Until I die, this land is mine.

The resulting song was an immediate success and was recorded over and again, by such artists as Pat Boone, Ferrante and Teicher, Mantovani, Eddie Harris, and Edith Piaf.

The 1967 Arab-Israeli War

Further evidence for the continuation of these attitudes can be found in American popular reactions to the "'67 War." Of all the conflicts subsequent to the establishment of the State of Israel, the 1967 War is the one most thoroughly researched as to American attitudes.

This research shows that media coverage continued to reflect a bipolar worldview. As Professor Michael Suleiman, an expert on American perceptions of the Middle East, put it, "hardly any 'good' qualities were attributed to the Arabs generally, whereas the Israelis were portrayed as practically without fault."[4] His survey of popular news magazines, including the *Sunday New York Times Magazine,* found that in 1967, Arabs were consistently portrayed as poor, backward, undemocratic, dishonest, and contentious. Israelis, on the other hand, were seen as the opposite: modern, honest, hardworking, and "Western oriented."[5] In addition, the Israelis were characterized as "kind and generous to the Arabs whom 'fate' had entrusted to their care." Suleiman concludes that "the arguments [used by the magazines] sound much like those of colonialists— arguments that were supposedly rejected by liberals and intellectuals of the West about twenty years ago."[6]

Newspaper Coverage of the War

The 1967 coverage by the four newspapers used in this book show the same bipolar stereotypes found by Professor Suleiman in his study of news magazines. The *New York Times* traced the origins of the 1967 war to "conflicting claims [to Palestine] that go back to biblical days."[7] America's "bond" with the Zionist state is, according to a *Times* editorial, "somewhat mystical" and stems from "Puritan ideas and Bible fundamentalism." These have proved more powerful than America's "pragmatic" interests in oil investments.[8] Other *Times* editorials and op-ed pieces described the Arab Middle East as "lands with great illiteracy," which made the Arabs susceptible to "myth" and "propaganda" put out by their governments about Israel and the West.[9]

Despite the fact that the Arabs were consistently described by the *New York Times* as aggressors capable of threatening the very existence of Israel,[10] they were also portrayed as congenitally incompetent. As a *Times* editorial of June 9, 1967, put it, "Arabs have never shown the advanced training or technology necessary to conduct a mechanized war of maneuver." They are "essentially incapable of fighting modern mobile war." The Israelis, on the other hand, have "a modern army."[11] How a people seemingly incapable of fighting "a modern mobile war" were at the same time capable of destroying a country with "a modern army" was not explained.

The *Washington Post* in 1967 described the Arabs as a "volatile and excitable people."[12] Their leaders were caricatured as "feudal dictators"[13] who had set the Middle East "aflame against pro-Western Israel."[14] Elsewhere both the Arabs and the Soviet Union, which supported the Arab position in 1967, were equated with Hitler.[15]

Israel, on the other hand, was variably described as a "rich and hopeful Jewish nation"[16] in danger of being "drowned in a Moslem sea"[17] and "a ghetto . . . ringed by enemies."[18] While Arab violence was that of "terrorists," Zionist violence was carried on by "commandos,"[19] and Moshe Dayan's appointment as defense minister in 1967 was likened to Winston Churchill's appointment to the prime ministership of Great Britain in 1939.[20]

According to a *Post* editorial of June 6, 1967, Israel had a "moral claim upon the Western world," and this made it "unthinkable for this country [the U.S.] or its allies, to permit the Jewish state to be destroyed."[21] Another of the paper's editorials asserted that upholding "peace and security" in the Middle East was a function of the "power and sense of responsibility of the Anglo-Saxon world."[22]

For the *Los Angeles Times* the 1967 Arab-Israeli crisis was basically a "tribal and religious conflict"[23] which had grown to "pit East against West."[24] Arab behavior in the crisis even seemed to have the potential to spark World War III.[25] Elsewhere, the Arabs were described as death-wielding nomads,[26] aggressors threatening to "destroy Israel,"[27] and latter-day Nazis.[28] As a consequence, Israel, "a modern nation," was threatened with extinction by primitive "hostile neighbors."[29]

A *Los Angeles Times* editorial of June 6, 1967, tied the Arabs to the communists and declared that the "U.S. commitment to maintain the territorial integrity and independence of Israel . . . obviously must be upheld."[30] Elsewhere, the paper quoted a leading Los Angeles rabbi as explaining that "the Arab-Israeli crisis will put to the test the Christian-Jewish dialog which has been an important feature of American life in recent years."[31]

Finally, the *Chicago Tribune* also portrayed the Arabs as aggressors and tied them to a Soviet Union eager to create "irritants to Western positions in the Middle East."[32] In political cartoons appearing in the *Tribune,* "fiery" Arab leaders, particularly Gamal Abdel Nasser, were depicted as "camel drivers" leading their people to war[33] and extremists poisoning the water holes of the Middle East.[34]

The *Tribune* devoted four articles to Jerusalem, describing the city as "the capital of the new Israel,"[35] "Israel's only frontier city,"[36] and "a city of synagogs [*sic*]."[37] No attention was paid to the Arab section of Jerusalem except to tell readers that, because of the division of the city, Jews had been prevented from worshipping at the Wailing Wall and "for 19 years the buildings of Hebrew University and Hadassah hospital, the finest in the Middle East, have stood empty and useless atop nearby Mount Scopus."[38] For a readership conditioned by a century of bipolar perceptions, this observation could only reinforce the notion that the Arabs were a backward people compared to the "progressive" Israelis. Having laid this context, the *Tribune* proceeded to run an article on June 3, 1967, laying out "prophesies" of the "return" of Arab East Jerusalem to Israeli control.[39]

In a mocking op-ed piece appearing in the *Tribune* on May 28, 1967, the syndicated columnist Russell Baker suggested that Egypt's Suez Canal was "built by Tyrone Power, produced by Darryl F. Zanuck, and seized in 1956 by Gamel Abdel Nasser." The Egyptians were angry at the Israelis because "Joseph, the youngest son of Jacob the Israelite . . . saved the Egyptians by advising the pharoah to lay in plenty of food. . . . If there is one thing they [the Egyptians] dislike, it is a nation that saved their necks."[40] While all this can be seen as humor in bad taste, it also identified two of the main sources of information that, since the nineteenth century, had supplied Americans with their information on the Middle East: the media in its various forms, and the Bible.

Thus, the imagery found in the newspapers in 1967 is quite similar to that which we found in the same papers in the 1920s, 1930s, and 1940s. This, along with the data concerning news magazine coverage in the late 1960s, supports the conclusion that, in regard to Palestine/Israel, the bipolar worldview and its corollary of altruistic imperialism survived at least through the 1960s.

The Zionists' Modern Dilemma

The reliance on colonialist attitudes should result in a dilemma for Zionists and their supporters in the modern era. When it comes to the Zionist venture in Palestine, attitudes continue to be held which are no longer accepted by most people in most places. How have American Zionists reacted to this predicament? They seem to have adopted two complementary approaches. The first is revealed by Rafael Medoff's research on American Zionist responses to Arab demands for democracy in Palestine. Medoff's work suggests that most American Zionists have refused to accept as relevant to Israel any democratic reforms that might undermine Jewish dominance,[41] yet they also ignored the issue that Zionism is a form of colonialism. Today, faced with Israeli actions such as occupation of conquered territories, Jewish settlement in the West Bank, Gaza Strip, and Golan Heights, and "legal" torture of Palestinians, Zionists still deny the applicability to Israel and its occupied territories of the standards of equity, civil and political rights, and treatment of minorities that have evolved in the postcolonial Western world.[42]

This position appears tenable because the majority of American Jews, as well as non-Jewish supporters of Zionism, give Israel a unique status, exempt from the normal critique that they would apply to other countries. Israel is the homeland of a people, the European (that is Western) branch of which came close to extermination, and therefore any means to protect and maintain the Jewish character of Israel is deemed acceptable.

Because the notion of a Jewish Palestine/Israel was and is seen as unique and perpetually vulnerable, American Zionists were never content with just countering their critics, but rather attacked them as mortal foes. Nor, as we have seen, were they ever comfortable with people who took a neutral stand toward their cause. To the extent that one can convert more and more Americans to Zionism, there will be fewer critics and less people willing to listen to what little criticism there is. Denial is easiest to maintain in an environment dominated by true believers.

Therefore, the second approach taken by American Zionists is, whenever possible, to reinforce the classic bipolar perceptions and interpretation of Palestine/Israel, and use them in the ongoing effort to recruit American politicians, civic leaders, and the general public to the Zionist cause. Arabs continue to be described as backward and fanatical foes of the West. Within this context, the denigration of Arabs and Muslims in contemporary American culture is, in part, a product of a continuing vigorous campaign on the part of American Zionists to monopolize American perceptions of Palestine/Israel in particular, and the Middle East in general.

Assimilation of the State Department

In the years prior to 1948 the American Zionists were successful in their effort to win over Congress and the American people, but the State Department and NEA eluded them. However, when in 1948 the White House became thoroughly pro-Zionist, the Zionists became even more determined to see a change in this last bastion of resistance. With their enhanced influence within the government, they were now able to successfully alter the position of diplomats.

Wallace Murray had left NEA in early 1945 to become the ambassador to Iran. His replacement was Loy Henderson, who, assisted by Gordon Merriam, had offered the greatest resistance to Zionist plans during the first Truman administration. It is likely that Truman, Clifford, and Niles would have liked to push Henderson out of the State Department altogether. This proved difficult, because Henderson's reputation within the department was excellent, and he usually had the support of the secretary of state. However, by mid 1948 Henderson was due to be rotated back to a field position. The State Department recommended that he be appointed ambassador to Turkey, but the Zionists did not want Henderson anywhere in the Middle East. They used their influence in the Senate to block Henderson from that post. Instead, he was made ambassador to India.[43] Gordon Merriam developed ulcers and took early retirement in 1949.

The changing of the guard at NEA meant a quick accommodation to the pro-Zionist position that now characterized the rest of the U.S. government. Thus, Kathleen Christison in her book *Perceptions of Palestine* tells us that by June of 1948 the State Department had "accepted the new Israeli state" and "abandoned any notion of supporting the formation of an independent Arab state" in non-Israeli Palestine.[44] She adds that "when the State Department came around to accepting Israel, it quickly lost patience with the Arabs for not following suit." She quotes a "high level State [Department] official" as declaring that he did not "care a dried

camel's hump" about what the Arabs thought or felt. They were just "fanatical and overwrought people" who were now endangering U.S. strategic interests.[45]

Never again would the State Department seriously challenge America's pro-Zionist foreign policy in the Middle East.[46] Even semi-indepen-
dent interpretations, seemingly consistent with White House policy, were
frowned upon. For instance, on June 5, 1967, a journalist asked a State
Department spokesman to affirm that the United States' position in the
UN relative to the Arab-Israeli crisis then occurring was one of neutrality.
The spokesman replied, "Indeed I would. . . . neutral in thought, word and
deed." Almost immediately the White House announced that that State
Department statement was "not a formal declaration of neutrality." By
the end of the day on June 5, Secretary of State Dean Rusk was explaining
that the correct way of describing the American position was one of "non
belligerency."[47] The *Washington Post* suggested that the Johnson administration desired to avoid the use of the term "neutral" because it had too
many "other connotations."[48] While the paper did not define what those
"other connotations" might be, it can be surmised that fear of Zionist
criticism was one of them. Even at the best of times such criticism could
prove politically costly, but with the Vietnam War raging and congressional "doves" suddenly becoming "hawkish" about supporting Israel,[49]
the Johnson administration was loath to confront them. Indeed, accommodating the Zionists might help win their support for the Vietnam War.

Yet even if there had been no Vietnam War, it is doubtful if the Johnson
administration would have adopted policies that ran counter to the desires
of American Zionists. President Lyndon Johnson's perceptions of and attitudes toward Israel were classically bipolar. As one scholar has described
it, "Johnson personally felt great affinity with Israel and Israelis in part
[based] on his religious upbringing and reading of the Old Testament, and
in part [based] on his identification with the Israelis as a frontier people, 'a
modern day version of the Texans fighting the Mexicans.'"[50] These were
more than just personal views. They were part of the historical worldview
we have been examining and so were essentially the same views as those of
Woodrow Wilson and Franklin Roosevelt.

Decolonizing the American Mind

As persistent as has been the bipolar worldview and its influence on
American perceptions of Palestine, it is not necessary to assume that its
continuation is inevitable. Since 1967 the evidence for popular American

perceptions of the Middle East, and Arabs generally, has been less consistent than in the past. In fact, some have seen these perceptions as swinging "like a pendulum . . . between positive and negative depending upon the perceived interests of the United States in the region."[51] To be sure, the stereotype of the Arab as a terrorist has persisted. Thus, immediately following the 1995 bombing of the federal building in Oklahoma City, much of the media assumed, without evidence, an Arab/Muslim connection. On the other hand, Palestinian agreement to the 1993 Oslo Accords, and their ongoing participation in the "peace process," has resulted in a certain amount of "good press" for them and their cause. The brutal response of the Israelis to the Palestinian Intifada of the late 1980s, shown nightly on American television, also brought into public view a picture of Israel and Zionism that gave pause to many Americans. It may be that the persistence of a brutal Israeli military occupation of the West Bank and Gaza Strip—the second-longest military occupation of the twentieth century—plus Palestinian willingness to enter into negotiations, has somewhat undermined popular American assumptions of the bipolar worldview in regard to the occupied territories.

And indeed, there has been a certain wavering in the overwhelming support Zionists have come to expect from the American people. This can be seen in polling data collected from the 1970s onward. In an exhaustive study of the available polling data from the 1970s to 1987, Elia Zureik and Fouad Moughrabi conclude that "there is solid support among the American public for the idea of an independent state for the Palestinian people (roughly 2 to 1 majority favours such an option)."[52] This position is supported by a national poll conducted in May of 1999 that reported 53 percent of Americans "favor . . . the establishment of an independent Palestinian state on the West Bank and the Gaza Strip."[53] Approaching the data in a different way, one can note that amidst crisis in 1967, 56 percent of Americans expressed sympathy for Israel (25 percent had sympathy for neither Israel nor the Arabs, and 15 percent had no opinion).[54] In the fall of 2000, again amidst growing tension between Palestinians and Israelis that would soon lead to prolonged violence, a similar poll conducted by Gallup reported sympathies for Israel at 41 percent (with 18 percent having sympathies for neither Israel nor the Palestinians, and 21 percent no opinion). There would seem to have been an erosion of support for Israeli domination of the Palestinians over the past thirty-three years.

However, does this really translate into "solid support" among present-day Americans for a Palestinian state? It depends how one chooses to read the data. It is probably safe to go so far as to say that an increasing number

222 I America's Palestine

of Americans feel that self-determination for the Palestinians is a prerequisite for a just and lasting peace in the Middle East.

Unfortunately, it is unclear what impact this evolving new attitude can or will have. It runs parallel with a still-solid popular American commitment to Israel's continued existence.[55] And more importantly, it has not resulted in any meaningful shift in the attitudes of U.S. government leaders in either the legislative or executive branches.[56] Thus, while more Americans show a willingness to see the Palestinians as a people with real national and human rights, the U.S. government remains committed to the Zionist interpretation of events. Of course, various administrations, both Democratic and Republican, make the claim that they act as "honest brokers" and "objective mediators" between Israelis and Palestinians. Perhaps this is a rhetorical recognition of a subtle shift in American public opinion in favor of Palestinian rights. However, American diplomatic action, and inaction, has in reality helped the Israelis restrict the Palestinians to "Bantustan-like" enclaves while Zionist settlers continue the colonization of the West Bank and Gaza Strip.

The future therefore is uncertain, both as to the fate of Palestine and the fate of Zionism as an Americanized ideology. In 1915 Louis Brandeis published a pamphlet entitled *The Jewish Problem and How to Solve It*. In this work he called on Americans to support Zionist colonization of Palestine. He asserted that "every American Jew who aids in advancing the Jewish settlement in Palestine . . . will be a better man and a better American for doing so."[57] Brandeis, and the American Zionists who followed him in urging this connection, turned out to be supremely persuasive. As a result, for over eighty years the Zionists have colonized not only Palestine, but the American mind as well. They were able to do so successfully because the Zionist message was seen as consistent with America's bipolar picture of Palestine. However, if, at some point, Zionist behavior becomes popularly perceived as incompatible with the assumed altruistic nature of the West and its world mission, then, like most of the West's other colonial endeavors, Zionism too may lose its appeal to the American mind.

Notes

Abbreviations

CT   *Chicago Tribune*
FRUS   *Foreign Relations of the United States*
LAT   *Los Angeles Times*
NEA   Division of Near Eastern Affairs of the State Department
NYT   *New York Times*
RDS   Records of the Department of State, Record Group 59
WP   *Washington Post*

1. Our Palestine

1. See Weinberg, *Manifest Destiny.*

2. See Phillips, *Protestant America and the Pagan World.*

3. Ibid., 1–31.

4. For an excellent account of this endeavor see Grabill, *Protestant Diplomacy and the Near East,* 3ff.

5. Ibid., chap. 1.

6. For an elaboration of this point of view see Sha'ban, *Islam and Arabs in Early American Thought,* chap. 5.

7. Phillips, *Protestant America and the Pagan World,* 243.

8. President William McKinley explained that "after walking the floor of the White House night after night until midnight" and going down "on my knees and pray[ing] to Almighty God for light and guidance," he came to the following decision as to the Philippines. "That there was nothing left for us to do but to take them all and to educate the Filipinos and uplift and civilize and Christianize them, and by God's grace do the very best we could by them, as our fellow men for whom Christ also died." Cited in Zinn, *A People's History of the United States,* 305–6.

9. Grabill, *Protestant Diplomacy and the Near East,* 14.

10. Merkley, *The Politics of Christian Zionism,* 57.

11. Grabill, *Protestant Diplomacy and the Near East,* 6.

12. The missionary William Thomson's two-volume *View of Syria* published in 1859 was a nationwide best-seller. Grabill estimates that it sold more copies than any other work except *Uncle Tom's Cabin.* Ibid., 39.

13. Earle, "American Missions," 417.

14. For a sense of the Muslim view of the actual state of Palestine, consult Khalidi, *Before Their Diaspora.*

15. See Sha'ban, *Islam and Arabs in Early American Thought,* and also Whitelam, *The Invention of Ancient Israel.*

16. Sha'ban, *Islam and Arabs in Early American Thought,* 91.

17. Grabill, *Protestant Diplomacy and the Near East,* 7.

18. See Shepherd, *The Zealous Intruders.*

19. Cited in DeNovo, *American Interests,* 11

20. See Grabill, *Protestant Diplomacy and the Near East,* 8.

21. Earle, "American Missions," 408, explained the Muslim reaction through the following analogy: "One can imagine the reception which would have been accorded to Moslem missionaries in this country if the situation had been reversed—that is, if New England had been invaded by Moslem missionaries, supplied with adequate funds to erect mosques and Moslem schools, determined to educate young Americans in the ways of the Orient, and protected by treaties of capitulation preventing regulation by American civil authorities."

22. DeNovo, *American Interests,* 21.

23. Ibid., 92–93.

24. Earle, "American Missions," 417.

25. See Fishman, *American Protestantism and a Jewish State,* 17ff.

26. Merkley, *The Politics of Christian Zionism,* 68

27. See Sandeen, *The Roots of Fundamentalism,* 234.

28. Grabill, *Protestant Diplomacy and the Near East,* 178.

2. America and the Balfour Declaration

1. Ingrams, *Palestine Papers,* 18.

2. Ibid., 173.

3. Tessler, *A History,* 146. See also the following State Department documents referring to the Husayn-McMahon correspondence: RDS 867n.01/897; 1251; 1444; 1476; 1501; and 1507.

4. Ingrams, *Palestine Papers,* 174.

5. Great Britain, Foreign Office Papers FO371/3053 (4/27/17), and FO371/3053 (4/28/17).

6. Grose, *Israel in the Mind of America,* 62–63.

7. Ibid., 63.

8. A summary of documents referring to the Balfour Declaration and compiled by the Division of Near Eastern Affairs. See RDS 867n.01/757 (6/6/37).

9. Urofsky, *American Zionism from Herzl to the Holocaust,* 208–9.

10. Grose, *Israel in the Mind of America,* 64.

11. For Wilson's support of Zionism, see Schulte Nordholt, *Woodrow Wilson,* 261; Heckscher, *Woodrow Wilson,* 540; and Ahmed, "Roots of Denial," 29.

12. Wise, *Challenging Years,* 186–87.

13. See Urofsky, *American Zionism from Herzl to the Holocaust,* 217, 230.

14. Link, *The Papers of Woodrow Wilson,* 164–65.

15. Ibid., 298. The Zionists mistakenly thought of House as an ally. In fact, he led them on with sympathetic words while advising Wilson to be cautious of their demands.

16. Ibid., 371.

17. Grose, *Israel in the Mind of America*, 69–70.

18. RDS 867n.01/757, p. 8. See also RDS 867n.01/758.

19. Grabill, *Protestant Diplomacy and the Near East*, 81.

20. Ibid., 116.

21. DeNovo, *American Interests*, 108.

22. Grabill, *Protestant Diplomacy and the Near East*, 92.

23. RDS 867n.01/758, p. 7. The State Department considered these statements of Wilson to be private sentiments and not official U.S. policy. However, Brandeis and the Zionists declared that from that point on an American opposed to Zionism was disloyal to the United States. See Urofsky, *American Zionism from Herzl to the Holocaust*, 218.

24. RDS 867n.01/16.

25. Manuel, *The Realities*, 172.

26. Cited in Ingrams, *Palestine Papers*, 32.

27. Cited in Voss, ed., *Stephen S. Wise: Servant of the People, Selected Letters*, 99.

28. For an explanation of how American Zionists rationalized their opposition to democracy and the liberal Jewish reaction, see Medoff, *Zionism and the Arabs*, 1–28, 43–59.

29. Bustami, "American Foreign Policy," 200. For Lansing, see Grabill, *Protestant Diplomacy and the Near East*, 126.

30. Polk, *The United States and the Arab World*, 120.

31. Urofsky, *American Zionism from Herzl to the Holocaust*, 230.

32. Grose, *Israel in the Mind of America*, 72.

33. Eleven years later the *CT* was using the same comparisons. On the occasion of General Allenby's visit to the United States in October of 1928, the *CT* wrote, "Viscount Allenby . . . who fulfilled ancient prophecies and achieved the dream of the crusaders eleven years ago when he wrested Jerusalem from the Turks." *CT* 10/4/28, 14.

34. As with the *CT*, the *LAT* also saw Allenby's actions in light of the Crusader heritage, eleven years after the war. Commenting on the occasion of Allenby's U.S. visit in the fall of 1928, the *LAT* said that when he captured Jerusalem "the whole of Christendom and Zion thrilled to [an] . . . inspiring campaign in the last of the crusades against the usurpers of ancient Zion." *LAT* 10/12/28, part II, 4.

35. *WP* 10/28/17, 4.

36. Ibid., 11/20/17, 6.

37. Ibid., 12/11/17, 6.

38. Ibid., 12/24/17, 4.

39. *LAT* 11/11/17, 2.

40. Ibid., 12/12/17, 4.

41. *CT* 11/19/17, 1.

42. Ibid., 11/27/17, 2.

43. *NYT* 3/9/17, 6.

44. Ibid., 3/14/17, 8.

45. Ibid., 12/11/17, 2.

46. Additional articles that mirror this stereotyped picture can be found as follows: For the *LAT:* 11/22, part II, 4; 11/25, 2; 11/27, part II, 4; 12/11, 1–2, and part II, 4; 12/24, 4. For the *CT:* 11/25, part II, 7; 11/27, 2. For the *WP:* 11/16, 2; 11/22, 3; 12/11, 6, 11; 12/21, 1; 12/23, sec. III, 7; 12/24, 4; 12/26, 5. For the *NYT:* 3/6, 10; 3/18, sec. VII, 6; 4/15, sec. I, 14; 4/25, 2; 5/29, 3; 6/25, 20; 11/9, 3; 11/25, sec. VII, 8; 11/30, 6; 12/10, 4; 12/15, 12; 12/17, 5; 12/19, 10; 12/24, 9.

47. *NYT* 12/11/17, 1.

48. Articles identifying Arabs as allies, associated with the Sherif Husayn's revolt, appear in 1917 mostly in the *NYT,* and do so between the months of January and October. After that they disappear altogether. See *NYT* 1/13, 2; 2/19, 4; 3/4, sec. V, 10; 3/10, 6; 6/24, sec. I, 3; 7/13, 2; 10/5, 2. See also *WP* 9/2, 1.

49. The one exception was the *LAT,* which devoted only two pieces to Zionism: 11/27, part II, 4, and 12/24, 4. The *CT* published six pieces: 10/15, 2; 11/9, 7; 11/14, 9; 11/24, 1, 2; 11/26, 4; The *WP* put out twelve articles: 11/9, 5; 11/25, 15; 11/28, 11; 11/29, 2; 11/30, 6; 12/12, two pieces, both on 2; 12/17, 4; 12/23, 3; 12/24, 7, 9; 12/30, sec. III, 3. Finally, the *NYT* published thirteen pieces: 11/9, 3; 11/14, 3; 11/16, 22; 11/19, 5; 11/30, 6; 12/3, 4; 12/6, 14; 12/10, 4; 12/15, 11; 12/17, 5, 11; 12/21, 6; 12/24, 3.

50. *CT* 11/24/17, 1.

51. *WP* 11/29/17, 2.

52. *WP* 12/12/17, 1–2. See also *WP* 11/25/17, 15, and 12/12/17, 2.

53. *NYT* 3/9/17, 6.

54. Ibid., 3/18/17, sec. VII, 6. See also *NYT* 11/25/17, sec. VII, 8.

55. Ibid., 12/12/17, 5.

56. See *NYT:* 5/4, 7; 5/6, sec. I, 3, 5; 5/17, 5; 5/19, 4; 5/20, sec. I, 7; 5/21, 12; 5/22, 11; 5/23, 5; 5/27, sec. II, 5; 5/31, 12; 6/3, sec. II, 3; 6/5, 3; 6/13, 8.

57. *NYT* 6/9/17, 20.

58. *NYT* 6/19/17, 11. See also *NYT* 7/18/17, an article dealing with El-kus's impressions of Turkish-Jewish relations in Palestine; *WP* 9/30/17, 11, and 10/8/17, 1.

59. See *NYT:* 6/19, 20; 7/13, 9; 9/2, sec. I, 12; 11/2, 7; 11/25, sec. I, 4; 12/6, 2.

60. *NYT* 12/10/17, 13.

61. Ibid.

62. See *NYT:* 3/18/17, 4; 3/30, 3; 8/24, 15; 11/4, 2; 12/11, 1; 12/13, 5; 12/18, 2; 12/20, 1.

63. See note 49 above.

64. *NYT* 6/25/17, 20.

65. Ibid., 4/25/17, 2.

66. Rafael Medoff argues that "although Arabs constituted more than 80% of

Palestine's population in 1917" they failed to be recognized as a "national group with national rights—largely because the Palestinian Arabs themselves did not claim the status of a specific national grouping." Medoff, *Zionism and the Arabs,* 23. One can only understand this blame-the-victim argument within the context of the Eurocentric assumption that colonialist powers had the right to reshape lands and peoples outside of Europe according to Western concepts such as nationalism.

67. See *NYT*: 5/7/17, 8; 5/14, 9; 5/29, 3; 11/19, 5; 11/30, 6; 12/6, 14; 12/10, 4; 12/21, 6; 12/24, 9.

68. *NYT* 12/15/17, 11.

69. *NYT* 12/13/17, 4. See also 12/17, 5. This latter article describes a $100 million fund "for constructive and administrative work in the new Jewish state."

70. *WP* 11/25/17, 15.

71. Ibid., 11/29/17, 2.

72. *WP*: 11/16, 2; 11/22, 3; 12/11, 6, 11; 12/21, 1; 12/23, sec. III, 7; 12/24, 4; 12/26, 5.

73. For the additional quote for Coffee, see *CT* 10/15/17, 2. See also *CT* 11/7/17, 7, and 11/14/17, 9.

74. *NYT* 12/17/17, 5. The same convention was covered by the *WP* 12/17/17, 4.

75. *NYT* 12/24/17, 17.

76. Ibid., 12/12/17, 14.

77. Ibid., 5/24/17, 16.

78. *Times* (London), 6/18/17, 5.

79. *NYT* 11/25/17, sec IX, 3. See also *NYT* 12/16/17, sec. IV, 4, and 12/5/17, 24. Similar sentiments were expressed by Rabbi Louis Grossmann of the Plum Street Temple in Cincinnati, Ohio, in a letter to President Wilson received at the White House in September 1918. Trying to warn Wilson away from Zionism, he writes "Nor may Christian romanticism which looks in this Zionistic Nationalism for a fulfillment of biblical prophecies delude you, Mr. President. . . . you know that prophecies and their theological implications are not historic fact. As the President of the United States, I am sure, you are not disposed to bend state policy to satisfy biblical hermeneutics. . . . Romanticism can have no standing in so sober a matter as the permanence and unassailability of citizenship." RDS 867n.01/28. It is impossible to know if the President ever read this. However, the writer may have been wrong in his assumption that Wilson could keep his "Christian romanticism" out of politics. When it came to Palestine, the American public and press proved incapable of doing so.

80. *NYT* 6/10/17, 16.

81. Ibid., 11/24/17, 12.

82. *LAT* 11/27/17, part XI, 4.

83. Ibid., 12/24/17, 4.

84. For evidence that such misgivings persisted right up until the founding of Israel, see Kolsky, *Jews against Zionism.*

85. See Khalidi, *Before Their Diaspora,* and Doumani, *Rediscovering Palestine.*

3. Early Perceptions of Mandate Palestine

1. Medoff, *Zionism and the Arabs,* 34. To put it crudely, in 1920, the League functioned as a "front" for the Allies.

2. Grose, *Israel in the Mind of America,* 91.

3. *NYT* 5/12/20, 16.

4. *LAT* 2/6/21, part II, 32.

5. The *NYT* published the King-Crane Report on 11/4/22, 13, 14, and 12/3/22, sec. II, 2. In an editorial, the *Times* commented that "If this exhumed report could have been given to the public when it was submitted, or soon after, it might have helped to prevent the inauguration or continuance of three policies that go counter to the commission's findings: a divided Syria, a Zionistic program in Palestine, and the control of upper Syria by a power [France] that was persona non grata to a large part of the population." *NYT* 8/30/22, sec. II, 4.

6. As the rest of Balfour's speech shows, the British desire to obtain League ratification of the Palestine mandate had nothing to do with any recognition of League authority over mandate territory. Rather, it had to do with British recognition of the fact that international loans for economic development in Palestine would come easier after ratification. See *NYT* 6/18/22, sec. VI, 6.

7. *NYT* 4/2/21, 2.

8. *NYT* 6/18/22, sec. VI, 6.

9. *NYT* 4/26/20, 1.

10. Quoted in the *NYT* 7/5/20, 17.

11. *NYT* 7/18/20, 22.

12. *NYT* 10/26/20, 21.

13. *NYT* 7/20/20, 15.

14. *NYT* 4/17/20, 1.

15. *NYT* 4/18/20, 17. See also *NYT* 4/9/20, 25.

16. *NYT* 5/3/21, 19. See also *NYT* 5/4/21, 7; 5/5/21, 2; 5/6/21, 5; 5/8/21, 17; 6/4/21, 2.

17. *NYT* 4/17/20, 1.

18. *NYT* 2/5/21, 11.

19. *NYT* 2/6/21, sec. II, 2.

20. *NYT* 4/27/20, 2, and 5/4/22, 19.

21. *WP* 2/11/21, 6.

22. Throughout this period the owner of the *NYT* was Adolph Ochs, the sophisticated and successful son of Jewish immigrants. Ochs was not a Zionist and once remarked, "I know no other definition for a Jew except religion." Cited in Salisbury, *Without Fear or Favor: The "New York Times" and Its Times,* 29.

23. Besides those cited below, see also, for example, *NYT* 10/7/21, 3; 8/18/21, 16; 12/4/21, part X, 20.

24. *NYT* 2/17/21, 2.

25. *NYT* 5/11/21, 18.

26. *NYT* 12/25/21, part II, 3.

27. An August 1922 dispatch from the American consulate in Jerusalem describes "the militant sections of the dissatisfied Arab populace" as engaging in "covert attacks on the Jewry of Palestine by assassination in retaliation for the Zionist encroachment on their land." George C. Cobb, the vice consul writing the report, describes these actions as follows: "In each of the crimes reported a cold deliberation of the most callous Apache character has been apparent." RDS 867n.01/308 (8/26/22).

28. *NYT* 6/11/22, sec. VII, 7.

29. *NYT* 6/25/22, sec. VII, 7.

30. See *NYT* 5/7/22, 6, and 5/21, sec. VI, 12.

31. See *NYT* 1/9/22, 18; 11/26, sec. VIII, 5; 11/9, 12; 12/24, sec. VIII, 4.

32. See *NYT* 1/1/22, 3; 3/13, 15; 4/3, 15; 4/17, 36; 5/15, 6; 6/14, 2; 9/18, 8; and 12/22, 25.

33. In 1923 the *NYT* published 41 articles, 23 of which were favorable to Zionism or the Palestine mandate. Most of the remainder can be seen as reporting of fact without comment. In 1924 there were 18 articles, of which 13 were pro-Zionist and 5 can be judged as critical of Zionism or the mandate.

34. *NYT* 8/11/20, 15.

35. *NYT* 4/13/21, 5.

36. *NYT* 7/10/21, part II, 3.

37. Ibid.

38. See the *NYT* 7/14/22, 25; 7/15/22, 4; 7/16/22, 14; and 9/12/22, 4.

39. *LAT* 8/22/22, part II, 4.

40. *NYT* 3/31/22, 6.

41. Ibid. The *NYT* took Lodge to task for his about-face. See 4/14/22, 16.

42. RDS 867n.01/199 (4/10/22).

43. On May 22, 1922, Allen Dulles wrote to Assistant Secretary of State Leland Harrison stating that he felt "strongly that the Department should avoid any action which would indicate official support of any one of the various theses regarding Palestine, either the Zionist, the anti-Zionist or the Arabs." He went on to describe the Zionists as "an influential and noisy group" whose claims had "a certain sentimental appeal" but had to be measured against the "cold fact . . . that the Jews in Palestine constitute about 10% of the population." He concluded that "If our policy is to let alone the political and territorial phases of that settlement [the Great Power division of Near Eastern territory after World War I] I see no reason why we should become pro-Zionists. . . . I thought it best to bring this matter to your attention in view of the Senate Resolution . . . which may result in added pressure on the Department to take some stand in the matter." RDS 867n.01/214 (5/22/22).

44. RDS 867n.01/1714 (6/17/40).

45. This is not the opinion of pro-Zionist historians. For instance, Manuel, *The Realities*, 271, states that the State Department's attitude toward the 1922 resolu-

tion was one of "covert hostility" and that "the foreign service careerists . . . did all they could to prevent the resolutions from passing." In reality, all Dulles and his staff did was write a number of internal memos. They never went outside the State Department in voicing their concerns.

46. *NYT* 6/14/22, 3.

47. House Foreign Affairs Committee, *Establishment of a National Home in Palestine,* 67th Cong., 2nd sess., House Congressional Resolution 52, April 18–21, 1922, 161.

48. Ibid.

49. Ibid., 156.

50. Lydon, "American Images of the Arabs," 156.

51. *NYT* 9/22/22, 2. Harding had long been sympathetic to the Zionist cause. On June 1, 1921, he had written to ZOA leaders that "It is impossible for one who has studied at all the services of the Hebrew people to avoid the faith that they will one day be restored to their historic national home, and there enter on a new and yet greater phase of their contribution to the advance of humanity." Quoted in House Committee, *Establishment of a National Home in Palestine,* 11.

52. *NYT* 1/9/23, 23. The theme of Arab violence was a major category of American perceptions of that people. See Hammons, "'A Wild Ass of a Man,'" chap. 3.

53. Laqueur, *History of Zionism,* 270.

54. Y. Shapiro, *The Formative Years,* 58.

55. Edelman, *David,* 61.

56. Y. Shapiro, *The Formative Years,* 13.

57. See *NYT* 12/18/27, sec. III, 8.

58. See Urofsky, "Zionism," 224.

59. *NYT* 7/21/20, 17; 2/17/21, 2; 5/4/21, 7; 2/18/23, 10; 5/1/26, 16; 3/25/28, 4; 4/22/28, sec. III, 6; 5/27/28, sec. III, 3; 6/10/28, sec. III, 6; 10/14/28, 29; 1/27/29, sec. III, 7; 3/30/29, 17. The press got much of their information from the Zionist Organization of America and the Jewish Telegraphic Agency.

60. *NYT* 5/1/26, 16.

61. RDS 867n.00/4 (5/2/21).

62. RDS 867n.01/153.

63. Handlin, "American Views," 1–21.

64. *NYT* 11/26/22, 5.

65. See Weizmann, *Trial and Error,* 58.

66. Ibid., 301.

67. Manuel, *The Realities,* 275–76. Though Manuel does not put it this way, Congress and the president can be seen in a public orbit subject to electoral politics. The State Department "careerists" were in a private orbit not subject to such pressure.

68. Grose, *Israel in the Mind of America,* 99.

69. N. Cohen, *The Year after the Riots,* 17ff.

70. RDS 867n.01/227 (5/26/22).

71. RDS 867n.01/214 (5/22/22).

72. RDS 867n.01/362. Rabbi Glazer had been promoting the Zionist cause among the Washington political elite for several years.

73. RDS 867n.01/362.

74. Ibid.

75. Ibid. See also consular report entitled "The Palestinian Census," RDS 867n.5011/2 (1/23/23). According to Zaha Bustami, Hughes's reply to Slemp was drafted by Allen Dulles. See Bustami, "American Foreign Policy," 299.

76. See DeNovo, *American Interests,* 38–40.

77. *CT* 2/23/21, 4. See also *NYT* 5/10/22, 1, and *WP* 2/24/21, 6.

78. *WP* 2/24/21, 6.

79. *NYT* 5/10/22, 1. See also *CT* 7/18/22, 7, and *LAT* 7/18/22, 7.

80. RDS 867n.6363/2 (8/12/21). See also Manuel, *The Realities,* 267ff.

81. RDS 867n.6363/8 (10/27/21).

82. RDS 867n.6363/10 (11/17/21).

83. RDS 867n.6363/10 (11/30/21).

84. RDS 867n.6363/11 (10/27/21).

85. RDS 867n.6363/23 (12/28/21).

86. RDS 867n.6363/31 (1/20/22).

87. RDS 867n.6363/25 (1/21/22).

88. RDS 867n.6363/41 (4/6/22).

89. RDS 867n.6363/49 (3/28/22).

90. Ibid.

91. RDS 867n.6363/62 (10/29/23).

92. RDS 867n.6363/69 (2/26/24).

93. Ibid.

94. RDS 867n.6363/65 (11/28/23).

4. The Calm before the Storm

1. See Merkley, *The Politics of Christian Zionism.*

2. Katibah, *The Case against Zionism,* 46. A copy of this work is in the New York Public Library. Also see the Arab American newspaper *The Syrian World,* published in New York City, for the spring of 1929; and Suleiman, "Arab Americans and the Political Process," 37–60. Finally, a *NYT* piece of 1/13/29, sec. III, 8, tells of the demand for a "Palestine Parliament" made by the Arabs in Palestine.

3. *NYT* 1/7/26, 25.

4. See, for example, 1/31, 16; 2/8, sec. VIII, 7; 3/2, 10; 4/1, 10; 4/25, 22; 5/4, 6; 5/23, 14; 6/12, 29; 6/22, 17; 7/5, sec. II, 3; 7/28, 39; 8/11, 23; 8/24, 12; 10/6, 2; 10/25, 29; 11/3, 37; 11/29, sec. IX, 6; 12/9, 20; 12/20, 2. The *NYT* printed 43 articles on Palestine and Zionism in 1926, 35 of which were favorable to the Zionist movement. In 1927 there were 33 articles, 29 of which were pro-Zionist. In 1928 there were 32, of which 23 were favorable to Zionism. The minority of articles that were not obviously pro-Zionist were most often factual pieces depicting troubles in Palestine. For the thoughtful reader these might have called into ques-

tion the rosy picture of those articles favoring the Zionists. These few were not, however, overtly favorable to the Palestinian Arabs.

5. *NYT* 7/28/25, 39.

6. *NYT* 12/20/25, 2.

7. *NYT* 5/3/25, sec. II, 16.

8. Ibid.

9. *NYT* 11/29/25, sec. IX, 6.

10. *NYT* 8/11/25, 23. See also *NYT* 4/12/25, 2.

11. *NYT* 1/16/25, 8, and 2/1/25, sec. VIII, 4. Several other *NYT* pieces reported on Arab disturbances over the visit of Arthur Balfour to Palestine in March 1925. These, however, were not accompanied by an explanation of the Arab position. See 3/25, 2; 3/27, 3; 3/8, 2; 3/29, 3; 4/9, 2; 4/10, 2; and 4/14, 2.

12. *NYT* 1/16/25, 8.

13. *NYT* 1/19/25, 15.

14. See, for example, the following 1926 *NYT* articles: 1/15, 12; 2/21, 13; 4/1, 7; 5/16, sec. II, 20; 5/23, sec. II, 20; 6/1, 16; 6/28, 7; 6/29, 12; 7/16, 9; 8/8, sec. VIII, 14; 9/19, 27; 9/28, 4; 11/9, 28; 11/12, 8; 11/19, 25; 12/1, 26; 12/6, 20; 12/13, 40.

15. *NYT* 8/8/26, sec. VIII, 14.

16. *NYT* 11/9/26, 17.

17. *NYT* 1/15/26, 12.

18. *NYT* 4/1/26, 7.

19. *NYT* 4/15/26, sec. II, 4.

20. *NYT* 9/6/26, p. 17.

21. See Tessler, *A History*, 179, and Shafir, *Land, Labor, and the Origins*, chap. 3.

22. Cited in the report of Vice Consul Aldridge to the State Department, RDS 867n.01/467.5 (9/27/26).

23. RDS 867n.01/467.5 (11/5/26).

24. See a corroborating *NYT* piece of 3/12/26, 5, entitled "15,000 Poles Go to Palestine."

25. RDS 867n.01/467.5 (11/5/26). Aldridge noted in his report that "the Arab elements in Palestine, needless to say, find unusual solace and comfort in the difficulties now facing Zionist endeavors."

26. *NYT* 5/9/26, sec. II, 20.

27. *NYT* 9/12/26, sec. II, 4. Most of these "motor vehicles" were American made. See *NYT* 4/25/26, sec. II, 4.

28. *NYT* 9/19/26, 27.

29. *NYT* 5/11/27, 19. See also *NYT* 7/18/26, sec. II, 18, and 11/19/26, 25.

30. See, for instance, *NYT* 6/1/26, 16, and 6/9/26, 38. The latter piece detailed "nearly $49 million of Jewish capital invested in Palestine from October 1, 1917 until March 31, 1926."

31. RDS 867n.01/467.5 (9/26/26).

32. *NYT* 12/18/27, sec. III, 8.

33. Weizmann, *Trial and Error*, 126.

34. *NYT* 12/18/27, sec. III, 8.
35. *NYT* 1/29/28, sec. III, 6.
36. *NYT* 6/10/28, sec. III, 1. See also 11/4/28, sec. III, 6.
37. Shafir, *Land, Labor, and the Origins,* 89.
38. See *NYT* 3/25/28, 4; 4/22/28, sec. III, 6; 5/27/28, sec. III, 3; and 6/10/28, sec. III, 6.
39. *NYT* 11/29/26, 1.
40. Pritchett, "Observations," 519–20.
41. *NYT* 11/30/26, 11.
42. Wise was surely being disingenuous here. The Zionists were so sure that such would not be the case in a democratic vote that they stood opposed to democracy in Palestine. See Medoff, *Zionism and the Arabs,* 43–44.
43. *NYT* 12/6/26, 20.
44. Tessler, *A History,* 174ff.
45. *NYT* 11/30/26, 28.
46. *NYT* 12/5/26, sec. II, 1.
47. *NYT* 4/12/27, 17. See also Felix Warburg's comment that "the problems between Arab and Jew are rapidly diminishing." *NYT* 6/18/27, 20.
48. See *NYT* 7/6/27, 43.
49. Ibid.
50. *NYT* 9/2/27, 15.
51. In 1928 the British would actually begin to restrict Jewish immigration because of the high unemployment. See *NYT* 11/4/28, sec. III, 6, and 12/18/28, 4.
52. *NYT* 10/31/27, 8.
53. *NYT* 9/8/27, 5.
54. For the background to the tension between European and American Zionists at this time, see Y. Shapiro, *Leadership.*
55. *NYT* 9/11/27, 30.
56. See Kolinsky, *Law, Order, and Riots,* 11. Kolinsky observes that "the concept of the 'Jewish National Home' was interpreted differently by successive British administrations. What they had in common was a rejection of the idea that the Jewish National Home should lead to statehood."
57. *NYT* 8/12/28, sec. II, 2.
58. *NYT* 9/2/28, sec. II, 21.
59. *NYT* 5/9/26, sec. II, 20.
60. *NYT* 5/10/22, 1.
61. *NYT* 12/30/28, sec. III, 6.
62. RDS 867n.156/81 (7/24/28).
63. RDS 867n.156/10 (10/20/28).
64. Ibid. See also RDS 867n.156/11.
65. RDS 867n.156/10.
66. RDS 867n.156/11.
67. Ibid.
68. RDS 867n.156/15 (6/25/29).

69. Ibid.

70. Ibid.

71. Ibid.

72. *NYT* 11/15/25, 15.

73. RDS 867n.404/21 (9/28/28).

74. Ibid.

75. *WP* 10/3/28, 4.

76. RDS 867n.404/21.

77. Ibid.

78. *NYT* 10/28/28, sec. III, 8.

79. Ibid.

80. Ibid.

81. Klatzker, "British Jerusalem in the News," 38.

82. *LAT* 9/26/28, part I, 8.

5. Storm: The 1929 Rebellion

1. *NYT* 1/20/29, sec. III, 6, and 3/30/29, 17.

2. *NYT* 1/11/29, 38; 3/10/29, 40; 7/4/29, 5.

3. *NYT* 1/20/29, sec. III, 6.

4. *NYT* 1/20/29, sec. III, 6, and 7/4/29, 5.

5. *NYT* 6/12/29, 30.

6. The figure is for the period of October 1917 to March 1926. See *NYT* 6/9/26, 30.

7. *NYT* 1/20/29, sec. III, 6.

8. *NYT* 4/7/29, sec. X, 17.

9. Ibid.

10. See also *NYT* 4/17/29, 26; 5/1/29, 6; and 5/24/29, 16.

11. *NYT* 3/11/29, 31.

12. RDS 867n.01/1398 (1/10/39), p. 3.

13. *NYT* 4/7/29, sec. X, 17.

14. *NYT* 1/13/29, sec. III, 8.

15. *NYT* 8/4/29, sec. II, 6. See also the Levy articles of 9/16/29, 6; 11/1/29, 9; and 11/4/29, 10.

16. *NYT* 4/12/25, 2.

17. Alternatively, it has been argued that they are not necessarily reduced to invisibility but rather to museum pieces. See Mitchell, *Colonizing Egypt.*

18. Urofsky, *American Zionism from Herzl to the Holocaust,* 241–42.

19. For a detailed discussion of the 1929 rebellion, see Kolinsky, *Law, Order, and Riots,* chap. 3.

20. *NYT* 6/12/29, 30.

21. *LAT* 8/26/29, 4. Occurring before the Nazis rose to power, Sheean's use of the term "Fascisti" referred to similarities he drew between the behavior of elements of the Revisionist movement and the Italian Fascists. For this connection, see Laqueur, *History of Zionism,* 361–65. Sheean's piece was printed not only in

the *LAT*, but also in other papers, such as the *New York World*. In the case of the *World*, the piece brought so many protest letters that Sheean's reports were dropped. According to Klatzker, "British Jerusalem in the News," 38, Sheean's critical treatment of the Zionsts meant that, when it came to Palestine, he "never again covered events for the daily press."

22. *NYT* 8/18/29, 1.
23. *NYT* 9/3/29, 1. See also 8/25/29, 1.
24. *LAT* 8/24/29, 1.
25. *LAT* 8/30/29, 1.
26. *CT* 8/27/29, 1.
27. *WP* 8/24/29, 4. See also 8/25/29, 10.
28. These words were used to describe the Palestinian Arabs by Congressman William Isovich in an August 26, 1929, telegram to the State Department. RDS 867n.404WW/18.
29. *CT* 8/27/29, 14.
30. *CT* 8/29/29, 14.
31. *CT* 8/31/29, 8.
32. *NYT* 8/29/29, 22.
33. *NYT* 8/28/29, 24.
34. *NYT* 9/1/29, sec. III, 4.
35. *NYT* 8/27/29, 26.
36. *LAT* 8/30/29, sec. II, 4.
37. *LAT* 9/4/29, sec. II, 4.
38. *LAT* 8/30/29, sec. II, 4.
39. *WP* 8/28/29, 6.
40. *WP* 8/29/29, 8.
41. *WP* 8/28/29, 6. See also 8/27/29, 6.
42. *CT* 8/29/29, 14.
43. RDS 867n.404WW/23 (8/23/29).
44. The term was used by, among others, Congressman Emanuel Celler in a communication to Secretary of State Stimson, RDS 867n.404WW/3 (8/23/29). See also Louis Gross to Stimson, RDS 867n.404WW/10 (8/24/29).
45. Paul Knabenshue based much of his opinion in this regard on the investigations of journalist Vincent Sheean (see note 21 of this chapter, above), whom he knew very well. He had even forwarded copies of Sheean's dispatches to the State Department. See RDS 867n.404WW/264 (10/19/29), p. 2 as well as 867n.404WW/268 (11/2/29) and 867n.404WW/276 (1/2/30).
46. RDS 867n.404WW/268 (11/2/29), p. 1.
47. RDS 867n.404WW/269 (12/9/29), p. 15. The Article 22, paragraph 4, referred to reads "Certain communities formerly belonging to the Turkish Empire have reached a stage of development where their existence as independent nations can be provisionally recognized subject to the rendering of administrative advice and assistance by a Mandatory until such time as they are able to stand alone." Knabenshue felt that this clause "must be recognized as giving legal validity to the

establishment of representative government in Palestine under the advice and assistance of the Mandatory" and anything that conflicted with it was "null and void." RDS 867n.404WW/269, p. 13.

48. RDS 867n.404WW/269 (12/9/29), p. 14. The emphasis is in the original.

49. RDS 867n.404WW/268 (11/2/29), p. 5.

50. Ibid., p. 12.

51. RDS 867n.404WW/273 (11/16/29), p. 4.

52. Ibid., p. 5.

53. Ibid. Compare Knabenshue's position to Naomi Cohen's assertion that the consul general's views, as expressed to the State Department, were both "anti-Zionist and anti-Semitic." N. Cohen, *The Year after the Riots*, 28.

54. RDS 867n.404WW/273 (11/16/29), p. 3.

55. Ibid., p. 6.

56. See RDS 867n.404WW/169, 252, 253, and 257.

57. RDS 867n.404WW/273 (11/16/29), p. 6.

58. For instance, on the banners (which read "America Act") carried at the protest march of "15,000 to 20,000" in New York City on August 26, 1929 (see *NYT* 8/27/29, 3), and the resolutions of the protest meeting of Chicago Jews on August 26, 1929 (see *CT* 8/27/29, 4). See also report of Washington, D.C., protest meeting in *WP* 9/2/12, 12.

59. Most of the letters and telegrams to the State Department can be found between RDS 867n.404WW/3 and 165. According to *NYT* 9/4/29, 9, the department had received "1,000 letters" by this date.

60. RDS 867n.404WW/13. See also a similar appeal from Representative Hamilton Fish reported in *NYT* 8/29/29, 3.

61. RDS 867n.404WW/80 (8/28/29).

62. RDS 867n.404WW/84 (8/24/29).

63. For press accounts emphasizing American citizen involvement and investment in Palestine, see *NYT* 8/26/29, 1; 8/29/29, 3; 8/30/29, 1, 5; 9/1/29, 2; 9/2/29, 1; 9/3/29, 20; 9/5/29, 9; 9/10/29, 6; 10/5/29, 22; 11/4/29, 15; 11/18/29, 6; *CT* 8/26/29, 1; 8/27/29, 1, 14; 8/29/29, 10, 11, 14; 8/31/29, 2; 9/13/29, 22; *WP* 8/26/29, 1; 8/29/29, 8; 9/11/29, 4; 9/21/29, 5; *LAT* 8/27/29, 1; 8/30/29, 2; 9/3/29, 1.

64. RDS 867n.404WW/80 (8/28/29).

65. RDS 867n.404WW/14 (8/26/29).

66. RDS 867n.404WW/156 (9/3/29).

67. RDS 867n.404WW/14 (8/26/29).

68. RDS 867n.404WW/156 (9/3/29).

69. *NYT* 9/2/29, 2.

70. Medoff, *Zionism and the Arabs*, 58.

71. *NYT* 8/29/29, 2. The *Syrian World* described the same meeting as a "national convention" of the "three organized bodies." See vol. IV, no. 1 (September 1929), 51–52.

72. *NYT* 9/7/29, 3.

73. Ibid.

74. *NYT* 8/30/29, 1, and *NYT* 9/4/29, 8.

75. *NYT* 8/28/29, 1.

76. See Bustami, "American Foreign Policy," 328. Under pressure from Hoover and the State Department, the Zionists toned down a letter of protest to the British government. See *WP* 8/28/29, 2.

77. RDS 867n.404WW/52; 61; 228; etc.

78. RDS 867n.01/543 (11/5/30). See also Bustami, "American Foreign Policy," 356.

79. For examples, see RDS 867n.01/90 (2/5/20); 867n.01/214 (5/2/22); 867n.01/199 (9/19/22); 86n.01/474.5 (12/1/26); 867n.404WW/255 (9/23/29); 8677n.404WW/257 (10/21/29); and 867n.01/539.5 (10/23/30).

80. This conclusion can be compared with those of Baram in *Department of State*, 248. Here Baram describes the American Zionists as "frequently weak from the standpoint of . . . public relations." It is to be noted that Baram does not pay much attention to the popular press in his research.

81. *LAT* 8/30/29, sec. II, 4.

82. Again, one can contrast this conclusion with the point of view of Baram, *Department of State*, 248. Here Baram asserts that the American Zionists were "increasingly the losers from the mid-1920s on" in the "duel between the State Department and the American Zionists."

6. The 1930s: New Storm and Subtle Changes

1. This pressure came not only from Jewish sources, but also from anti-Semitic governments such as that in Poland. For instance, on October 10, 1936, the U.S. embassy in Geneva informed the State Department that "During the mandates discussion . . . the Polish representative [on the Mandates Commission of the League of Nations] stated that the over-population of Poland obliged the Jews, whose economic structure did not readily fit in with the social evolution of the country, to seek emigration outlets and he therefore hoped that the troubles in Palestine would not . . . cause any change in the immigration policy." RDS 867n.00/397 (10/6/36). See also RDS 867n.01/800 and *NYT* 3/5/37, 2.

2. See Tessler, *A History,* 237.

3. *NYT* 6/21/36, 15. There were a few informed Americans who agreed. William Ernest Hocking, a well-known Harvard professor of philosophy, wrote into the *NYT* to observe that the Zionist effort "amounts to an unenlightened proposal to bring one group an impractical relief, without regard to the entailed sufferings of another group, and the certainty of further inflaming discord and hatred." *NYT* 6/14/36, sec. IV, 9. See also letters in the *NYT* 6/28/38, sec. IV, 9, and 6/5/36, 20.

4. RDS 867n.00/329, p. 1. See also *NYT* 12/22/35, 24.

5. *NYT* 12/23/35, 9; 12/29/35, sec. IV, 5; and 2/17/36, 10.

6. *NYT* 2/5/36, 15.

7. *NYT* 3/25/36, 15

8. RDS 867n.00/715, p. 2. It was this sort of experience that led Dr. Hussein Khalidi, mayor of Jerusalem, to comment, "When Arabs read speeches and de-

bates of the British Parliament they are filled with despair because not a word is spoken in their favor." *NYT* 1/17/37, 27.

9. *CT* 5/26/36, 1. For a description of how Palestinian Arabs saw their resistance during the years 1936–39, see Swedenburg, *Memories of Revolt*.

10. See, for example, *NYT* 4/18/36, 1; 6/22/36, 1; 6/28/36, 12; *CT* 5/27/36, 1; 5/30/36, 6; *LAT* 5/22/36, 1; 5/30/36, 1; *WP* 4/20/36, 4; 5/24/36, sec. III, 4; 5/27/36, 5.

11. *WP* 5/27/36, 8.

12. *LAT* 5/20/36, part II, 4; and 5/30/36, 1.

13. *CT* 4/21/36, 7; 4/28/36, 5; and 5/15/36, 16.

14. *NYT* 5/15/36, 16.

15. *NYT* 1/19/36, sec. IV, 5. An earlier *WP* editorial asserted that Americans did not fear the fact that "the white races are losing ground numerically in comparison to the dark races" because "the white race, the builder of civilization, will exercise intelligence enough to remain supreme." *WP* 9/28/28, 6.

16. *NYT* 5/31/36, 14. For more information on the Pro-Palestine Federation, see Merkley, *The Politics of Christian Zionism*, 106ff.

17. *NYT* 6/21/36, sec. IV, 9.

18. *NYT* 6/17/36, 22.

19. *NYT* 6/8/36, 12, and 6/17/36, 22.

20. *NYT* 4/21/36, 22.

21. *WP* 5/27/36, 8.

22. *NYT* 5/31/36, sec. IV, 4.

23. *NYT* 6/28/36, 12.

24. *NYT* 6/30/36, 14.

25. *NYT* 6/17/36, 18.

26. Ibid.

27. *WP* 5/24/36, sec. III, 4.

28. *WP* 5/28/36, 1.

29. *LAT* 5/30/36, 1.

30. *LAT* 5/20/36, 1.

31. *LAT* 5/20/36, part II, 4.

32. *CT* 5/15/36, 16. See also 4/28/36, 5, and 4/21/36, 7.

33. *CT* 5/30/36, 6.

34. *CT* 4/30/36, 10.

35. *CT* 4/29/36, 10.

36. *LAT* 5/15/36, 6.

37. *LAT* 5/16/36, part II, 4.

38. *CT* 5/15/36, 20.

39. *WP* 5/16/36, 6.

40. *NYT* 5/15/36, 24.

41. *NYT* 5/19/36, 22.

42. RDS 867n.00/334 and 867n.01/1180 (10/15/38).

43. Ibid. Rosenblatt to Rifkind.

44. Ibid. Rifkind to Sam Rosenman.

45. Ibid. Rosenman to Franklin D. Roosevelt (7/16/36).

46. Ibid. FDR to Moore (7/21/36).

47. Ibid. Murray to Hull (7/25/36). See also 867n.01/744 (1/18/37).

48. For an assessment of Secretary of State Hull, see Drummond, "Cordell Hull," 184–209.

49. RDS 867n.00/334 (7/27/36).

50. Ibid. Hull to FDR (7/27/36).

51. Ibid. Murray to Phillips (8/6/36).

52. See, for instance, the dismissive judgment of Peter Grose, that "the State Department made only perfunctory attempts to learn the scope and nature of Jewish investment in Palestine." Grose, *Israel in the Mind of America*, 100.

53. RDS 867n.01/728 (9/16/36). In August 1937 Wadsworth had an interview with the mufti of Jerusalem and told him that "our concern in these matters [the happenings in the Middle East] was limited to the American interests involved which, in the case of Palestine, were as he would readily understand, in large measure Jewish." RDS 867n.01/860.

54. RDS 867n.00/420.

55. Ibid., p. 34. In the State Department's assessment of U.S. economic relations with Palestine, such investments were noted as "invisible items" and recognized as significant additions to what was otherwise a minuscule rate of economic exchange between the United States and Palestine. See RDS 867n.01/928 (9/17/37).

56. Actually, the Zionists knew this argument was "unsound" and later, in 1944, admitted so to State Department personnel. See RDS 867n.01/2337F (4/20/44).

57. RDS 867n.01/928 (9/17/37), p. 36.

58. *NYT* 9/7/36, 4.

59. See RDS 867n.00/343–382 for letters received by the State Department on violence in Palestine and the issue of possible suspension of Jewish immigration.

60. RDS 867n.01/709 (5/16/36).

61. Ibid.

62. RDS 867n.00/403 (10/16/36). The resolutions were also sent to "our Congressmen and Senators." For other Arab American communications, see RDS 867n.00/427.

63. Ibid.

64. *NYT* 6/6/37, 37.

65. *NYT* 6/9/37, 30.

66. RDS 867n.00/430. A group of American academics and clergymen acting in support of the Arab Palestinian cause visited Hull on July 20, 1937 (see RDS 867n.01/807). Also, in discussions with Wallace Murray prior to seeing Secretary of State Hull, Peter George informed the chief of the Division of Near Eastern Affairs that Ameen Rihani was to tour "84 schools" presenting the Arab point of view. He also said that discussions with American Jewish "intellectual groups" were ongoing. See RDS 867n.00/434.

67. See RDS 867n.00/430 (2/1/37) and also 867n.00/434.

68. RDS 867n.00/431.

69. *NYT* 2/2/37, 12.

70. RDS 867n.00/430.

71. RDS 867n.00/811.

72. Ibid. See also RDS 867n.01/860.5.

73. Ibid.

74. The Division of Near Eastern Affairs closely followed the debate among American Zionists over partition and came to the conclusion that Wise really "represents only a small minority viewpoint" (see RDS 867n.01/907.5). Also, Wallace Murray distributed to his superiors an article taken from the *New York Herald Tribune* in July of 1937 which reported on an opinion poll conducted by the *Jewish Morning Journal*. The poll claimed that 73 percent of those Jews contacted were in favor of the British partition plan (see RDS 867n.01/813 and /946). None of this information seems to have caused either Murray or Hull to hesitate in using Wise's position as representative of American Jewry when it came to presenting those views to the British. Perhaps this was because Wise seems to have had much more influence in Congress and the White House than did Lipsky or any other American Jewish leader.

75. *CT* 7/9/37, 14.

76. RDS 867n.01/737 (2/24/37).

77. RDS 867n.01/445 (4/5/37).

78. RDS 867n.01/466 (6/8/37). See also 867n.00/465 (6/4/37). For information on Wise's relationship with FDR, see Merkley, *The Politics of Christian Zionism,* 121ff. Just how "deep" FDR's concern was is a matter of debate. See Adler, "The Roosevelt Administration and Zionism," 132–48.

79. RDS 867n.00/480 (7/2/37). Wise met with Hull on July 12. See *LAT* 7/13/37, 2.

80. RDS 867n.01/847.

81. Manuel, *The Realities,* 305.

82. RDS 867n.01/741, Hull to Tydings (4/5/37).

83. RDS 867n.00/465 and 867n.00/466 (6/12/37).

84. RDS 867n.00/453 (5/3/37). See also 867n.01/759 and 8867n.01/758.5 (6/22/37).

85. Many of the newspapers under consideration worked under the same assumption, namely, that the U.S. government had a real legal basis from which to veto British decisions that impacted the Palestine mandate. See *CT* 7/8/37, 5, and 7/12/37, 10; and *WP* 7/9/37, 1.

86. RDS 867n.01/759 (6/10/37). See also 867n.01/780.5 (7/8/37), p. 3.

87. RDS 867n.01/879.

88. RDS 867n.01/769 (6/14/37).

89. The possibility of such a confrontation was conjured up in the tough talk that came from some ZOA supporters. For instance, Senator Copeland of New York told the *WP,* "I am not in favor of going to war with Great Britain over the

question [of Palestine], but I think this government, in solemn and set terms, should make clear to the British that it would be a violation of our treaty . . . if they fail to take into consideration the views which we hold." *WP* 7/9/37, 2.

90. RDS 867n.01/791a (7/12/37–7/16/37). To this can be added the fact that in mid July, Secretary of State Hull had personally arranged for Stephen Wise to be presented to Anthony Eden, the British foreign secretary, through the U.S. embassy in London. The meeting failed to take place because of a change in Wise's traveling plans. Then, on July 30 in Geneva, Wise also had a "long talk" with William Ormsby-Gore, the British colonial secretary. See *CT* 7/31/37, 5, and RDS 867n.01/851.

91. RDS 867n.01/753.5 (9/17/37).

92. RDS 867n.01/787 (7/12/37). Another site for State Department documents on Standard Oil is RDS 890f.6363 Standard Oil.

93. RDS 867n.01/807, Murray to Hull (7/19/37). See also 867n.01/951, a letter from the International Missionary Council, dated October 20, 1937, stating concerns over the preservation of American missionary rights in any future Jewish state created by partition.

94. For Husayni's letter, see RDS 867n.01/919. The mufti's interview with Wadsworth is found in the same file.

95. See, for example, *NYT* 1/13, 9; 1/7, 10; 1/14, 11; 1/17, 27; 1/19, 11; and 1/24, sec. IV, 5.

96. *NYT* 1/13/37, 9.

97. *NYT* 1/19/37, 11.

98. *WP* 7/9/37, 8.

99. For 1937 see, for example, *NYT* 2/23, 16; 2/27, 8; 3/7, 20; 3/8, 9; 3/14, 38; 3/15, 12; 3/17, 15; 3/18, 14; 3/19, 8; 3/22, 10; 4/11, 17; 4/12, 10; 4/16, 16; 5/8, 22; and 6/14, 11. See also *CT* 7/31/37, 5, and *WP* 7/8/37, 3.

100. *NYT* 2/8/37, 18.

101. Ibid.

102. *NYT* 6/30/37, 17.

103. *NYT* 7/26/37, 2.

104. Magnes's ideas would be laid out in the *NYT* ten days later, 7/18/37, sec. IV, 8. But the similarity to the *NYT*'s position indicates an earlier communication.

105. *NYT* 7/8/37, 22. The *LAT* editorialized against partition on 7/10/37, part II, 4, and the *WP* on 7/9/37, 8.

106. *NYT* 7/10/37, 14.

107. *LAT* 7/8/37, 12.

108. *NYT* 7/10/37, 14.

109. Ibid.

110. *CT* 7/13/37, 12.

111. *WP* 7/8/37, 3.

112. *NYT* 7/25/37, 22.

113. *NYT* 1/14/37, 11.

114. *NYT* 7/22/37, 1. The *LAT* gave the same interpretation as the *NYT* when

it reported that the Peel Commission report "will be submitted shortly to the League of Nations, which has the final word." *LAT* 7/8/37, 12.

115. *NYT* 7/22/37, 11.

116. *WP* 7/9/37, 2.

117. RDS 867n.01/836A.

118. *NYT* 5/9/37, sec. II, 4, and 5/10/37, 11.

7. The War Years

1. Smith, *Palestine and the Arab-Israeli Conflict,* 102–3.

2. RDS 867n.01/1583, p. 3.

3. Ibid., 8–10.

4. Urofsky, *American Zionism from Herzl to the Holocaust,* 414.

5. RDS 867n.01/1600.

6. RDS 867n.01/1542 (4/39).

7. RDS 867n.01/1564 (5/22/39).

8. For both King's letter and the House and Senate statements, see RDS 867n.01/1542 (5/4/39).

9. Ibid. See also the State Department press release of October 14, 1938 (number 499).

10. Adler, "The Roosevelt Administration and Zionism," 133. See also Adler, "Franklin D. Roosevelt and Zionism," 265–76.

11. See Tschirgi, *The Politics of Indecision,* 74.

12. RDS 867n.01/1548 (5/4/39).

13. RDS 867n.01/1542B (5/10/39).

14. RDS 867n.01/1556.5 (5/17/39).

15. *NYT* 5/18/39, 24. See also the op-ed column by Anne O'Hare McCormick, *NYT* 8/19/39, 14.

16. See, for example, *NYT* 5/19/39, 6; 5/20/39, 2; and 5/22/39, 8.

17. *NYT* 5/26/39, 15.

18. *WP* 5/19/39, 12.

19. *WP* 5/13/39, 3, and 5/23/39, 3.

20. *LAT* 5/19/39, part II, 4.

21. *CT* 5/23/39, 12.

22. Manuel, *The Realities,* 305.

23. Baram, *Department of State,* 53, 254.

24. N. Cohen, *The Year after the Riots,* 21.

25. The works of Adler and Urofsky have been cited above. Michael Cohen's point of view is found in his book *Truman and Israel.* On the other hand, there are some notable exceptions to this rule. See Stevens, *American Zionism,* and Christison, *Perceptions of Palestine.*

26. RDS 867n.01/1431.5 (2/9/39). See also 867n.01/1603 (6/14/39) and 867n.01/1602.5 (5/25/39).

27. RDS 867n.01/1714 (6/17/40).

28. RDS 867n.01/1729.5 (4/14/41).

29. RDS 867n.01/1739 (4/15/41).
30. RDS 867n.00/627 (3/3/43).
31. Ibid.
32. RDS 867n.01/1707 (3/28/40). See also 867n.01/20–1343 (10/13/43).
33. RDS 867n.00/[last numbers indecipherable] (11/26/43).
34. RDS 867n.01/12–442 (12/4/42).
35. Ibid., (12/17/42).
36. RDS 867n.00/592 (7/15/42).
37. RDS 867n.01/1–1943 (1/19/43).
38. RDS 867n.01/1–2643 (1/26/43).
39. RDS 867n.01/1–2643 (2/4/43).
40. RDS 890F.00/89 (5/26/43).
41. In agreeing to this aspect of the Atlantic Charter, Churchill exempted the peoples of the British Empire. However, Palestine was not a formal part of the empire.
42. RDS 867n.00/89 (4/30/43). See also a memorandum on an interview given by Ibn Saud to a correspondent of *Life* magazine in March 1943. RDS 867n.01/5–1243 (5/12/43).
43. RDS 867n.00/632 (5/6/43).
44. RDS 867n.01/1765A (6/12/43).
45. RDS 867n.01/1993.5 (6/12/43).
46. Ibid., RDS 867n.01/1765A.
47. RDS 867n.01/1877 (7/7/43).
48. RDS 867n.01/1997.5 (9/27/43).
49. Ibid.
50. Grose, *Israel in the Mind of America*, 152.
51. William A. Eddy, *FDR Meets Ibn Saud*, Kohinur Series, no. 1 (New York: American Friends of the Middle East, Inc., 1954), excerpted in Khalidi, *From Haven to Conquest*, 509–10.
52. Quoted in Grose, *Israel in the Mind of America*, 153.
53. RDS 867n.01/10–1845. See also Neff, *Fallen Pillars*, 25.
54. Quoted in Grose, *Israel in the Mind of America*, 154.
55. Quoted in Schectman, *United States*, 110. The attitude of many in Congress who saw Palestine only in terms of a "Jewish question" can be compared to the broader view of NEA. As Wallace Murray had observed in December of 1942, "the problem of the establishment in Palestine of a national home for the Jews has become an Arab question as well as a Jewish one." RDS 867n.01/12–442 (12/17/42).
56. *NYT* 10/24/45, 20.
57. RDS 867n.01/2251 (3/11/45).
58. RDS 867n.01/1055 and 1330.
59. RDS 867n.01/1496 (7/27/38).
60. RDS 867n.00/592 (7/15/42) and RDS 867n.01/1797 (2/11/42).
61. RDS 867n.01/2017.5 (10/28/43).

62. RDS 867n.4016/100 (4/18/41) and RDS 867n.01/1634.

63. RDS 867n.01/12–1242 (12/12/42).

64. See *NYT* 5/28/39, sec. IV, 8. See also the *Baltimore Sun* of 3/7/40.

65. *Life* 6/28/43, 11.

66. RDS 867n.01/11–2342 (11/23/42).

67. D. Shapiro, "Political Background," 166–77.

68. *NYT* 5/11/42, 6.

69. *NYT* 5/12/42, 12.

70. RDS 867n.01/1734 (4/21/41).

71. *NYT* 3/28/41 [page number indecipherable].

72. RDS 867n.01/1741 (4/21/41).

73. RDS 867n.01/1735 (4/22/41).

74. RDS 867n.01/1807 (4/23/42). The quote is from the "Statement of Aims and Principles of the APC." How an organization, the ends of which had to result in the denial of self-determination for the Arab majority of Palestine, could portray itself as promoting an "experiment in democracy" was never explained by the APC or its congressional supporters.

75. Starting in 1942, and running through the war years, thousands of letters and telegrams poured into Washington every year. See RDS 867n.01/2080 onward.

76. RDS 867n.01/1918 (8/18/43).

77. RDS 867n.01/2172.

78. *NYT* 2/2/44, 25.

79. *NYT* 2/16/44, 10. See also *NYT* 2/17/44, 11, wherein Faris Malouf, an American citizen, is headlined as "Syrian Fights Bill on Palestine Issue."

80. *NYT* 2/12/44, 12.

81. RDS 867n.01/2–744.

82. Ibid.

83. *NYT* 3/1/44, 2. NEA agreed with this position. See RDS 867n.01/2315.

84. *NYT* 3/8/44, 4.

85. *NYT* 3/2/44, 4.

86. *NYT* 3/22/44, 5.

87. *NYT* 3/10/44, 1.

88. See RDS 867n.01/2222 (3/28/44).

89. RDS 867n.01/2300 (3/27/44).

90. *NYT* 3/29/44, 3. Taft, Wagner, and the other supporters took this position despite Roosevelt's statement of March 29, 1944, indicating support for Stimson and Marshall's request that the resolutions be shelved. See *NYT* 3/29/44, 3.

91. See *NYT* 6/28/44, 14, and 7/21/44, 12.

92. See RDS 867n.01/12–144 (12/1/44), pp. 7, 8.

93. RDS 867n.01/12–1144 (12/11/44).

94. RDS 867n.01/2384 (5/19/44). Even while passing the blame onto Silver, Goldman sought to apportion a share to the State Department. Goldman told Murray that Silver had acted "under the erroneous impression that the Secretary

[of State] in his interview of January 13 with Silver had given approval for the resolutions." Thus the whole thing was rendered a "misunderstanding." See RDS 867n.01/234 (5/26/44).

95. RDS 867n.00/687 (2/10/44).

96. *NYT* 3/29/44, 3.

97. See, for instance, Wyman, *The Abandonment of the Jews*; Morse, *While Six Million Died*; and Laqueur, *The Terrible Secret.*

98. Brody, "American Jewry, the Refugees, and Immigration Restriction," 321.

99. Finger, *American Jewry during the Holocaust*, 7.

100. *NYT* 11/1/44, 6, and 2/5/44, 28.

101. Wyman, *The Abandonment of the Jews*, 190.

102. Ibid.

103. Schoenbaum, *The United States and the State of Israel*, 22. A 1942 poll asking if more Jewish refugees from Germany should be admitted to the United States brought a negative response of 77 percent. In 1946, another poll showed 72 percent registering opposition to Truman's request of Congress that more refugees be allowed into the country. See Suleiman, *Arabs in the Mind of America*, 114–15.

104. Brody, "American Jewry, the Refugees, and Immigration Restriction," 324–25. An exception here is the non-Zionist Jewish Labor Committee, which advocated the "right of free immigration" into the United States.

105. Ibid., 330. Henry Morgenthau Jr., secretary of the treasury, also consistently battled against the policies of Long.

106. Ibid., 331.

107. Ibid., 348.

108. Adler, Grose, Urofsky, and Wyman all write as if there were no distinctions between the two divisions.

109. RDS 867n.01/1718.5 (9/18/40).

110. See RDS 867n.01/1196 (10/13/38); 867n.01/1402 (1/20/39); 867n.01/1740 (4/29/41).

111. See RDS 867n.01/1169 and 1209 (10/13/38); letters dated 10/21/38 (no RDS number); RDS 867n.01/1512 (4/3/39); RDS 867n.01/12–444 (12/4/39); RDS 867n.01/1754 (6/21/41); RDS 867n.01/624.5 (3/8/43); RDS 867n.01/12–1244 (12/20/44).

112. See RDS 867n.01/1402 (1/20/39). See also Shatara's letter to Hull, dated 10/13/38, RDS 867n.01/1169.

113. See RDS 867n.00/619 (2/3/43); also RDS 867n.00/89 (4/30/43).

114. See RDS 867n.01/812.5 and following correspondence running 1942–1944.

115. RDS 867n.01/1740 (4/10/41).

116. Ibid.

117. See *LAT* 5/22/39, 3.

118. RDS 867n.01/1737.5; also RDS 867n.01/1744.

119. RDS 867n.4016/140 (4/13/43).

120. See *NYT* 11/28/44, 17.

121. RDS 867n.01/11–2744 (11/27/44).

122. For a recent account of the rendering invisible of the Palestinians, see Christison, *Perceptions of Palestine*.

8. 1945–1948: Zionism Triumphant

1. RDS 867n.01/3–545 (3/14/45). Also see Burns, *Roosevelt*, 397–98.

2. Cited in Truman, *Years of Trial and Hope*, 132–33.

3. Truman, *Year of Decisions*, 69.

4. See M. Cohen, *Truman and Israel*, 27; Christison, *Perceptions of Palestine*, 67–68; Lawson, "The Truman Administration and the Palestinians," 59–80.

5. Cited in Evensen, *Truman, Palestine, and the Press*, 129.

6. Ibid., 115.

7. M. Cohen, *Truman and Israel*, 28ff.

8. See Truman's second and third State of the Union addresses, in Israel, *State of the Union Messages*, 2948, 2957–58.

9. Truman, *Years of Trial and Hope*, 159.

10. Christison, *Perceptions of Palestine*, 63.

11. Evensen, *Truman, Palestine, and the Press*, 115.

12. Christison, *Truman, Palestine, and the Press*, 70.

13. Ibid., 72.

14. Ibid., 72.

15. Ibid., 70.

16. Clifford, *Counsel to the President*, 14, 24.

17. *FRUS* (1948), 1501.

18. *FRUS* (1945), 728. Pro-Zionist historians find these arguments irrelevant. For many of them foreign policy is indistinguishable from domestic concerns. Thus, according to Michael Cohen, Truman was "elected by the whole nation, including a sizable Jewish minority. Therefore, he was bound to serve the interests of his Jewish constituency too, not only because of political self-interest but also on good moral and constitutional grounds." Such arguments, of course, reduce both the president and "national interest" to the servitude of strong domestic interest groups. Under such circumstances it is difficult to know what Cohen means when he says the president was "elected by the whole nation." See M. Cohen, *Truman and Israel*, 90.

19. Neff, *Fallen Pillars*, 31.

20. See Grose, "The President versus the Diplomats," 41.

21. Neff, *Fallen Pillars*, 32. See also RDS 867n.01/10–145 (10/1/45). Compare Ibn Saud's position to that of Stephen Wise, who in 1945 stated that "a Jewish national home was a reparation due to the Jewish people for their sufferings in the war." *NYT* 5/11/45, 13.

22. *FRUS* (1945), 745 n. 42.

23. RDS 867n.01/10–145 (10/1/45). See also Acheson, *Present at the Creation*, 170–72.

24. RDS 867n.01/10–245 (10/2/45). See also Neff, *Fallen Pillars*, 33.

25. Neff, *Fallen Pillars*, 33.

26. Ibid. Other historians, such as Michael Cohen, see the British offer as a response to "a mounting crescendo of anti-British agitation in the U.S. that dwelt on the humanitarian aspect of the Jewish DP problem." M. Cohen, *Truman and Israel*, 122.

27. *FRUS* (1945), 837. See also Neff, *Fallen Pillars*, 34.

28. *FRUS* (1945), 722.

29. *FRUS* (1945), 841–42.

30. *FRUS* (1945), 828–29. Thus, when in May 1946, Arab governments were invited by the United States to submit views on the Anglo-American Inquiry's report (as part of "prior consultations"), the Palestinian Arabs refused to do so. See Neff, *Fallen Pillars*, 39.

31. RDS 867n.01/4–3046 (4/30/46). See also *NYT* 5/12/46, 17; 5/13/46, 15; and 6/7/46, 11.

32. RDS 867n.01/5–346 (5/8/46).

33. RDS 867n.01/6–346 (6/3/46).

34. *FRUS* (1946), 654. Truman had already declared himself willing to seek congressional permission for 50,000 DPs to enter the United States.

35. Neff, *Fallen Pillars*, 40.

36. *FRUS* (1946), 673–74. See also Neff, *Fallen Pillars*, 41.

37. *FRUS* (1946), 679–82. See also Laqueur, *History of Zionism*, 572–73.

38. *FRUS* (1946), 701–3.

39. *FRUS* (1946), 604–5.

40. Neff, *Fallen Pillars*, 42.

41. *FRUS* (1946), 708–9.

42. *FRUS* (1946), 717–20.

43. Cited in Wilson, *Decision on Palestine*, 99–100.

44. *FRUS* (1946), 732–35.

45. Wilson, *Decision on Palestine*, 100.

46. See Gallup poll published in *WP* 11/19/47, 12.

47. See *NYT* 7/4/46, 1, and 7/7/46, 10.

48. *NYT* 7/23/46, 1. According to Judah Magnes, there were a sizable number of American Jews who were materially aiding Zionist terrorism in Palestine. See *NYT* 10/30/47, 18.

49. Neff, *Fallen Pillars*, 45.

50. RDS 867n.01/11–2447 (11/24/47). See also *FRUS* (1947), 1154ff. Many of the newspaper editors around the country had also focused on the issue of Soviet penetration of the Middle East. See Evensen, *Truman, Palestine, and the Press*, 127–32. On the other hand, there was some recognition of the fact that American-Soviet agreement on partition had helped the issue succeed at the UN. See *NYT* 11/30/47, 1, 63.

51. Cited in Eddy, *FDR Meets Ibn Saud*, 37.

52. See Evensen, *Truman, Palestine, and the Press*, 114–15.

53. *NYT* 10/19/47, 1. Naively, the Americans discounted Arab warnings. U.S.

representative at the UN Herschel Johnson made a speech in November 1947 in which he said, "My government refuses to believe that any member of the UN, whatever may be their opinions on this highly controversial and bitter question, will attempt to defy the decision which may be taken by this organization." *CT* 11/23/47, 13.

54. *NYT* 10/19/47, 1.
55. Flapan, *The Birth of Israel*, 32.
56. *NYT* 10/12/47, 2. For the incident where Silver yelled at Truman, see Christison, *Perceptions of Palestine*, 68.
57. Neff, *Fallen Pillars*, 49. See also *CT* editorial of 5/18/48, 12.
58. Christison, *Perceptions of Palestine*, 73.
59. RDS 867n.01/11–2441 (11/24/47).
60. Tschirgi, *The Politics of Indecision*, 237.
61. Truman, *Years of Trial and Hope*, 158. See also Urofsky, "Ha Ma'avek," 294ff.
62. Neff, *Fallen Pillars*, 50. See also *NYT* 12/24/45, 9.
63. See RDS 867n.00/1–1848 (1/18/48) for suggestive evidence.
64. See Neff, *Fallen Pillars*, 51, and also Wilson, *Decision on Palestine*, 124–26.
65. *FRUS* (1947), 1153–58.
66. See Khalidi, *From Haven to Conquest*, lxxix. Also, for texts of these plans, see *Journal of Palestine Studies* 18, no. 1 (autumn 1988): 20–38.
67. Truman, *Years of Trial and Hope*, 158–59.
68. Neff, *Fallen Pillars*, 57.
69. *FRUS* (1948), 666–68.
70. Neff, *Fallen Pillars*, 58.
71. Truman, *Years of Trial and Hope*, 160.
72. Ibid., 163.
73. Tschirgi, *The Politics of Indecision*, 245.
74. Neff, *Fallen Pillars*, 59.
75. Truman, *Years of Trial and Hope*, 160.
76. *FRUS* (1948), 690–95. Clifford was not the only one going about slandering the Arabs. Members of Congress were also doing it. See *NYT* 5/12/46, 17.
77. *FRUS* (1948), 697, 749.
78. Wilson, *Decision on Palestine*, 135.
79. *FRUS* (1948), 697, 749.
80. See, for instance, Wilson, *Decision on Palestine*, 58–59, 135; and Spiegel, *The Other Arab-Israeli Conflict*, 33.
81. Truman, *Years of Trial and Hope*, 161.
82. Weizmann, *Trial and Error*, 458–59.
83. Truman, *Years of Trial and Hope*, 161.
84. *FRUS* (1948), 742–43.
85. See Gallup poll in *WP* 11/19/47, 12.
86. Grose, *Israel in the Mind of America*, 276.

87. Spiegel, *The Other Arab-Israeli Conflict*, 33.

88. *NYT* 3/21/48, 10, and 3/25/48, 1. See also Evensen, *Truman, Palestine, and the Press*, 154–57.

89. See Evensen, *Truman, Palestine, and the Press*, 158ff.

90. Tschirgi, *The Politics of Indecision*, 250.

91. Ibid., 252–53. See also M. Cohen, *Truman and Israel*, 228–29; *NYT* 8/22/46, 8, and 8/24/46, 5. For evidence that Henderson's anti-Zionist stand was not motivated by anti-Semitism, but rather "by the instincts of a patriot" who "fought his cause with dignity and courage" as well as "the code of a gentleman," see Podet, "Anti-Zionism in a Key U.S. Diplomat," 155–87. The quote is taken from 187.

92. Neff, *Fallen Pillars*, 63.

93. *FRUS* (1948), 972–76. Marshall would later tell the president that he would not publicly oppose him on the issue of recognition. For Truman this was the equivalent of a green light from the State Department. See Weisberger, "Present at the Creation Again?" 30.

94. See Grose, "The President versus the Diplomats," 51. By May 10 it was clear that the UN would not approve trusteeship. See Wilson, *Decision on Palestine*, 146.

95. Neff, *Fallen Pillars*, 63.

96. RDS 867n.01/5–1748 (5/17/48).

97. Ibid.

98. See *NYT* 12/1/47, 9. See also headline for *LAT* 12/1/47, 1: "Arabs Rip U.S. Flag, Burn Embassy."

99. Neff, *Fallen Pillars*, 64.

100. *FRUS* (1948), 1036–37. See also Wilson, *Decision on Palestine*, 147.

101. Truman, *Years of Trial and Hope*, 165.

102. See M. Cohen, *Truman and Israel*, 258–59.

103. See Evensen, *Truman, Palestine, and the Press*, 151ff.

104. See ibid., 130–32, and Christison, *Perceptions of Palestine*, 78.

105. Evensen, *Truman, Palestine, and the Press*, 10.

106. *NYT* 12/18/45, 1.

107. *NYT* 12/19/45, 14.

108. *NYT* 11/14/45, 18.

109. *NYT* 12/18/45, 15.

110. *WP* 11/19/47, 19.

111. *NYT* 1/6/45, 10.

112. *NYT* 4/4/46, 7.

113. *NYT* 8/14/46, 6.

114. *NYT* 10/30/46, 14.

115. *NYT* 10/27/46, 21.

116. *NYT* 5/1/46, 1, 3.

117. *NYT* 10/7/46, 1.

118. *NYT* 8/22/46, 8, and 8/24/46, 5.

119. *NYT* 6/13/46, 1, 4.
120. *NYT* 9/4/46, 22.
121. *WP* 11/22/47, 8.
122. *CT* 5/6/48, 22.
123. *NYT* 9/16/46, 5.
124. *NYT* 7/28/46, part IV, 2E. Also *NYT* 7/23/46, 1, 3. Ironically, the hotel was owned by the Palestine Economic Corporation, an American Zionist organization headed by Robert Szold.
125. Evensen, *Truman, Palestine, and the Press,* 130–32.
126. *NYT* 11/30/47, 1, 63, and 11/28/47, 10. See also *WP* 11/24/47, 2.
127. *CT* 11/28/47, 4.
128. *WP* 11/28/47, 10.
129. *WP* 11/23/47, 9.
130. *NYT* 11/30/47, 68.
131. *LAT* 11/30/47, 1.
132. *LAT* 11/20/47, 8.
133. *LAT* 12/1/47, 1.
134. *NYT* 11/30/47, part IV, 10.
135. *NYT* 11/30/47, 68.
136. Ibid.
137. *NYT* 12/1/47, 6.
138. *NYT* 5/15/48, 14.
139. *WP* 5/14/48, 22.
140. *WP* 5/16/48, 4B.
141. *CT* 5/18/48, 12.
142. *LAT* 5/18/48, part II, 4.
143. *CT* 5/13/48, 8.
144. *CT* 5/18/48, 12.
145. *LAT* 5/14/48, 8.
146. *NYT* 9/30/45, sec. IV, 8. See also RDS 867n.01/1045 (2/10/45), which gives an analysis by NEA staffers of the first annual convention of the American Council for Judaism.
147. *NYT* 7/7/46, 18.
148. *NYT* 10/30/47, 18.
149. *NYT* 12/17/46, 17.
150. *NYT* 8/3/46, 8.
151. *NYT* 8/31/46, 6.
152. *NYT* 5/15/48, 3.
153. *NYT* 10/7/45, sec. IV, 8.
154. *NYT* 9/30/45, sec. IV, 8.
155. See Lazaron's letter to Loy Henderson, RDS 867n.01/1247 (6/12/47).
156. See letter from the institute to President Truman dated 3/19/45, in RDS 867n.01/3–1945.
157. Ibid.

158. *NYT* 8/23/45, 10.

159. *NYT* 10/7/45, 30.

160. *NYT* 4/20/46, 8. Ibn Saud pointed out to the U.S. government that there existed "vast empty territories . . . in Australia, New Zealand and the two Americas and elsewhere that could absorb and support several times the total number of Jews in the world." Ibid. See also *NYT* 7/9/46, 3, and 10/4/46, 8.

161. *NYT* 6/13/46, 5.

162. *NYT* 4/14/46, 9.

163. *NYT* 11/17/46, 26.

164. *NYT* 9/5/46, 26. See also the Hourani letter, in *NYT* 12/18/46, 28.

165. See *NYT* 11/21/47, 26, and *NYT* 11/25/47, 8, 166. Christison, *Perceptions of Palestine*, 25, 56, 74.

166. See Davidson, "Debating Palestine," 237.

9. Colonizing the American Mind

1. *NYT* 4/4/46, 7.

2. *WP* 5/14/48, 14.

3. *WP* 5/16/48, 4B.

4. Suleiman, *Arabs in the Mind of America*, 41.

5. Ibid., 43.

6. Ibid., 44.

7. *NYT* 6/6/67, 20.

8. *NYT* 6/9/67, 44.

9. *NYT* 6/8/67, 46.

10. See, for example, *NYT* 5/27/67, 1; 5/30/67, 3; 5/31/67, 42; and 6/7/67, 46.

11. *NYT* 6/9/67, 44.

12. *WP* 6/7/67, A24.

13. *WP* 6/1/67, A18.

14. *WP* 5/27/67, A13.

15. *WP* 6/5/67, A21.

16. *WP* 6/7/67, A25.

17. *WP* 6/5/67, A22.

18. *WP* 6/1/67, A21.

19. *WP* 6/6/67, A10.

20. *WP* 6/5/67, A21.

21. *WP* 6/6/67, A16.

22. *WP* 5/27/67, A13.

23. *LAT* 5/28/67, sec. E, 1.

24. *LAT* 5/26/67, part II, 4.

25. *LAT* 5/25/67, part II, 4.

26. *LAT* 5/28/67, sec. E, 7.

27. *LAT* 5/27/67, part I, 1.

28. *LAT* 6/2/67, part II, 4.

29. *LAT* 6/4/67, sec. A, 2.

30. *LAT* 6/6/67, part II, 4.
31. *LAT* 6/4/67, sec. A, 4.
32. *CT* 5/26/67, 10.
33. *CT* 5/27/67, 1.
34. *CT* 5/28/67, 4.
35. *CT* 6/1/67, 12.
36. *CT* 5/30/67, 6.
37. *CT* 6/4/67, 10.
38. *CT* 6/3/67, 4.
39. Ibid.
40. *CT* 5/28/67, 4.
41. Medoff, *Zionism and the Arabs*, 161–64.
42. This denial is pictured in Tivnan, *The Lobby*.
43. Wilson, *Decision on Palestine*, 59, 154–55.
44. Christison, *Perceptions of Palestine*, 86–87. See also *FRUS* (1948), 1133–37.
45. Christison, *Perceptions of Palestine*, 89. See also *FRUS* (1948), 1173, 1184.
46. For a good review of the evolution of that foreign policy, see Suleiman, *U.S. Policy on Palestine*.
47. *WP* 6/6/67, A1, A8.
48. *WP* 6/6/67, A8.
49. See *CT* 6/4/67, sec. I, 9.
50. Smith, *Palestine and the Arab-Israeli Conflict*, 196.
51. Ables, "Changing Images," 301.
52. Zureik and Moughrabi, *Public Opinion and the Palestine Question*, 45.
53. *Newsweek* poll conducted by the Princeton Survey Research Associates and reported on www.pollingreport.com/israel.htm.
54. Zureik and Moughrabi, *Public Opinion and the Palestine Question*, 25.
55. See the *Gallup Poll Monthly*, no. 407 (August 1999): 3.
56. Zureik and Moughrabi, *Public Opinion and the Palestine Question*, 13–19, 45.
57. Cited in Urofsky, "Zionism," 223.

Bibliography

Ables, Gisela Renate. "Changing Images of the Arab World in the American Popular Mind." Ph.D. diss., University of Houston, 1998.

Acheson, Dean. *Present at the Creation: My Years in the State Department.* New York: Norton, 1969.

Adler, Selig. "Franklin D. Roosevelt and Zionism, the Wartime Record." *Judaism* 21 (summer 1972): 265–76.

———. "The Roosevelt Administration and Zionism: The Pre-War Years, 1933–1939." In *Essays in American Zionism, 1917–1948,* ed. Melvin Urofsky, 132–48. New York: Herzl Press, 1976.

Ahmed, Hisham. "Roots of Denial: American Stand on Palestinian Self-Determination from the Balfour Declaration to World War Two." In *U.S. Policy on Palestine: From Wilson to Clinton,* ed. Michael Suleiman, 27–57. Normal, Ill.: Association of Arab-American University Graduates, 1995.

Baram, Phillip. *The Department of State in the Middle East, 1919–1945.* Philadelphia: University of Pennsylvania Press, 1978.

Brody, David. "American Jewry, the Refugees, and Immigration Restriction, 1932–1942." In *The Jewish Experience in America: Selected Studies from the Publications of the American Jewish Historical Society,* ed. Abraham J. Karp, 2:219–247. Waltham, Mass.: American Jewish Historical Society, 1969.

Burns, J. M. *Roosevelt: The Soldier of Freedom.* New York: Harcourt, Brace, 1970.

Bustami, Zaha. "American Foreign Policy and the Question of Palestine, 1856–1939." Ph.D. diss., Georgetown University, 1989.

Christison, Kathleen. *Perceptions of Palestine: Their Influence on U.S. Foreign Policy.* Berkeley: University of California Press, 1999.

Clifford, Clark. *Counsel to the President: A Memoir.* New York: Random House, 1991.

Cohen, Michael. *Truman and Israel.* Berkeley: University of California Press, 1990.

Cohen, Naomi. *The Year after the Riots: American Responses to the Palestine Crisis of 1929–1930.* Detroit: Wayne State University Press, 1988.

Davidson, Lawrence. "Debating Palestine: Arab-American Challenges to Zionism, 1917–1932." In *Arabs in America: Building a New Future,* ed. Michael Suleiman, 227–40. Philadelphia: Temple University Press, 1999.

DeNovo, John A. *American Interests and Policies in the Middle East, 1900–1939.* Minneapolis: University of Minnesota Press, 1963.

Doumani, Beshara. *Rediscovering Palestine*. Berkeley: University of California Press, 1995.

Drummond, Donald F. "Cordell Hull (1933–1944)." In *An Uncertain Tradition: American Secretaries of State in the Twentieth Century,* ed. Norman Graebner, 184–209. New York: McGraw-Hill, 1961.

Earle, Edward Mead. "American Missions in the Near East." *Foreign Affairs* 7, no. 3 (April 1929): 398–417.

Eddy, William A. *FDR Meets Ibn Saud*. New York: American Friends of the Middle East, 1954.

Edelman, Maurice. *David: The Story of Ben Gurion*. New York: Putnam, 1965.

Evensen, Bruce J. *Truman, Palestine, and the Press: Shaping Conventional Wisdom at the Beginning of the Cold War*. New York: Greenwood Press, 1992.

Finger, Seymour Maxwell. *American Jewry during the Holocaust*. New York: Holmes and Meier/American Jewish Commission on the Holocaust, 1984.

Fishman, Hertzel, *American Protestantism and a Jewish State*. Detroit: Wayne State University Press, 1973.

Flapan, Simha. *The Birth of Israel*. New York: Pantheon Books, 1987.

Foreign Relations of the United States. 1945, vol. 5; 1946, vol. 7; 1947, vol. 5; 1948, vol. 5, pt. 2. Washington, D.C.: Government Printing Office.

Ghareeb, Edmund. *Split Vision: The Portrayal of Arabs in the American Media*. Washington, D.C.: American-Arab Affairs Council, 1983.

Grabill, Joseph. *Protestant Diplomacy and the Near East: Missionary Influence on American Policy, 1810–1927*. Minneapolis: University of Minnesota Press, 1971.

Graebner, Norman, ed. *An Uncertain Tradition: American Secretaries of State in the Twentieth Century*. New York: McGraw-Hill, 1961.

Grose, Peter. *Israel in the Mind of America*. New York: Knopf, 1983.

———. "The President versus the Diplomats." In *The End of the Palestine Mandate*, ed. William Louis and Robert Stookey, 32–57. Austin: University of Texas Press, 1988.

Hammons, Terry Brooks. "'A Wild Ass of a Man': American Images of Arabs to 1948." Ph.D. diss., University of Oklahoma, 1978.

Handlin, Oscar. "American Views of the Jew at the Opening of the Twentieth Century." In *The Jewish Experience in America: Selected Studies from the Publications of the American Jewish Historical Society,* ed. Abraham Karp, 5:1–21. Waltham, Mass.: American Jewish Historical Society, 1969.

Heckscher, August. *Woodrow Wilson*. New York: Scribner, 1991.

Ingrams, Doreen, ed. *Palestine Papers, 1917–1922*. New York: George Braziller, 1973.

Israel, Fred, ed. *The State of the Union Messages of the Presidents, 1790–1966*. New York: Chelsea House–Robert Hector, 1966.

Katibah, Habib. *The Case against Zionism*. New York: Syrian-American Press, 1921.

Khalidi, Walid, ed. *Before Their Diaspora: A Photographic History of the Palestinians, 1876–1948*. Washington, D.C.: Institute for Palestine Studies, 1996.

———. *From Haven to Conquest: Readings in Zionism and the Palestine Problem until 1948.* Beirut, Lebanon: Institute for Palestine Studies, 1970.

Klatzker, David. "British Jerusalem in the News." *Middle East Quarterly* 1, no. 4 (December 1994): 35–47.

Kolinsky, Martin. *Law, Order, and Riots in Mandatory Palestine, 1928–1935.* London: St. Martin's Press, 1993.

Kolsky, Thomas. *Jews against Zionism: The American Council for Judaism, 1942–1948.* Philadelphia: Temple University Press, 1990.

Laqueur, Walter. *A History of Zionism.* New York: Schocken, 1989.

———. *The Terrible Secret.* New York: Henry Holt, 1998.

Lawson, Fred. "The Truman Administration and the Palestinians." In *U.S. Policy on Palestine: From Wilson to Clinton,* ed. Michael Suleiman, 59–80. Normal, Ill.: Association of Arab-American University Graduates, 1995.

Link, Arthur, ed. *The Papers of Woodrow Wilson.* Princeton: Princeton University Press, 1983.

Lydon, Cindy. "American Images of the Arabs." *Mid East* vol. 9, no.3 (May–June 1969): 156.

Manuel, Frank. *The Realities of American-Palestine Relations.* Washington, D.C.: Public Affairs Press, 1949.

Medoff, Rafael. *Zionism and the Arabs: An American Jewish Dilemma, 1898–1948.* Westport, Conn.: Praeger, 1997.

Merkley, Paul C. *The Politics of Christian Zionism, 1891–1948.* London: Frank Cass, 1998.

Mitchell, Timothy. *Colonizing Egypt.* Berkeley: University of California Press, 1991.

Morse, Arthur D. *While Six Million Died: A Chronicle of American Apathy.* New York: Random House, 1968.

Neff, Donald. *Fallen Pillars: U.S. Policy towards Palestine and Israel since 1945.* Washington, D.C.: Institute for Palestine Studies, 1995.

Phillips, Clifton. *Protestant America and the Pagan World: The First Half Century of the American Board of Commissioners for Foreign Missions, 1810–1860.* Cambridge, Mass.: Harvard University Press, 1969.

Podet, Allen. "Anti-Zionism in a Key U.S. Diplomat: Loy Henderson at the End of World War II." *American Jewish Archives* 30 (1978): 155–87.

Polk, William R. *The United States and the Arab World.* Cambridge, Mass.: Harvard University Press, 1975.

Pritchett, Henry. "Observations in Egypt, Palestine and Greece." *International Conciliation,* no. 225 (December 1926): 519–20.

"Records of the Department of State Relating to the Internal Affairs of Turkey, 1910–29." Record Group 59. The National Archives and Record Service, General Services Administration, Washington, D.C.

"Records of the Department of State Relating to the Internal Affairs of Palestine, 1930–44." Record Group 59. The National Archives and Record Service, General Services Administration, Washington, D.C.

"Records of the Department of State Relating to the Internal Affairs of Palestine, 1945–49." Record Group 59. The National Archives and Record Service, General Services Administration, Washington, D.C.

Rubenberg, Cheryl. *Israel and the American National Interest.* Chicago: University of Illinois Press, 1986.

Said, Edward. *Covering Islam: How the Media and the Experts Determine How We See the Rest of the World.* New York: Pantheon Books, 1981.

Salisbury, Harrison. *Without Fear or Favor: The "New York Times" and Its Times.* New York: Times Books, 1980.

Sandeen, Ernest. *The Roots of Fundamentalism: British and American Millenarianism, 1800–1930.* Chicago: University of Chicago Press, 1970.

Schectman, Joseph. *The United States and the Jewish State Movement.* South Brunswick, N.J.: A. S. Barnes, 1966.

Schoenbaum, David. *The United States and the State of Israel.* New York: Oxford University Press, 1993.

Schulte Nordholt, Jan. *Woodrow Wilson: A Life for World Peace.* Berkeley: University of California Press, 1991.

Sha'ban, Fuad, *Islam and Arabs in Early American Thought.* Durham, N.C.: Acorn Press, 1991.

Shafir, Gershon. *Land, Labor and the Origins of the Israeli-Palestinian Conflict, 1882–1914.* Berkeley: University of California Press, 1989.

Shaheen, Jack. *The TV Arab.* Bowling Green, Ohio: Bowling Green State University Popular Press, 1984.

Shapiro, David. "The Political Background of the 1942 Biltmore Resolution." *Essays in American Zionism, 1917–1948,* ed. Melvin Urofsky, 166–77. New York: Herzl Press, 1978.

Shapiro, Yonathan. *The Formative Years of the Israeli Labour Party: The Organization of Power, 1919–1930.* London: Sage Publications, 1976.

———. *Leadership of the American Zionist Organization, 1897–1930.* Urbana: University of Illinois Press, 1971.

Shepard, Naomi. *The Zealous Intruders.* San Francisco: Harper and Row, 1987.

Smith, Charles. *Palestine and the Arab-Israeli Conflict.* New York: St. Martin's Press, 1988.

Spiegel, Steven. *The Other Arab-Israeli Conflict: Making America's Middle East Policy, from Truman to Reagan.* Chicago: University of Chicago Press, 1986.

Stevens, Richard. *American Zionism and U.S. Foreign Policy, 1942–1947.* Beirut, Lebanon: Institute for Palestine Studies, 1970.

Suleiman, Michael. *The Arabs in the Mind of America.* Battleboro, Vt.: Amana Press, 1988.

———. "Arab Americans and the Political Process." In *The Development of Arab-American Identity,* ed. Ernest McCarus, 34–60. Ann Arbor: University of Michigan Press, 1994.

———, ed. *U.S. Policy on Palestine: From Wilson to Clinton.* Normal, Ill.: Association of Arab-American University Graduates, 1995.

Swedenburg, Ted. *Memories of Revolt: The 1936–1939 Rebellion and the Palestinian National Past.* Minneapolis: University of Minnesota Press, 1995.

Tessler, Mark. *A History of the Israeli-Palestinian Conflict.* Bloomington: Indiana University Press, 1994.

Tivnan, Edward. *The Lobby: Jewish Political Power and American Foreign Policy.* New York: Simon and Schuster, 1987.

Truman, Harry. *Year of Decisions.* New York: Doubleday, 1956.

———. *Years of Trial and Hope.* New York: Doubleday, 1956.

Tschirgi, Dan. *The Politics of Indecision.* Prager Publishers, 1983.

Urofsky, Melvin. *American Zionism from Herzl to the Holocaust.* Lincoln: University of Nebraska Press, 1975.

———. "Ha Ma'avek: American Zionists, Partition and Recognition, 1947–1948." In *Essays in American Zionism, 1917–1948,* ed. Melvin Urofsky, 215–43. New York: Herzl Press, 1978.

———. "Zionism: An American Experience." *American Jewish Historical Quarterly* (March 1974).

Voss, Carl Hermann. *Stephen S. Wise: Servant of the People, Selected Letters.* Philadelphia: Jewish Publication Society of America, 1970.

Weinberg, Albert. *Manifest Destiny: A Study of Nationalist Expansionism in American History.* Chicago: Quadrangle Books, 1963.

Weisberger, B. "Present at the Creation Again?" *American Heritage* vol. 45, no. 2 (April 1994): 28–30.

Weizmann, Chaim. *Trial and Error.* New York: Harper, 1944.

Whitelam, Keith. *The Invention of Ancient Israel: The Silencing of Palestinian History.* New York: Routledge Press, 1996.

Wilson, Evan. *Decision on Palestine: How the U.S. Came to Recognize Israel.* Stanford, Ca.: Hoover Institution Press, 1979.

Wise, Stephen. *Challenging Years: The Autobiography of Stephen Wise.* New York: Putnam, 1949.

Wyman, David. *The Abandonment of the Jews: America and the Holocaust, 1941–1945.* New York: Pantheon Books, 1984.

Zinn, Howard. *A People's History of the United States.* New York: Harper and Row, 1980.

Zureik, Elia, and Fouad Moughrabi, eds. *Public Opinion and the Palestine Question.* New York: St. Martin's Press, 1987.

Index

Lawrence Davidson is professor of history at West Chester University, which is part of the Pennsylvania state university system. He teaches Middle East history and his research is in the area of U.S. relations with and perceptions of the Middle East. He has published more than fifteen articles and a book, *Islamic Fundamentalism* (1998). His current work is a history of the Division of Near Eastern Affairs of the State Department.